MY *Love* FOR
NAPLES

The Food, the History, the Life

The **HIPPOCRENE** Cookbook Library

MY *Love* FOR

NAPLES

The Food, the History, the Life

Anna Teresa Callen

HIPPOCRENE BOOKS
NEW YORK

Book and jacket design by Brad Rickman.
Photography by KennethChenPhotography.com and Krisztina Simsa-Crane.
Styling by Brett Kurzweil.

For more information, address:

HIPPOCRENE BOOKS, INC.
171 Madison Avenue
New York, NY 10016

Library of Congress Cataloging-in-Publication Data

Callen, Anna Teresa.
  My love for Naples : the food, the history, the life / Anna Teresa Callen.
      p. cm.
  Includes bibliographical references and index.
  ISBN-13: 978-0-7818-1205-4 (alk. paper)
  ISBN-10: 0-7818-1205-4 (alk. paper)
  1. Cookery, Italian--Neapolitan style. 2. Cookery--Italy--Naples. 3.
Naples (Italy)--Social life and customs. I. Title.
  TX723.2.S65C35 2008
  641.5945--dc22
                    2007033097

Printed in the United States of America.

Contents

My family at our home in Abruzzo in 1933. Standing, from left to right, are Uncle Filippo, Mamma, Aunt Cettina, Papa, and Aunt Ela. My brother and I sit at our grandmother's knee.

introduction

This book is dedicated to the food of Campania, its capital Naples, the islands of Capri and Ischia, and the magical coastal strip of the Amalfi Drive with its villages climbing up and down the steep hills overlooking the splendid bay.

The cuisine of this southern region of Italy is that of *cucina povera*, which does not mean "poor cuisine" but "cooking of the poor." In view of their limited resources, the people of Campania had to be inventive, both in their everyday food, and for holidays and festivities. Thus foods that were readily available, first and foremost tomatoes, have been used in many dishes, in imaginative and delicious ways, from *antipasto alla Caprese*, made with the unique *mozzarella di bufala* and ripe red tomatoes, to the humble *spaghetti cu' 'a pummarola 'ncoppa* to seafood dishes, such as *brodetto di pesce*.

During its long history, Naples was occupied by the Greeks, Romans, Arabs, Spanish, Normans, and French. All of these invaders left traces of their civilizations, bringing new traditions, customs, art, and introducing new plants, grains, and fruit trees, which made the food of the region so varied and colorful and enhanced the Neapolitans' diet.

Those who first experimented with the new ingredients were the cooks of the nobility, who were mostly from France. They became known as the *Monzù* (from the French *Monsieur*). Eager to impress their masters, they created a new kind of cuisine, the one of the aristocracy. Their banquets and parties were the talk of the town and were imitated all over southern Italy. The Monzù invented sophisticated dishes such as Crepes Stuffed with Ricotta, and Prosciutto and Parmesan Cheese, many of which are still part of Neapolitan menus today. But it was in the field of desserts that these new cooks became especially extravagant. They deserve credit for

My father and mother in Campania.

having invented the Orange Ice, which gets its flavor from a generous shot of orange liqueur, and the *pastiera*, a symbol-laden Easter cake whose main ingredient is wheat. Chocolate became a passion, and it was used in the most unusual forms. In Amalfi, for instance, there still is a concoction made with eggplants and chocolate.

Each region of Italy has its own specialty. For Campania it is pizza, which has conquered the world in a more lasting way than any army ever conquered Naples. There is some uniformity in the basic ingredients used in Italian cuisine, but there are also major differences. For instance, in the North polenta is a staple, whereas in the South vegetables grown in the soil (*terra*), such as tomatoes, form the basic ingredients of the regional cuisine. Hence we Italians jokingly call Northerners *polentoni* and Southerners *terroni*.

This book explores the cuisine of Campania in all its facets.

A LITTLE HISTORY

Campania, an ancient region in the south of Italy, has a long and eventful history. Continuous waves of conquerors set foot on this land, leaving their imprints, which are still visible in the splendid architecture, the customs, and of course, the food. The English word *Lucullan* for "sumptuous, lavish" goes back to the banquets that the Roman General Lucius Licinius Lucullus held for his guests on the shore of the bay of Naples.

But before the Romans there were the Etruscans, the Samnites, and the Greeks, who founded *Neapolis* (Naples), building magnificent temples whose ruins you can still visit all over the region. Paestum, at the tip of the peninsula, a place that thrilled the German poet Goethe, is the best example of this past splendor.

For the Romans, Campania was one of their most prestigious conquests. The Emperor Tiberius had a villa, the ruins of which still exist, built for himself on Capri. The beauty of Campania pleased these Romans so much that they called it *Campania Felix* ("happy country"), a name that is often used for Campania to the present day.

After the Roman conquest of Campania, the Goths, Byzantines, Lombards, Arabs, and Normans from France invaded this region at various times with its heterogeneous population that included Italians, Greeks, and Muslim Arabs. Under the firm and benevolent rule of the Normans, Campania prospered in the twelfth century and became one of the most civilized nations in Europe under Emperor Frederick II. He founded universities, allowed Muslims to practice their religion, and wrote poetry. He was also a passionate hunter and wrote a famous book about hunting. He is often represented in regal position holding a falcon in his right hand. He was

Me and my twin brother, Mimmo, age 5.

an extraordinary character, and in his time he was called *Stupor Mundi*, the amazement of the world. Because of his opposition to the dogmata of the Pope, who had sovereignty over many parts of Italy, he was excommunicated twice, but his popularity did not diminish.

The list of conquerors and invaders continues with the Angiovins, Aragons, Spaniards, and Bourbons. What motivated many of the foreign conquerors to stay was the fertility of the land surrounding Mount Vesuvius. The country was dotted with small farms. The landscape was full of shepherds with their flocks, and coops lodging all sorts of birds. Vineyards started to cover the flanks of Campania's gentle mountains. The Italian patriot and general Giuseppe Garibaldi started the unification of Italy with the conquest of Sicily and Campania in 1860.

Campania still remains a fertile region today. Mythical olive trees, sacred to the goddess Minerva, decorate the gentle slopes of the hills. The farms around Caserta, Benevento, and Avellino produce the best vegetables of the region: cabbage, beans, broccoli, tomatoes, only to name a few. Zucchini grow to a length of six feet. A great variety of fruit—pears, apples, peaches, plums, pomegranates, figs and more—are available practically year-round. Orange and lemon

My brother and me on a ski vacation in the Italian Alps. Like many Italian men, my brother was an avid sportsman who enjoyed the outdoors.

trees grow along the breathtaking Amalfi Drive, with Sorrento showing off its magnificent walnut trees.

Food is an important part of Campania's culture. The emphasis is on the quality and freshness of the ingredients. The tomato is king in Naples but it is used to dress food, not to obliterate it. When I came to the United States, the last restaurant I wanted to eat in was an Italian restaurant where so-called Neapolitan fare was served. Everything was drowned in tomato sauce, smelling of garlic, hot pepper, and too many herbs. But with the arrival of new chefs from Italy, cookbooks, and cooking schools, Campania's food has returned to its authentic flavor and consistency even far away from Naples.

I hope in this book I have been able to capture the true tastes of this region with its long, rich history and wonderfully diverse culinary heritage.

MY LIFE IN NAPLES

I have always had a passion for Naples, a city with natural beauty, majestic grand palaces, panoramic avenues, and intriguing, winding narrow streets in the heart of the city, where it's fun to get lost. I did that when my devilish twin brother Mimmo and his friends organized a *filone*, which means that we skipped school. We would go to *Spaccanapoli*, a narrow street that, as its name implies, splits Naples in two. To fully admire this phenomenon you have to climb up the hill of San Martino that overlooks the city. The street of Spaccanapoli looks like a long snake stretched out through downtown Naples. From this street, countless busy little lanes go in every direction.

This is the place to savor the spirit of the Neapolitans. When I was a child, there were vendors at every corner, watching their merchandise like hawks—pushcarts full of food, knickknacks, and clothing. But my favorite were the basement shops selling all sorts of things, including

English and American books, which were shunned by the fascist government. It was in one of these shops that I found a beautiful edition of Mark Twain's *The Adventures of Tom Sawyer*, in English. I read it with the help of a dictionary. Because of my father's work, we moved to Naples in 1939. In September, World War II broke out. It didn't take us by surprise, in view of the political relationship between Mussolini and Hitler. But we felt relatively safe, since we lived in a residential area called Il Vomero that was far from any military facilities.

My brother, me, my mother and my father on a *passeggiata* by the bay in Naples, 1942. Italians love nothing better than to walk by the sea.

At that time, we could still take our late-afternoon stroll, a *passeggiata*, that was almost a ritual everywhere in Italy. We would go to the main street of our neighborhood, Via Scarlatti, nicely dressed, meet friends, and end up at a *caffè*. While the grownups sipped their *aperitivo*, we children had ice cream, which didn't spoil our appetite since the *cena*, the evening meal, was usually small. On Sundays, we enjoyed a real adventure—a trip by *funicolare*, a cable railway that slides down the hill of the Vomero to downtown Naples. We took long walks on the beautiful, panoramic Via Caracciolo to admire the islands of Capri and Ischia floating in the blue waters of the bay. We always ended the evening in a pizzeria, where we would enjoy our favorite pizza with soft drinks for us and beer for my father. On holidays, we would go for picnics with friends to Posillipo, a residential area with magnificent villas on the hill that encloses the gulf. There is also a pine forest in Posillipo that is an ideal place to spend a holiday.

Naples had always been a place where varied and delicious foods were available, but when the war started, food was rationed, and staples like pasta, bread, and meat became scarce. Sometimes a friend who lived in the country would bring us a *mozzarella di bufala*, a real treat, or a precious chicken—they were impossible to find. The eggs were also invaluable. The chicken was used from top to bottom, with me always getting the head, and Mimmo the feet. Mother would concoct several meals with a chicken, starting with a stew and vegetables. Half of the

Me (center) on board the *Christopher Columbus* in 1961, returning to America to get married.

breast was reserved for salad, to which celery, carrots, tomatoes, and, if we had it, a boiled egg were added. No mayonnaise—who had the oil to make it? There was no Hellmann's in those days. The salad was flavored just with a good squeeze of local lemons. The bones, never discarded, were turned into a flavorful broth that was used for some sort of *minestra* with vegetables, and, if we were lucky, a little bit of rice or pastina. We had to be inventive.

Nowadays, with my two cousins Gianna and Franca, who are married to Neapolitans, I am relearning the cuisine of the past, as well as new developments. Cooking is never static. Every time I visit my cousins, I learn more. The places where they prefer to take me are the farmhouses. Some of them now accommodate guests and prepare wonderful authentic food, usually served on a communal table set in a garden or a charming courtyard. I highly recommend them. Staying at an *agriturismo* also gives you the opportunity to visit the many holiday resorts on the coast, and places like Ravello and Positano, or, for a bit of culture, the ancient Roman town of Paestum.

THE WINES OF CAMPANIA

Since antiquity, the wines of Campania have been highly respected. The ancient Romans considered the vineyards around Falerno the best of their empire. The Falerno wine is still produced today in its red and white varieties, and like some of the other wines from the gulf, the islands, and around Mount Vesuvius, it is a DOC (*Denominazione di Origine Controllata*, roughly translated: "protected place name"). The DOC designation is given to over three hundred Italian wine-growing areas, and regulates factors such as area of production, permissible grape varietals, maximum yield of grapes per acre, minimum alcohol content, aging requirements, and even vineyard practices like pruning and trellising. To be eligible for a DOC designation, wines must also pass a taste test and a chemical analysis.

Other important wines are the white Greco di Tufo and Fiano di Avellino, and the red Aglianico (Hellenic) which arrived with the Greeks. The red Taurasi, one of the oldest wines of the region, is probably the best known outside Italy. The white Lachrima Christi ("the tear of Christ") from the Vesuvius area also dates back to antiquity. In fact, vats used to store this wine were found during archaeological excavations of Pompeii and Herculaneum, cities buried in the violent eruption of Mt. Vesuvius in 74 A.D. And let's not forget the quite fashionable Limoncello, a liqueur made from the sun-pampered lemons grown in the hills of Sorrento and Amalfi.

In the province of Aversa north of Naples, there is an unusual and tasty wine, not well known even in Italy, called Asprinio. It is cultivated in an unusual way. The vines wind around poles erected against a high wall that then appears all green and whose top is full of leaves moving in the wind. The white Falanghina, from around the Avenillo area, is cultivated in the same manner. Apparently, this is an ancient method of cultivation that attracted even the imagination of Pliny the Elder. Two thousand years ago he wrote quite poetically about these vines, comparing them to imaginary giants "climbing with wanton arms . . . among their branches . . . soaring aloft to such a height that a hired picker expressly stipulates in his contract for the cost of a funeral and a grave." As you can see, Pliny also had a sense of humor!

Although wine is highly respected and loved in this region, people look at it as an enhancer of food and a healthy appetite, and above all as part of a meal to be consumed with friends. And since we are talking of ancient philosophers, I would like to relate a passage from the appropriately named "Symposium" by Plato. He too, with a great sense of humor, describes how he served wine when entertaining friends: "I prepare but three craters for prudent men—one is for health and to drink first, the second is for love and pleasure, the third for sleep."

My father, who could not agree more with these sages, always gave me and my brother a "finger" of wine with our meals when we were children. I didn't particularly like it, unless it was sweet, but I drank it because it was good for me!

antipasti

In today's Neapolitan cuisine, the antipasto is unfortunately relegated to special occasions and festivities. The everyday meal immediately starts with a *minestra* (soup) or pasta—especially pasta, which is impossible to remove from a Neapolitan table. After all, the Neapolitans are not called *mangia maccheroni* (macaroni eaters) for nothing. However, a dinner for guests always includes an antipasto, which can be a simple *bruschetta*, a variety of *crostini*, or a sumptuous *insalata di mare* (seafood salad).

In Italy, and especially in the south, breakfast is almost non-existent. Neapolitans start their day with a *tazzulella du caffè* (small cup of strong espresso). On their way to work, they usually stop at a nearby bar for a second *tazzulella*, or maybe a cappuccino and a brioche. After all, one needs a *supponta* (Neapolitan for "support"). It is also common for people to have another snack at a local bar during midday repast, such as a *tramezzino* (small sandwich), or a few crostini accompanied by the obligatory *aperitivo*. In a way, this is a small antipasto. But in this chapter we will talk of real *antipasti* (plural of antipasto). Some of them are simple, and others are not so simple—there is an antipasto for everyone.

La Caprese

La Caprese is a simple antipasto from the island of Capri. It is made with fresh mozzarella, tomatoes, a dribbling of olive oil, and a garnish of basil. La Caprese has become quite popular in the United States, and for good reasons. It is easy to assemble and the colorful display of white mozzarella, red tomato, and fresh green basil looks beautiful, especially on a white serving plate.

When I was growing up in Naples, la Caprese was different, though. Most of the time tomatoes and mozzarella were assembled as a *crostino*, a slice of toasted crusty bread topped with tomato and mozzarella, with or without basil. The beginning of pizza? Not quite, as you will see later.

Often the crostino was baked until the mozzarella started to melt. For us children, this was *la merenda*, a mid-afternoon snack. Before dinner, the grown-ups had an aperitif with a *stuzzichino* (a small bite to wet the appetite).

You really don't need a recipe for la Caprese and crostino. Just follow the above formula, use fresh buffalo mozzarella and make sure to have enough to satisfy the eaters. *Buon appetito!*

Grilled Garlic Bread | **BRUSCHETTA**

It is amazing to me to see how humble snacks like bruschetta and crostini have taken the United States by storm. Chefs have found ways to embellish them with many wonderful innovations. At times, a few slices on a plate can become a meal.

Bruschetta are slices of toasted bread rubbed with fresh garlic and sprinkled with olive oil. They originated in Abruzzo and expanded to the bordering regions of Umbria and Lazio and the rest of Italy. Very simple to prepare, bruschetta in its simplest form is also a wonderful accompaniment for soups, stews, and other foods.

It is difficult to say how many people can be served with a loaf of bread. You should calculate at least two slices per person.

1 loaf long or round Italian bread, cut into ½-inch thick slices

½ cup extra-virgin olive oil

1 large garlic clove

½ to 1 *diavoletto* (dried Italian hot red pepper), to taste (optional)

Preheat the oven to 400 degrees F.

Place the slices of bread on baking sheets and set aside.

Thoroughly blend the olive oil with the garlic and hot pepper in a food processor. Brush the bread with the oil mixture and place in the oven.

Reduce the oven temperature to 200 degrees F and bake for 10 minutes. Turn off the oven and let the bruschetta cool in the oven until ready to serve.

NOTE *The best topping for bruschetta is chopped tomatoes dressed with a little oil, oregano, or basil. They are also delicious with a spread of chopped chicken liver. However, for the Neapolitans, the traditional topping is mozzarella and anchovies.*

Bruschetta with Ricotta and Herbs

BRUSCHETTA ALLA RICOTTA E ERBE

This is one of the most popular bruschetta in Campania, especially in the hills around Benevento where sheep roam guarded by a dutiful dog. It is light, nutritious and for this reason is often fed to children after they return from school. For the grownups who love anchovies, it is a good idea to add a few of them to the ricotta. I also suggest anchovy paste, which has a more delicate flavor.

12 servings

12 (½-inch thick) slices crusty Italian whole-wheat bread

¼ cup extra-virgin olive oil

1 garlic clove, halved

2 cups whole-milk ricotta, drained

1 teaspoon anchovy paste, or 3 or 4 chopped anchovies packed in oil (optional)

1 teaspoon chopped fresh oregano

¼ teaspoon chopped fresh basil

¼ teaspoon chopped fresh sage

1½ tablespoons grated Parmesan cheese

Preheat the oven to 400 degrees F.

Brush the bread on both sides with the olive oil. Rub one side with the garlic. Place the slices, garlic-side up, on baking sheets and bake for 5 to 10 minutes. Turn off the oven and let the bread crisp and cool in the oven.

In a mixing bowl combine the ricotta, anchovies, and herbs. Spread on the bread slices and sprinkle with the Parmesan cheese.

Reduce the heat to 370 degrees F and bake the bruschetta for 10 to 15 minutes, or until the tops are crusty and slightly brown. Serve hot.

Mozzarella and Anchovy Crostini

CROSTINI DI MOZZARELLA CON ACCIUGHE

Crostini are similar to bruschetta, but while the latter are also served as an accompaniment, crostini are always antipasti or snacks. They can be topped with cheeses, salami, a spread of chicken livers, or cooked and finely chopped vegetables.

These crostini are typical Neapolitan. The flavors of mozzarella and anchovies are a perfect match.

6 servings

12 thin slices of Italian *sfilatini* or baguette

12 slices whole-milk mozzarella

12 anchovies packed in oil, drained

Preheat the oven to 375 degrees F.

Place the bread on baking sheets and bake in the oven until lightly toasted.

Top each slice of bread with a slice of mozzarella and an anchovy.

Put the slices back in the oven and bake until the mozzarella starts to melt, about 10 to 15 minutes.

NOTE *As a variation, add a slice of tomato and a basil leaf to each* crostino *before baking.*

Baked Eggplant with Mozzarella "In a Coach"

MELANZANE IN CARROZZA

The name of this recipe is a little bit of a joke. But the Neapolitans are famous for their sense of humor. The food is layered like a sandwich, and *in carrozza* means "in a coach."

In the original Neapolitan recipe, the slices of eggplants are deep-fried, but I bake mine. When it is feasible without compromising the flavor, I make my food as healthy as possible, and I think that baking works beautifully in this dish. But do not tell a Neapolitan—he or she will not believe you. Grazie!

6 servings

4 pounds medium eggplants

2 tablespoons kosher salt

¼ cup extra-virgin olive oil

3 or 4 large balls whole-milk mozzarella cheese (about 3 pounds)

Cut eggplants crosswise into ½-inch thick slices. Discard the ends or reserve for another use. Place the slices in a colander, sprinkle with the salt, and let drain for about 20 minutes.

Heat the oven to 375 degrees F. Lightly oil two baking sheets.

Cut the mozzarella into ½-inch slices. (You should have twice as many eggplant slices as mozzarella slices.)

Dry the eggplant slices with paper towels, brushing off as much salt as possible, and place them on the prepared baking sheets. Brush each slice with oil. Bake for 10 minutes, turn each slice and bake for 10 more minutes.

Remove the baking sheets from the oven. Place a slice of mozzarella on a slice of eggplant and top with another eggplant slice. Repeat until all eggplant slices are used. Put both baking sheets back in the oven and bake for 15 minutes, or until the mozzarella starts to melt.

Transfer the "sandwiches" with a spatula to a serving platter and serve hot.

Breaded Mozzarella "In a Coach" | MOZZARELLA IN CARROZZA

A typical *trattoria* dish that can be found in and around Naples, this is a rustic repast, eaten as an antipasto, a snack, or for an impromptu *cena* (dinner). The mozzarella, sandwiched between two pieces of bread, is *in carrozza*, "in a coach!"

6 servings

12 slices crusty Italian bread, cut as thinly as possible

1¾ pounds whole-milk mozzarella

1 (2-ounce) can anchovies packed in oil

3 eggs

3 tablespoons milk

Canola oil for deep frying (see note)

All-purpose flour for dredging

Cut each slice of bread in half. Cut the mozzarella into 12 slices, matching the shape of the bread as much as possible. Place a slice of mozzarella and a small strip of anchovy between two slices of bread. Secure with a toothpick to keep the pieces together.

Beat the eggs with the milk.

Heat 2 to 3 inches of oil in a skillet to the smoking point (see note). Dredge the "sandwiches" in the flour and dip them into the beaten eggs. Fry a few pieces at a time until golden on both sides. Drain on paper towels and serve hot.

NOTE *Add a shot of olive oil to the canola oil for added flavor.*

Before you start frying, lightly soak a small piece of bread in vinegar, and when you think that the oil is hot, add this bread. If the bread floats up immediately, the oil is ready. Also, this bread will absorb any unwanted flavor from the oil. This is very important if you are reusing oil in which you have fried before.

Mortadella with Marinated Mushrooms

MORTADELLA A SORPRESA

A simple antipasto, delicate and flavorful. Mortadella is a kind of salami loved all over Italy but especially in Campania. It is often given to children for their afternoon snack stuffed in a crusty *panino*.

6 servings

1 (5-ounce) jar marinated mushrooms, drained

1 pound whole-milk mozzarella, cubed

6 large thin slices mortadella

Place the mushrooms and mozzarella in the bowl of a food processor and chop finely.

Spread mixture on the slices of mortadella. Roll each slice into a cigar-shaped cylinder and cut in half. Serve.

NOTE *You can also use canned artichokes instead of mushrooms.*

Mortadella and Artichoke Rolls

ROLLATINE DI MORTADELLA CON CARCIOFI

When we were children we loved to have these *rollatine* for our afternoon snack, especially when they were put in a *panino*. You can also use good American ham in place of the mortadella.

6 servings

14 slices mortadella

1 (6-ounce) jar marinated artichokes, drained

2 tablespoons mayonnaise

1 teaspoon dry or fresh unflavored bread crumbs

6 lettuce leaves (any variety)

In the bowl of a food processor place 2 slices of mortadella and the artichokes. Puree and transfer to a bowl. Add the mayonnaise and bread crumbs and mix well.

Spread a small amount of the mixture on each of the remaining mortadella slices and roll them. Place a lettuce leaf on each individual plate, arrange two rolls on each and serve.

NOTE *For cocktails, cut the rolls in half and secure with toothpicks.*

Mushrooms Stuffed with Cheese

FUNGHI RIPIENI DI FORMAGGIO

Mushrooms, whether just grilled, or using your imagination stuffed with a myriad of ingredients, make great antipasti. These are filled with a mixture of ricotta and mozzarella flavored with Parmesan cheese.

6 servings

20 medium to large Portobello mushrooms

2 tablespoons extra-virgin olive oil

1 garlic clove

1 (15-ounce) container whole-milk ricotta, drained

1 pound whole-milk mozzarella, shredded

3 tablespoons freshly grated Parmesan cheese

1 tablespoon chopped fresh Italian parsley

Freshly milled pepper to taste

Preheat the oven to 375 degrees F.

Quickly wash the mushrooms under running water and dry them. Remove and chop the stems. Set the caps aside.

In a large skillet heat 1 tablespoon olive oil and add the chopped mushroom stems and garlic clove. Sauté for a few minutes. Remove from the heat and cool. Remove the garlic and discard.

In a mixing bowl, combine the mushroom stems, ricotta, mozzarella, Parmesan, parsley, and pepper.

Lightly oil a baking sheet with sides in which the caps can fit snugly.

Fill the mushroom caps with the prepared cheese mixture and place the caps on the baking sheet. Bake for 30 minutes and serve hot.

Marinated Anchovies | **ALICI MARINATE**

This is a typical summer antipasto, which the Neapolitans enjoy before lunch sitting on one of their panoramic terraces or gardens overlooking the beautiful Gulf of Naples.

6 servings

1 pound fresh anchovies, heads and bones removed

½ cup white vinegar

1 teaspoon sugar

2 garlic cloves, chopped

2 to 3 teaspoons chopped fresh Italian parsley

Salt to taste

¼ cup extra-virgin olive oil

Wash the anchovies well and dry with paper towels. Layer them in a noncorrosive dish with sides.

Combine the vinegar and sugar and pour over the anchovies. This vinegar marinade pickles, or "cooks," the fish without heat. Cover and refrigerate for 4 hours.

Take the anchovies out of the marinade and pat them dry. Discard the marinade.

Place a layer of anchovies in a serving dish and sprinkle some of the garlic, parsley, and salt over them. Continue layering the rest of the anchovies the same way.

Pour the olive oil over the anchovies 30 minutes before serving.

NOTE *Sometimes a small amount of chopped hot red pepper is also sprinkled on each layer (about one small pepper).*

Tuna-Stuffed Tomatoes | **POMODORI RIPIENI DI TONNO**

When fresh fish is not available, Neapolitans will use canned fish which is excellent in Italy. Tuna is undoubtedly a favorite. Buy the largest plum tomatoes you can find for this recipe.

6 servings

6 large plum tomatoes

1 (6-ounce) can tuna packed in olive oil

2 hard-boiled eggs, chopped

1 tablespoon capers, drained

2 tablespoons chopped fresh Italian parsley

2 tablespoons mayonnaise

Juice of half a lemon

Lettuce leaves for garnish

Cut the tomatoes in half. Gently squeeze out the seeds. Place the tomato halves on a plate cut-side down to drain.

In a bowl, mix the tuna with its oil and the eggs until well combined. Add the capers, parsley, mayonnaise, and lemon juice. Mix well.

Fill the tomato halves with the tuna mixture and serve on a bed of lettuce.

Seafood Salad "Lubrense Style"

INSALATA DI MARE ALLA LUBRENSE

Massa Lubrense is one of the charming towns along the Amalfi Coast, a few miles south of Sorrento. From there, you have a view down to Marina della Lobbia, the small port from where the town gets its fresh seafood. This colorful salad requires a little work but the reward is a delicious, beautifully presented dish. You can do many steps in advance, so don't panic! Use the leftovers to stuff tomatoes.

FISH

1 onion, peeled and with a crisscross cut at the root end

1 carrot

1 celery stalk, trimmed and cut in half

2 sprigs Italian parsley

2 bay leaves

10 peppercorns

Salt to taste

1 slice cod (about 1 pound)

8 ounces scrod

3 whitings, heads on but gutted and cleaned

1 monkfish (about 1 pound)

2 or 3 squids with tentacles

DRESSING

3 tablespoons extra-virgin olive oil

1 tablespoon red wine vinegar

1 hard-boiled egg, quartered

Place the onion, carrot, celery stalk, parsley, bay leaves, peppercorns, and salt in a large pot that can also accommodate the fish. Add enough water to come up 5 to 6 inches above the solids. Bring to a boil, reduce the heat and cook for about 15 minutes.

Add the cod, scrod, whitings, and monkfish. Bring to a boil again and boil for about 15 minutes. Add the squids including their tentacles and cook for 5 minutes. Remove the squids with a slotted spoon and set aside. Remove the pot from the heat and let the fish cool in their own broth.

FOR THE DRESSING Put the oil and vinegar in the food processor and pulse a few times, then add the remaining ingredients for the dressing. Puree and set aside.

FOR THE GARNISH Dice 2 or 3 strips of the roasted peppers and set aside the rest. In a large mixing bowl combine the olive oil, garlic, and parsley. Mix well, then add the diced peppers, potatoes, and tomatoes. Mix again and set aside.

Remove the fish and carrot from the pot. Skin, bone and flake the fish. Cut the bodies of the squid into thin circles and add them to the mixing bowl with the garnish, reserving the tentacles. Add the flaked fish. Dice the carrot and add. Discard the onion and celery but reserve the broth for another use.

1 tablespoon anchovy paste

1 tablespoon dry or fresh unflavored bread crumbs

½ celery stalk, tender part only, finely chopped

½ cup fresh Italian parsley leaves, loosely packed

½ cup fresh basil leaves, loosely packed

1 small bunch chives

2 or 3 small cornichons

Juice of 1 lemon

GARNISH

2 or 3 bell peppers of varied colors, roasted, peeled, and cut into thin strips (see recipe for Roasted Peppers "Neapolitan-Style" on page 35)

2 tablespoons extra-virgin olive oil

1 garlic clove, chopped

1 tablespoon chopped fresh Italian parsley

2 medium unpeeled russet potatoes, boiled and diced

2 firm tomatoes, coarsely chopped

2 tablespoons capers, drained

4 radicchio leaves

Lemon wedges

Add the dressing to the mixing bowl and toss well. Put the mixture into an oval serving dish and sprinkle with capers. Place the tentacles in the middle of the dish as garnish and the radicchio leaves on each end. Place the pepper strips on either side of the dish. Serve with lemon wedges.

NOTE   *This dish can be prepared in advance (even the day before) and refrigerated. Take it out 10 minutes before serving.*

Cranberry Beans and Tuna

ANTIPASTO DI FAGIOLI FRESCHI E TONNO

This dish is usually made during the summer months when cranberry beans, called *spolichini* in Neapolitan dialect, are fresh. It is so nice to see them at the regional markets, spilling out of rustic baskets with their variegated shells shimmering in the sun.

6 to 8 servings

1 pound fresh cranberry beans in their pods, or 1 (16-ounce) can red kidney beans

1 dry bay leaf

1 sprig Italian parsley

Salt to taste

1 (6-ounce) can tuna packed in olive oil

2 tomatoes, diced

1 garlic clove, chopped (optional)

Juice of half a lemon

1 tablespoon extra-virgin olive oil

2 tablespoons balsamic vinegar

1 tablespoon chopped fresh parsley

Shell the cranberry beans and discard the shells. Wash the beans and place them in a large saucepan. Add water to cover, the bay leaf, and parsley. Bring to a boil and add salt. Reduce the heat and simmer for about 30 minutes, or until the beans are tender but not mushy.

Pour some of the oil from the can of tuna into a mixing bowl. Crumble the tuna and add to the bowl with all remaining ingredients. Mix well.

Drain the beans, discard the bay leaf and parsley. Cool and combine with the tuna mixture. Serve.

NOTE *This dish can be prepared in advance. It looks nice when the salad is arranged on a bed of green lettuce.*

Poached Tuna Roll | **SALAME DI TONNO**

Leave it to the Neapolitans to elevate humble fare to make delicious dishes. This tuna roll is a good example.

6 servings

1 (6-ounce) can tuna packed in olive oil

1 small potato, boiled and peeled

3 tablespoons dry or fresh unflavored bread crumbs

1 cornichon, chopped

1 tablespoon chopped fresh Italian parsley

2 eggs

Mayonnaise

6 lemon wedges

Place the tuna with its oil and the potato in a mixing bowl, mash and mix until well combined. Add the bread crumbs, cornichon, parsley, and eggs. Mix well.

With wet hands pick up the tuna mixture and give it the shape of a salami. If it seems too soft, add more bread crumbs.

Wet a piece of cheesecloth or a cloth napkin, wring it out well to extract the water, and place on a work surface. Place the tuna roll on it and carefully wrap the roll with it. Secure with kitchen twine and place into a saucepan where it can fit snugly. Cover with water and bring to a boil. Reduce the heat and simmer for 25 to 30 minutes.

Remove the roll from the water and untie it. Remove the cheesecloth or napkin. Chill the tuna roll, covered loosely with foil, in the refrigerator for at least 1 hour.

To serve, cut the roll in slices. Arrange them on a serving platter, garnish each slice with a dollop of mayonnaise and surround with lemon wedges.

Steamed Vegetables with Lemon Vinaigrette

GIARDINIERA CON SALSA AL LIMONE

A refreshing dish just right for summer, or any other season really. The capers give a special tanginess to the sauce. The Neapolitans prefer their capers in vinegar. If you use the salted ones, rinse them under cold water.

6 servings

LEMON DRESSING

2 celery stalks, trimmed and cut into chunks

5 or 6 sprigs Italian parsley

1 carrot, cut into chunks

1 garlic clove

2 scallions, trimmed but with some of the green parts left on, chopped

¼ cup extra-virgin olive oil

Freshly milled pepper to taste

Juice of half a lemon

2 tablespoons capers, drained

GIARDINIERA

12 asparagus stalks, trimmed, or 3 medium zucchini

8 ounces string beans, trimmed

1 small head cauliflower, cored and cut into florets

1 small bunch broccoli, trimmed and cut into florets

2 hard-boiled eggs, sliced

For the dressing, place all the ingredients except the capers in the bowl of a food processor. Chop finely, place in a serving bowl, stir in the capers, and set aside.

Steam or blanch all the vegetables but keep them crisp. If using zucchini cut each of them lengthwise into six strips.

Arrange the vegetables on a serving plate. Garnish with slices of the hard-boiled eggs. Serve the dressing on the side.

Squid Salad | **INSALATA DI CALAMARI**

Squid should be fresh. A Neapolitan will not eat them if they are one day old. Here, we have to trust our fish market. However, to give them back their sea flavor, brine the squid for 10 to 15 minutes in a bowl of water and 1 tablespoon salt, and then rinse the squid before you cook them.

6 servings

1¾ pounds squid, cleaned, and brined (see above)

½ cup wine vinegar (red or white)

¼ cup extra-virgin olive oil

Salt to taste

Freshly milled pepper to taste

Juice of 1 lemon

3 scallions, thinly sliced

1 clove garlic, chopped

1 tablespoon chopped fresh Italian parsley

Cut the squid into thin ringlets. Cut the tentacles in half if there are any.

In a large saucepan combine the vinegar, ¼ cup water, and 3 tablespoons of the olive oil and bring to a boil. Add the squid, stir well and cook until the liquid begins to boil again. Immediately drain the liquid, transfer the squid to a bowl, and cool completely.

One hour before serving add 1 tablespoon olive oil, salt and pepper, the lemon juice, scallions, garlic, and parsley. Toss well and then again before serving.

Octopus in Tomato Sauce "Luciana" | **POLIPO ALLA LUCIANA**

The name Luciana comes from Santa Lucia, one of the little marinas along the magnificent coastline of the City of Naples. The octopus is highly regarded in Naples and surrounded by superstitions. For instance, a wine cork must be cooked with the octopus to make it tender. I sometimes forget, yet my beast still comes out tender. I agree with the proverb *"Purpe se coce int'all'acqua soia"* ("The octopus cooks in its own juice") because the water released by the octopus is the real flavor.

Another superstition is to encourage men and women of marriageable age to eat octopus as an aphrodisiac. It is also said that in the old days, when Santa Lucia was still a port, prostitutes waiting for the exhausted fishermen to return from their busy workday, would push them upon their return to drink the water from the octopus to enhance their libidos.

6 servings

½ cup extra-virgin olive oil

3 garlic cloves, crushed

1 small hot red pepper, seeds removed (optional)

3 to 4 pounds octopus, washed and each cut into 2 to 3 pieces

1 (28-ounce) can peeled tomatoes, drained and chopped

2 tablespoons chopped fresh Italian parsley

In a large saucepan with a tight-fitting lid, combine the olive oil, garlic, and hot pepper, if used. Stir over medium heat until the garlic starts to color. Add the octopus pieces and stir for a few seconds.

When the water from the octopus starts to accumulate, add the tomatoes. Cover the pot with aluminum foil and the lid. The octopus should cook tightly covered. Bring to a boil and reduce the heat. Cook at a steady simmer for about 40 to 45 minutes.

Sprinkle with parsley and serve hot with a good Italian bread.

NOTE *The Neapolitans like this dish quite spicy; therefore they always use hot pepper. But I prefer a milder taste.*

Roasted Peppers "Neapolitan-Style" | **PEPERONI ALLA NAPOLETANA**

This antipasto is often served as a light dinner, usually on Sundays. In Italy and especially in Naples, the Sunday meal, which is served at lunchtime, is quite abundant.

6 to 8 servings

6 large bell peppers,
a mix of green, yellow and red

¼ cup extra-virgin olive oil

1 tablespoon chopped fresh
Italian parsley

1 tablespoon capers, drained

Salt to taste

Freshly milled pepper to taste

20 black olives, pitted and
coarsely chopped

3 or 4 anchovies packed in oil,
chopped, or 1 teaspoon anchovy
paste

Unflavored dry or fresh bread
crumbs

Roast the peppers by placing them directly on a gas flame or you can use your oven's broiler. Turn them often until their skins are charred. Drop the peppers in a brown bag and close it. This will make it easier to peel the peppers. When cool enough to handle, peel the peppers, core and cut into strips.

Combine the peppers with the olive oil, parsley, capers, salt, and pepper. Mix well and add the olives. If using anchovy paste, mix it with the peppers at this point.

Preheat the oven to 375 degrees F. Oil a 9-inch baking dish from which you can serve and sprinkle with bread crumbs.

Place half of the pepper mixture in one layer in the prepared dish. If using the chopped anchovies, scatter them over the peppers. Top with the remaining pepper mixture, level the top and sprinkle with bread crumbs. Bake for 15 to 20 minutes. Serve hot or at room temperature.

soups

ABOUT BROTH

If Sunday is the day for *ragù* (meat sauce) in Naples, Saturday is the day for *il brodo*. When Neapolitans say *brodo*, they mean broth. Unlike the English language, which does not have words for different types of soups, with the exception of chowder, in Italian there are different terms. We have *zuppa*, which is rather liquid; *minestra*, a soup with two or three ingredients that give a thicker consistency; *minestrone*, which means "big minestra" because usually it contains many ingredients; and *minestrina*, a broth in which some *pastina* (tiny pasta made with eggs) or semolina has been cooked. Angel hair pasta, *tagliolini* (thin homemade noodles), and, on special occasions, tortellini are also served in a fragrant, homemade chicken or beef broth and this soup is usually referred to as *minestra*.

There is nothing better than homemade broth, and it is so easy to prepare. Broth freezes well, so you can always have a supply of it for soups. You can also use it for risotto, pot roasts and stews, and other dishes.

I always buy whole chickens. Unless I am roasting it, I cut the chicken into pieces for the dish I am making, maybe a stew, and reserve the neck, giblets, back and wing tips and freeze them. When I have a good amount of these parts, I ask my butcher to give me a couple of veal bones, which add flavor and make the broth more gelatinous.

Nothing gets wasted when I make broth. After straining the liquid with a fine-mesh colander, I separate the vegetables from the meat and bones. I puree all the vegetables with a food mill for a delicate *crema di verdure* (cream of vegetable soup) that can also be used as a thickener for sauces and as a base for risotto. It also freezes well. I pick all the meat off the chicken bones and use it to make a small chicken salad.

I recommend that you make the broth in advance, strain it and refrigerate it. This way all the fat that has congealed at the top can be easily removed from the surface. Freeze some of the broth in an ice cube tray and then bag the cubes. They are a godsend when sautéing or braising and a healthy substitute for that extra oil or butter.

Often the terms "broth" and "stock" are used interchangeably, but they are in fact different. In a broth, the meat, vegetables, and liquid are placed all together in a large pot and simmered for several hours on the stove. Whereas to prepare a stock, the meat and vegetables are first roasted in the oven and then cooked in a large stockpot. Italians seldom make stocks, which are reserved for some elaborate dishes *alla francese* (French style) or restaurant cooking.

Chicken Broth | **BRODO DI POLLO**

Makes 8 cups of broth or more

3 pounds chicken pieces with bones, or the equivalent in backs, bones, necks, wings, giblets, etc.

2 veal bones

2 celery stalks, cut in half

1 carrot, cut into 4 pieces

1 onion, peeled, with a crisscross cut at the root end and studded with 2 cloves

3 sprigs Italian parsley

1 bunch fennel greens or dill

10 peppercorns

2 bay leaves

Salt to taste

Place all the ingredients in a stockpot. Cover with cold water to come up 2 inches above the solids. Bring to a boil, reduce heat and simmer for about 3 hours. Remove the meat and vegetables for another use, and discard bones. Strain the broth and store in the refrigerator or freezer.

Beef Broth | **BRODO DI MANZO**

The *brodo di manzo* is used to make a heart-warming *minestrone*, which contains a variety of vegetables and often some sort of pasta or rice. Like all broths, this too is better made in advance, strained, and chilled, so that the fat congealed at the top can be easily removed.

Makes 8 cups of broth or more

3 pounds beef with bone, preferably the shin or shoulder

2 veal bones, preferably with marrow

2 celery stalks, cut in half

1 large carrot, cut into 4 pieces

1 large onion, peeled, with a crisscross cut at the root end and studded with 2 cloves

3 sprigs Italian parsley

2 or 3 leaves fennel, including the greens

2 bay leaves

10 peppercorns

Salt to taste

Place all the ingredients in a stockpot and add water to come up 2 inches above the solids. Bring to a boil and simmer over very low heat for about 3 hours. (You can remove the chunk of beef after it has cooked for 2 hours and reserve it for another use.)

Strain the broth and discard the bones, but remove the marrow from the veal bones and reserve it as an addition to a soup. Store the broth in the refrigerator or freezer until ready to use.

NOTE *I pass the vegetables from the broth through a food mill and reserve the puree for another use.*

Mushroom Broth | **BRODO DI FUNGHI**

Never one to throw anything away, my mother used mushrooms that were not perfect and stems that were too big or tough for mushroom broth. She always added a good handful of dried porcini for a truly earthy aroma. To further enhance its flavor, she dropped into the broth a bouillon cube, which, especially during the lean war years, she considered a godsend. Nowadays, I like to use as a base my homemade chicken broth (recipe on page 39). But I would not hesitate to use the ubiquitous "Knorr" bouillon cube. As a matter of fact, I always have some around.

The mushroom broth was mostly used for soups and risotto, but also for fish and meat dishes to enhance their taste. I freeze some of this broth in ice cube trays, and when I am sautéing something and it starts to stick, I do not run for butter or oil, but for my little cube. Not only does it lubricate the pan but it also gives the food more flavor.

Makes 6 to 7 cups

¼ cup dried porcini mushrooms

1 pound mushrooms

1 garlic clove, crushed

1 bunch scallions, greens included, each cut into 4 pieces

1 carrot, sliced

1 celery stalk, cut into 8 pieces

2 sprigs Italian parsley plus more chopped for garnish

2 bay leaves

¾ teaspoon chopped fresh thyme, or ¼ teaspoon dried thyme

2 cloves

¼ teaspoon seven herbs (see note)

5 or 6 peppercorns

1 tablespoon tomato paste

8 cups chicken broth

Soak the dried porcini in a cup of lukewarm water for about 15 to 20 minutes.

Meanwhile, cut off the bottoms of the mushroom stems and discard. Chop the remaining mushrooms. In a large stockpot, place mushrooms and all remaining ingredients except the chopped parsley.

Gently, as not to upset the sediments at the bottom, lift the dried porcini mushrooms from the water and add to the pot. Strain the soaking water through a paper towel and add as well. Bring to a boil, reduce the heat and simmer for about 35 to 40 minutes. Strain the broth.

Remove the bay leaves, and puree all the solids in a food processor or pass through a food mill. Ladle the mixture into individual soup bowls, add some of the broth, sprinkle with the chopped parsley and serve. Store the remaining broth in the refrigerator or freezer until needed.

NOTE   *The seven herbs in this combination are sage, thyme, rosemary, basil, oregano, mint, and marjoram. The mixture can enhance any roast or sauce. Try it!*

The puree can also be used as a thickener or a base for a sauce. Both the puree and broth freeze well. You can also use canned artichokes instead of mushrooms.

Egg Drop Soup | **STRACCIATELLA**

This is a quick soup that is made all over Italy. All you need is a good broth, a few eggs, some Parmesan cheese, and a good (or nasty) cold! I am not joking. When we were children, this was the panacea to soothe all the pain and discomfort of influenza. It is also a good dish for a winter night, when you have had a big lunch. My father used to say that it was a digestive.

4 servings

5 cups chicken or beef broth

3 eggs

2 tablespoons freshly grated Parmesan cheese

Bring the broth to a boil.

In a bowl beat the eggs and add the cheese. Gently drop the mixture into the boiling broth, stirring it in with a whisk. Cook for 3 to 5 minutes and serve.

NOTE *My mother's friend Mrs. Contegno, an excellent cook who lived next door to us in Naples, used to add zucchini to this soup.*

Chicken Soup with Almonds | **ZUPPA RINASCIMENTALE**

An elegant soup—surely a creation of one of the foreign chefs serving the Neapolitan aristocrats during the past glorious times of the Kingdom of Naples.

4 servings

1 slice white bread

1 to 2 tablespoons milk

6 almonds, blanched

1 cooked chicken breast, skinned, boned and cubed

7 cups homemade chicken broth

Freshly grated Parmesan cheese

Tear the bread into small pieces and put in a mixing bowl. Add enough milk to wet the bread. Place in a food processor together with the almonds and chicken. Process until reduced to a creamy consistency. Add 1 cup of the broth and process for a few seconds. Transfer the mixture into a tureen.

Bring the rest of the broth to a boil and pour into the tureen. Serve with a bowl of Parmesan to sprinkle on top.

Hearty Soup | **ZUPPA ALLA SANTÉ**

A good chicken broth was a luxury in the old days, and especially during the war when food was scarce. Everybody raised chickens for the eggs, especially those with the good fortune of having a backyard or a terrace.

At the time my family lived in Naples, we had our washerwoman tending our chickens in her garden outside the city walls. She would bring us the eggs every time she came to pick up or return our laundry. But if she arrived with a chicken in her hand, it elicited a chorus of *che peccato!* (what a pity!), because it meant no more eggs. But for my brother and me it was happiness. It meant a hearty chicken broth, maybe with some beaten eggs and little meatballs for this delicious version of stracciatella, and of course a luxurious second course of boiled chicken with mother's superb green sauce. The word *santé* ("health" in French) in the name of this soup is another reminder of the influence of French cuisine in Naples.

6 servings

12 ounces ground meat, a combination of beef and veal

4 eggs

6 tablespoons freshly grated Parmesan cheese

2 tablespoons very fine unflavored dry bread crumbs

1 tablespoon chopped fresh Italian parsley

2 tablespoons extra-virgin olive oil

½ tablespoon unsalted butter

7 cups chicken broth

In a mixing bowl, combine the ground meat with 1 egg, 3 tablespoons of Parmesan, the bread crumbs, and parsley. Stir with a wooden spoon until well combined. Put about 1 teaspoon of this mixture in the palm of your hand and shape it into a little ball, the size of a cherry. Repeat until all the meat mixture is used.

In a large skillet, heat the oil and butter. Gently sauté the meatballs for a few minutes until brown. Set aside.

Bring the broth to a boil.

Add the meatballs to the broth and simmer for about 5 minutes. Beat 3 eggs with the remaining Parmesan and add to the pot. Stir vigorously with a whisk for 2 to 3 minutes. Serve hot with additional Parmesan if desired.

Thin Noodles in Broth | **TAGLIOLINI IN BRODO**

King Vittorio Emanuele II, called "the father of our country" for his important part in unifying Italy, loved *tagliolini*. When he stayed at his royal palace in Naples, his servants related that the king ate his *tagliolini* with great gusto, sporting a large napkin knotted behind his ears to protect his uniform and medals.

To make your *tagliolini* as fine as the tradition commands, you must stretch the *sfoglia* (sheet of dough) very thin. Keep in mind though, that you can stretch the dough with a pasta machine, but you have to cut the *tagliolini* by hand.

6 to 8 servings

Basic Pasta Dough prepared with 3 eggs (recipe on page 92)

7 to 8 cups homemade chicken broth

Freshly grated Parmesan cheese

Make the dough according to the recipe. Stretch the dough as thin as possible. If using a pasta machine, go to the last setting.

As soon as you finish one sheet, sprinkle it lightly with flour and roll it up. Cut it into very fine strands with a sharp knife. Unravel the strands and place them on trays lined with kitchen towels. Repeat until you finish all the dough.

Bring the broth to a boil. Add the *tagliolini* and stir gently. Let the broth come up to a boil, cook for 1 to 2 minutes and serve with Parmesan on the side.

NOTE *If I have a very good broth I prefer my* tagliolini *without cheese, but I always put a bowl of grated Parmesan at the table. Mrs. Cortelli Lucrezi, the Italian food writer, adds chicken livers sautéed with a little onion and 2 to 3 diced tomatoes to this soup.*

Noodle Soup with Meatballs

ZUPPA DI DITALINI CON BRODO E PALLINE DI CARNE

This elegant and nourishing soup, made with chicken broth, is one of the Saturday dishes usually served to guests, but is also very good just for the family.

6 servings

8 ounces ground meat, an equal mixture of beef, pork, and veal

1 egg, beaten

2 tablespoons finely chopped fresh Italian parsley

Salt to taste

Freshly milled pepper to taste

1 tablespoon extra-virgin olive oil

1 tablespoon unsalted butter

2 tablespoons dry Marsala wine

8 ounces ditalini pasta, or any other kind of small pasta

10 cups hot homemade chicken broth (recipe on page 39)

Freshly grated Parmesan cheese

Place the meat in a mixing bowl. Add the egg, 1 tablespoon parsley, salt, and pepper. Mix well and shape into very small meatballs the size of an olive.

In a skillet, heat the olive oil and butter and sauté the meatballs until brown, about 5 minutes. Pour off the fat from the skillet and return it to the heat. Add the Marsala and simmer until evaporated.

Cook the pasta in boiling salted water for 5 minutes. Meanwhile, bring the broth to a boil. Drain the pasta and add to the hot broth. Simmer until the pasta is almost cooked, about 10 minutes. Add the meatballs and 1 tablespoon parsley. Serve the soup with a bowl of Parmesan cheese on the side.

Pumpkin Soup with Pastina | **PASTINA E ZUCCA IN BRODO**

The Neapolitans are fond of pumpkin, and when they are in season, pumpkins appear in quite a few dishes. After seeing those marvelous pumpkins and squashes coloring the highways of America every fall, I searched for this recipe that I think is quite good. Do not discard the seeds of the pumpkin, they can be washed and dried in a slow oven. If you wish you can sprinkle them with a little salt. In Naples roasted pumpkin seeds are much appreciated and sold from pushcarts with the amusing name of *spassatiempo* (pastime).

6 servings

1 fresh yellow pumpkin, about 3 pounds, preferably a turban squash

1 tablespoon extra-virgin olive oil

1 tablespoon unsalted butter

1 large leek, white part only, well rinsed and chopped

Salt to taste

7 cups homemade chicken broth

¼ cup *acini di pepe* pastina

Freshly grated Parmesan cheese

Preheat the oven to 350 degrees F.

Cut the pumpkin in half and remove the seeds and filaments. Place the pumpkin halves on a baking sheet with a rim, cut side up, and add 1 cup water. Bake for 20 to 30 minutes. This will make the pumpkin softer and easy to cut. Cool, peel, and cut into small cubes.

In a large stockpot, place the olive oil and butter, add the leek and sauté for 5 to 6 minutes. Add the pumpkin cubes and salt and cook stirring for 5 to 6 minutes, then add enough broth to come up 1 inch above the solids. Bring to a boil, reduce heat and simmer for about 30 minutes or until pumpkin is tender. Allow to cool slightly.

Puree the soup in a food processor. Return mixture to the pot and add the remaining broth. Bring to a boil and add the pastina. Cook over medium heat for 8 to 10 minutes, or until the pastina is cooked. Serve with Parmesan cheese.

NOTE *Instead of using pumpkin, I also make this soup with grated zucchini or with spinach, peas or potatoes diced very small.*

Escarole Soup

MINESTRA DI SCAROLA

This soup, which is good in every season, is a favorite in Naples during the winter months.

6 servings or more

2 heads escarole or curly endive, about 1½ to 2 pounds total, trimmed and washed

2 tablespoons extra-virgin olive oil

2 garlic cloves, chopped

1 carrot, shredded

1 (16-ounce) can tomato puree

1½ teaspoons chopped fresh basil or oregano, or ½ teaspoon dried

5 to 6 cups homemade chicken or beef broth

30 *ciliegine* (see note), or 8 ounces fresh whole-milk mozzarella, cut into small cubes

Freshly grated Parmesan cheese

Blanch the escarole for 3 to 5 minutes in boiling water and drain, reserving 2 cups of the cooking water. When the escarole is cool enough to handle, chop coarsely.

Heat the olive oil in a large pot and add the garlic and shredded carrot, cook 5 minutes while stirring. Add the tomato puree. Fill the can half full with some of the reserved water from the escarole, swirl to rinse and add the water to the pot. Add the basil or oregano, bring to a boil and simmer for 10 minutes. Add the chopped escarole and cook for 5 minutes, stirring. Add the broth, stir again and cook for about 10 minutes. If you like your soup on the thinner side, add more of the escarole cooking water.

Ladle the soup into individual bowls, put 5 *ciliegine* or mozzarella cubes in each bowl and serve with Parmesan cheese.

NOTE Ciliegine *are small, fresh mozzarella balls sold in tubs in supermarkets.*

Bread Soup | **MINESTRA DI PANE**

This is another dish from the *cucina povera*. The addition of the bouillon cube was a stratagem used to pretend that the *minestra* was made with real broth. If you have broth, by all means use it. And, as you can see, legumes are a crucial ingredient.

6 servings

1 tablespoon extra-virgin olive oil

2 slices pancetta, coarsely chopped

1 carrot, coarsely chopped

1 medium onion, coarsely chopped

2 cups cooked beans (chickpeas, fava beans) or cooked lentils

4 ripe tomatoes, cubed

1 small bunch Swiss chard, cut into strips

1 or 2 chicken bouillon cubes (optional)

1 tablespoon chopped fresh Italian parsley

6 slices all-wheat or hard-crusted bread, toasted and cubed

Freshly grated Pecorino Romano cheese

In a large pot heat the olive oil and add the pancetta. Cook until the fat is rendered, then add the carrot and onion. Cook stirring until the onion is translucent, about 5 minutes. Add the beans, tomatoes, and chard. Cook stirring for about 5 minutes, then add 6 cups water and the bouillon cube(s). Bring to a boil, reduce the heat to a simmer and cook for about 30 minutes. Add the parsley at the end.

Divide the bread among 6 individual soup bowls. Ladle the soup into the bowls and serve with the grated cheese.

Minestrone with Meats and Greens | **MINESTRA MARITATA**

It is difficult to translate this name. *Maritata* literally means "married"—in this case, it is meat "marrying" the vegetables. Its origins go back to the Romans.

Nowadays this *minestra* is seldom made, and when you read the ingredients you will know why. But because it is so Neapolitan, I had to include it. However, I kept in mind today's nutrition demands and cut down the fat as much as possible. You must use fresh herbs for this *minestra*—we Italians call this herb combination *erbe aromatiche*.

I usually make the first four steps the day before serving the soup and refrigerate the meat and broth overnight. This way I can skim all the fat accumulated at the top and have a lean broth.

6 servings

1 bunch rosemary

10 to 12 sprigs Italian parsley, including stems

1 sprig sage

2 or 3 sprigs thyme

1 bunch broccoli rabe

1 bunch kale

1 head escarole, coarsely chopped

1 head chicory, root removed and coarsely chopped

1 large head Savoy cabbage, shredded

1 prosciutto bone

1 thick slice prosciutto (about 2 ounces), diced

1 pound dried sausage or Italian salami in one piece

Tie the rosemary, parsley, sage, and thyme into a bunch.

Wash, trim and cut the broccoli rabe and kale. Wash and combine all the greens in a bowl (see note).

In a large stockpot, preferably enameled cast iron, put the herbs, prosciutto bone, prosciutto, sausage, pancetta, and Parmesan rinds. Cover with water to come up 2 inches above the solids. Bring to a boil and simmer for about 2 hours. The meats should be always covered with water, so add more if necessary.

When the meats are tender, transfer them to a bowl with a little broth to keep them wet. Discard the herbs and Parmesan rinds. At this point, you can refrigerate the meats and broth until the next day, when you can remove the fat off the top of the broth.

When ready to put the minestra together, dice the meats and return to the pot. Add the broth and bring to a boil. Add the greens, making sure there is enough liquid. If not, add some water, depending on how thin you want the soup. Simmer for about 10 minutes, or until the greens are tender. Serve, passing the grated cheese around.

1 thick slice pancetta (about 2 ounces), diced

3 or 4 pieces Parmesan rinds, wax part scrubbed (see note)

Freshly grated Pecorino Romano cheese

NOTE   *To wash the combined greens, I put them in a bowl to which I add 1 tablespoon of kosher salt and water to cover. I let it stand 20 minutes before draining and rinsing. This removes any grit from the greens.*

I never throw away the rind of Parmesan cheese after using it. I save it for uses such as this. Scrub the wax off the rind with a knife, this is easier to do holding the rind under hot water.

Minestrone

This is a big minestra with a lot of vegetables, rounded off with some small pasta or rice. It is nourishing and filling, especially if one includes some legume, which the Neapolitans do all the time. This is a dish from the *cucina povera*, the cooking of the poor. If a prosciutto bone was available, it became a "regal soup," as my father used to call it. You can also use a bouillon cube, which I do here, for extra meat flavor.

6 to 8 servings

2 tablespoons extra-virgin olive oil

1 large onion, coarsely chopped

2 garlic cloves, chopped

2 carrots, diced

2 celery stalks, trimmed and diced

1 (28-ounce) can peeled tomatoes

2 large potatoes, peeled and diced

2 medium zucchini, diced

1 small Savoy cabbage, shredded

2 cups peas, fresh or frozen

2 chicken or beef bouillon cubes

Salt to taste

Freshly milled pepper to taste

1/2 cup rice, or 1/2 cup small pasta like *tubettini, quadrucci, orzo*

2 tablespoons chopped fresh Italian parsley

Freshly grated Parmesan cheese

In a large stockpot heat the olive oil and add the onion, garlic, carrots, and celery. Sauté for about 10 minutes, stirring often.

Drain the tomatoes, reserving the liquid. Chop the tomatoes and add them to the pot. Cook for 5 to 8 minutes, then add the vegetables. If using frozen peas, reserve them to add during the last 5 minutes. Add the liquid from the tomatoes, 8 cups water, the bouillon cubes, and salt and pepper to taste. Bring to a boil and simmer until the vegetables are almost tender, about 25 to 30 minutes. Add the rice or the pasta and cook until tender, about 10 to 12 minutes. Add the chopped parsley and serve with a bowl of Parmesan cheese on the side.

NOTE   *You can use other vegetables, such as string beans, cauliflower, broccoli, fresh fava beans, escarole, etc.*

Pasta and Bean Soup | **PASTA E FAGIOLI**

This minestra is probably the most Italian of all Italian soups. Of course the Tuscans brag about their version—after all aren't they called *mangia fagioli* (bean eaters)? The Venetians also think theirs is the best, but let's not forget the Neapolitans. The Italian actor Marcello Mastroianni swore that the best *pasta e fagioli* is the one made by his friend, the very Neapolitan Sophia Loren.

This soup is often made with a prosciutto bone. If you have one, by all means add it to the soup. In the summer the people from Campania use *spolichini* (fresh cranberry beans). The fresh noodles are cooked directly in the *minestra* since they do not need much cooking. However, if you prefer to use another kind of short dry pasta, I recommend cooking it for 5 minutes in a separate pot before adding it to the soup.

6 servings

1 ½ cups dried beans, preferably cannellini, borlotti, or chickpeas

1 ham bone, cut into 2 pieces

1 dry bay leaf

1 (16-ounce) can peeled tomatoes

3 to 4 tablespoons extra-virgin olive oil

1 onion, chopped

1 garlic clove, chopped

1 celery stalk, finely chopped

1 carrot, chopped

2 sprigs Italian parsley, chopped

1 tablespoon tomato paste

A touch of hot pepper (optional)

8 ounces wide flat egg noodles, preferably homemade, or *tubettini* or elbow macaroni

Salt to taste

Sort the beans to remove any possible impurity, rinse and plunge them in a pot of boiling water. Cook for 10 minutes then rinse under running cold water. This will remove the indigestible "patina" on the skin of the beans, which causes those unpleasant intestinal problems.

Place the beans in a large heavy pot, preferably enameled cast iron. Add the ham bones and water to come up to 3 inches above the beans. Add the bay leaf and bring to a boil. Reduce heat and simmer for 45 minutes, or until beans are almost tender.

Drain the liquid from the tomatoes and reserve. Cut the tomatoes in slices. Set aside.

Heat the oil in a large skillet and sauté the chopped vegetables for 5 to 8 minutes. Add the tomato slices, tomato paste, and hot pepper if used. Add a little of the reserved juice from the tomato can and cook for 15 to 20 minutes. Add this mixture to the pot with the beans. Continue cooking for about 10 minutes. Then add the remaining water from the tomato can, and if there is not enough liquid to cook the noodles, add 2 cups or more of hot water. Bring to a boil and add the noodles. Cook until the noodles are done, 5 to 8 minutes. Taste for flavor and if necessary, add a little salt. Remove the bay leaf and discard. Remove the ham bones, shred the meat from the bones and return the meat to the pot. Serve hot.

Cranberry Bean Soup with Pasta

PASTA E FAGIOLI FRESCHI (SPOLICHINI)

This flavorful *minestra* is made with fresh beans, which the Neapolitans call *spolichini*. They are fresh cranberry beans, which today appear more often in produce stores and green markets. The beans are sold unshelled, in their bright red-speckled pods. They cook faster than the dried type and are easier to digest.

6 to 8 servings

2 pounds fresh unshelled cranberry beans, or 1 (16-ounce) can red kidney beans

2 tablespoons extra-virgin olive oil

1 onion, chopped

1 (14.5-ounce) can peeled tomatoes

1 tablespoon tomato paste

1 garlic clove, chopped

Salt to taste

1 cup small pasta, such as shells, elbow macaroni, or *tubettini*

2 teaspoons chopped fresh Italian parsley

Remove the beans from the pods and drop the beans in a bowl of cold water. Set aside.

Heat the olive oil in a large pot with a heavy bottom. Add the onion and sauté for 5 minutes. Add the tomatoes with their liquid, tomato paste, garlic, and salt. If using the fresh beans, drain the beans and add to the pot. Cook, stirring, for 5 minutes.

Add 2 cups of water, cover and bring to a boil. Lower the heat and simmer until the beans are tender, about 30 minutes. Make sure there is enough liquid in the pot and add more if necessary.

Meanwhile, cook the pasta in boiling salted water for 5 to 6 minutes. Drain, reserving two cups of the cooking liquid, and add one cup to the pot with the soup. Let the mixture come back to a boil, then add the pasta. Simmer until the pasta is tender, about 5 minutes. You may need to add more of the cooking liquid.

If using the canned beans, drain and add them to the pot. Cook a few more minutes to warm the beans. This dish should be rather soupy. Add the chopped parsley, stir and serve.

Soup with Pasta, Potatoes and Tomatoes

ZUPPA DI PASTA E PATATE AL POMODORO

Pasta and potatoes may seem a strange combination, but in Naples this soup is very popular. My mother used to add little meatballs made with a mixture of beef, pork and veal to this soup. I prefer a mixture of cut-up chicken giblets and hearts. Both give a more succulent flavor to this dish.

6 servings

½ cup small pasta, like *tubettini* or elbow macaroni

3 tablespoons extra-virgin olive oil

1 onion, finely chopped

1 pound mixture of chicken giblets and hearts, chopped

1 (28-ounce) can peeled tomatoes

1 garlic clove

2 sprigs Italian parsley

½ cup loosely packed basil leaves

3 medium potatoes, peeled and cut into small cubes

2 bay leaves

Salt to taste

Freshly milled pepper to taste

Freshly grated Parmesan or Grana Padano cheese (see note)

Cook the pasta in salted boiling water for about 10 minutes. With a slotted spoon transfer the pasta to a bowl, add 1 tablespoon olive oil, stir and set aside. Discard water.

Return the pot in which the pasta cooked to the heat, add 2 tablespoons olive oil and the onion. Cook over low heat, stirring for about 5 to 8 minutes. Add the giblet and heart mixture and cook until brown, about 5 to 8 minutes. Add the tomatoes and their juice. Bring to a boil and simmer for 10 minutes.

Chop the garlic, parsley, and basil. Add half of this mixture to the pot. Add the potatoes, bay leaves, and 1 cup water. Stir and cook for 10 minutes. Season with salt and pepper, then add 4 cups water. Bring to a boil, lower heat, and simmer for about 30 to 40 minutes, or until the potatoes are soft, stirring once in a while. Add the pasta, stir and cook until tender. If you prefer this *minestra* soupier, add some hot water before adding the pasta.

Remove the bay leaves. Stir in the remaining garlic, parsley, and basil. Serve with the grated cheese.

NOTE *Parmesan and Grana Padano are similar cheeses. The Grana Padano is made in a different region than the Parmesan and can therefore not be called the same.*

Soup with Beets, Potatoes and Zucchini

ZUPPA DI RAPE ROSSE, PATATE E ZUCCHINE

This is a country soup, the true product of the peasants of "Campania Felix," as the Romans called this region. When I came to America, I started to call this soup "Italian Borscht" as it is made with bright red beets. The balsamic vinegar and the yogurt are my ideas.

6 servings

3 beets

8 cups chicken or beef broth

1 large potato, peeled and diced

1 or 2 zucchini, diced

3 scallions, green parts included, cut into ¼-inch pieces

3 tablespoons balsamic vinegar

Plain yogurt (optional)

Remove and discard the stems and leaves from the beets, if any. Wash and scrub the beets well. Place them in a pan, cover with water, bring to a boil, reduce the heat and cook until tender, 40 to 45 minutes. Cool in their own water. When cool enough to handle, remove the beets from the water, reserving the water. If necessary filter the water through a paper towel. Peel the beets, dice them and set aside.

In a large pot place the broth, and the water from the beets and bring to a boil. Add the diced potato. When the potato is almost tender, about 15 to 20 minutes, add the zucchini. Bring to a boil again and simmer for 5 to 8 minutes, then add the beets, scallions, and vinegar. Continue cooking 5 more minutes. Serve with a spoonful of yogurt, if you wish.

Clam and Mussel Soup

ZUPPA DI VONGOLE E COZZE

This soup is usually served with toasted or fried bread to absorb the flavorful sauce, which has a fresh sea taste, enriched by the tomatoes. In the summer, ripe juicy tomatoes should be substituted for canned tomatoes.

6 servings

2 pounds mussels

1 pound clams

1 tablespoon flour

3 tablespoons extra-virgin olive oil

2 garlic cloves, crushed

1 (28-ounce) can peeled tomatoes

1 tablespoon chopped fresh Italian parsley

Place the mussels and clams in a large bowl, cover with water and toss with the flour. This will release possible sand residue.

Heat the olive oil in a large saucepan. Add the garlic and cook until the oil starts to sizzle. Add the tomatoes with all their liquid from the can. Rinse the can with 1 cup water and add. Stir with a wooden spoon, crushing the tomatoes as much as possible. Cover, reduce the heat and simmer for about 10 minutes.

Rinse the mussels and clams and add them to the casserole. Raise the heat and cook until they open. Their juices will add flavor to the sauce. (Discard any mussels or clams that do not open.)

Serve in soup bowls and sprinkle with parsley.

NOTE *Nowadays mussels are sold with their beards removed, but check them, and if necessary, remove the beards.*

pizza

LORE AND HISTORY

In my book *The Wonderful World of Pizzas, Quiches and Savory Pies*, I wrote that the pizza we eat today is the sole invention of the Neapolitans. And in *The Food of Italy*, the late American writer Waverly Root pointed out that "the antiquity of pizza as a Neapolitan dish is firmly established." The Neapolitans spread their beloved pizza to all corners of the world.

But where and when did it start? In the Bible we find a story about a famished Elijah sleeping in the wilderness: "And as he lay and slept under a juniper tree … an angel touched him and said unto him 'Arise and eat.' And he looked, and, low and behold, there was a cake baked in the coals and a cruse of water at his head." The "cake" made with some sort of grain and water is called *focaccia* in the Italian version of the Bible. The term derives from the Latin "focus" which indicates that it appeared on top of a scorching stone.

Many of today's breads have Neolithic origins—the Mexican tortilla, the Scottish oatcake, the Egyptian ta, and even the johnnycakes whose preparation the American settlers learned from the Indians. In the *Aeneid*, the Roman poet Virgil writes about Aeneas and his chiefs and captains "cooking the 'cake' on swords, as on a grill . . . turn their teeth upon the slender cakes to profane with hand and jaw the fateful 'circle of crust'." That "fateful circle of crust" is undoubtedly a *focaccia* or flatbread.

The crown of the Neapolitan pizza has always been the tomato, which arrived from Peru. The Italian expression *vale un Perú* to describe something of great value reflects the importance of the tomato. Pizza *al pomodoro* (with tomato), undoubtedly the invention of the Neapolitans, *vale un Perú*!

Focaccia and Pizza Dough | **PASTA PER FOCACCIA E PIZZA**

There is not much difference between a pizza and a focaccia. They are made with the same dough, and both are flatbreads. They can be cooked completely unadorned, with only a sprinkling of salt and a drizzle of oil. For pizza, after the dough has risen once, it is usually stretched very thin (this is the way I like it) and topped with some condiment. The focaccia dough should rise twice, and it is shaped thicker than pizza. The focaccia takes very simple toppings: olive oil, kosher salt, rosemary or sage, a few chunks of fresh tomatoes or some anchovies.

This is a basic recipe. It can be done in a food processor, and it freezes well.

Makes 1 (9 × 12-inch) rectangular focaccia, or 2 (12-inch) pizzas

1 package active dry yeast

1 cup lukewarm water

1/2 teaspoon sugar

3 1/2 cups all-purpose or bread flour

1 1/2 teaspoons salt

3 tablespoons extra-virgin olive oil

Dissolve the yeast in the water, add the sugar and 1 teaspoon of the flour. Mix and let stand for 10 minutes. If a bubbly foam forms at the top, the yeast is alive and you can proceed with the recipe.

In a food processor combine 3 cups of the flour and the salt. Add the olive oil and yeast mixture. Process until a ball forms on the blades. If this doesn't happen, add a little more water. On the other hand, if the mixture is too wet, add more flour.

Place the dough on a floured pastry board. Knead and slap the dough on the board for about 10 to 15 minutes, adding more flour if necessary. The dough should be elastic, smooth, and pliable.

Gather the dough into a ball and place it in a lightly oiled bowl. Mark a crisscross cut on top of the dough with a knife, cover with plastic wrap and a few kitchen towels, set in a warm place and let the dough rise for 1 hour, or until doubled in size.

Before using, punch the dough down and knead a little. If the dough is to be used for a focaccia, let it rise a second time. After the first rising, the dough can be punched down, wrapped in plastic wrap and refrigerated or frozen. If frozen, thaw in the refrigerator overnight.

NOTE *For a crispier crust use 1 cup whole-wheat flour mixed with 2 cups of the all-purpose or bread flour. This dough can be used for any kind of pizza. It works well when stuffed, such as for a calzone.*

Whole-Wheat Pizza Dough | **PASTA PER FOCACCIA E PIZZA**

Makes 1 (9 × 12-inch) rectangular focaccia, or 2 (12-inch) pizzas

1 package active dry yeast

1 cup lukewarm water

1½ cups whole-wheat flour

2½ cups bread flour

2 teaspoons salt

3 tablespoons extra-virgin olive oil

Combine the yeast and water, stir and set aside for about 10 minutes, or until a foam rises to the top.

In a food processor combine the whole-wheat flour, 2 cups of the bread flour and the salt. Add the olive oil and yeast mixture. Process until a ball forms on the blades. If this doesn't happen, add a little more water. On the other hand, if the mixture is too wet, add more flour.

Place the dough on a floured board and knead for about 10 to 15 minutes, adding more flour if necessary. The dough should be elastic, smooth and pliable.

Gather the dough into a ball and place it in a lightly oiled bowl. Mark a crisscross cut on top of the dough with a knife, cover with plastic wrap and a few kitchen towels, set in a warm place and let the dough rise for 1 hour, or until doubled in size.

Before using, punch the dough down and knead a little. If the dough is to be used for a focaccia let it rise a second time. After the first rising, the dough can be punched down, wrapped in plastic wrap and refrigerated or frozen. If frozen, thaw in the refrigerator overnight.

Basic Focaccia

After you have mastered the pizza dough (see recipes pages 59 and 60), you can make all sorts of focaccias. However, the dough must rise a second time. The focaccia is not as thin as pizza, it should be at least 1½ inches high before baking it on a rectangular baking sheet.

The simplest of all focaccia recipes uses just a little olive oil and a sprinkle of salt.

In Naples the favorite focaccia is topped with herbs. Rosemary is the most popular, but it is up to your taste to try other flavors. It is then baked at 400 degrees F for 20 to 25 minutes. Serve the focaccia warm and cut into squares.

For stuffed focaccia, split a square in half horizontally, spread your favorite cold cuts, cheese or other ingredients on half of the square and cover with the remaining half.

Focaccia with Anchovies | **FOCACCIA DELLA VIGILIA**

This focaccia is traditionally eaten at lunch on Christmas Eve to break the fast practiced by Italian Catholics on this day. Of course for Americans, eating something like a pizza for lunch is not their idea of sacrifice, but do not forget that in Italy the main meal is at lunchtime. Then for the Christmas Eve evening meal, there is the famous *cenone*, a big dinner whose many courses consist mostly of fish.

8 or more servings

Extra-virgin olive oil

1 batch Focaccia and Pizza Dough (recipe on page 59)

5 or 6 anchovies packed in oil, cut into pieces

Kosher salt to taste

Freshly ground pepper to taste

Preheat the oven to 400 degrees F.

Lightly oil a 10 × 15-inch baking sheet. Place the dough on the prepared sheet. With oiled fingers, stretch the dough into a ¾-inch-thick rectangle the size of the baking sheet. Press your fingers into the dough and make little wells about 2 inches apart. Press the pieces of anchovy into them. Drizzle with olive oil and sprinkle with salt and pepper.

Bake until the edges of the focaccia start to brown, 15 to 20 minutes. Cut into squares and serve.

Herb Focaccia | **FOCACCIA ALLE HERBE**

This focaccia can be eaten alone or stuffed with delicate cheeses, such as Fontina, Robbiola or a good fresh mozzarella and a touch of prosciutto for a delicious lunch sandwich.

Makes 1 (9 × 12-inch)
rectangular focaccia

½ cup warm milk

2 packages active dry yeast

¼ cup extra-virgin olive oil plus more for brushing

½ teaspoon freshly milled black pepper

1 tablespoon chopped fresh rosemary, or 1 teaspoon dried

1 tablespoon chopped fresh thyme, or 1 teaspoon dried

1 tablespoon chopped fresh oregano, or 1 teaspoon dried

1 tablespoon chopped fresh basil, or 1 teaspoon dried

1 sprig Italian parsley

3 to 4 cups bread flour

½ teaspoon salt

Kosher salt for sprinkling

In a bowl combine the milk, yeast and ¼ cup olive oil.

In a food processor, combine the pepper and all the herbs. Process for a few seconds, then add 3½ cups of flour and the salt. Process to mix well, then start adding the milk-yeast mixture. Stop as soon as a ball forms on the blades. If this doesn't happen, add a little more milk. On the other hand, if the mixture is too wet, add more flour.

Place the dough on a floured board and knead, adding more flour when necessary until the dough is smooth and elastic, about 15 to 20 minutes. Place the dough in an oiled bowl, cover with plastic wrap and a few kitchen towels, set in a warm place and let the dough rise for 1 hour, or until doubled in size.

Preheat the oven to 350 degrees F and lightly oil a baking sheet.

Spread the dough about 1-inch thick on the baking sheet. Dimple the dough with your fingers, brush with olive oil and sprinkle with a little bit of kosher salt. Bake for 30 to 40 minutes or until the top is golden brown. Remove from the oven, brush again with a little olive oil, cool before cutting.

Pizza with Tomatoes

PIZZA CLASSICA NAPOLETANA

A Neapolitan will tell you that one can live with a piece of bread, a tomato, and a little olive oil. True! You will often see Italian children snack on a slab of thick bread smeared with olive oil and topped with a few slices of fresh, red tomatoes. It takes only one step and a little inventiveness to turn this simple repast into a succulent pizza. Bear in mind that in Italy, and especially in Naples, the pizzas are never very large. The 8-inch pizzas from this recipe are the usual size for an individual serving.

Makes 2 (8-inch) pizzas

1 batch Focaccia and Pizza Dough (recipe on page 59)

2 or 3 ripe, fresh tomatoes, cut in slices

1½ teaspoons chopped fresh oregano, or ½ teaspoon dried

2 tablespoons extra-virgin olive oil

Salt and pepper to taste

Preheat the oven to 400 degrees F and lightly oil two 8-inch pizza pans.

Divide the dough into two balls and place them in the prepared pans. With oiled hands, stretch the dough the size of the pan, as thin as possible. Shape a wall of dough all around the edges to better contain the topping.

In a mixing bowl, place the sliced tomatoes and oregano. Add the olive oil and toss. Set the tomatoes evenly on the dough. Sprinkle with a little salt and pepper.

Bake for 15 to 20 minutes, or until the edges of the dough start to brown. Cut into wedges and serve.

Pizza with Tomatoes, Mozzarella and Basil

PIZZA MARGHERITA

In my opinion, this is the pizza that conquered the world. A famous Neapolitan *pizzaiolo* (pizzamaker), a certain Mr. Esposito, was once invited to the royal palace to make pizza. In honor of the Italian Queen Margherita he decided to top the pizza with ingredients in the three colors of the Italian flag: tomatoes, mozzarella, and basil. He called it Margherita, and a legend was born. Remember though, that the basil must be fresh to truly represent the bright green of the Italian flag.

Makes 2 (8-inch) pizzas

1 batch Focaccia and Pizza Dough (recipe on page 59)

2 or 3 ripe, fresh tomatoes, sliced

1 pound whole-milk mozzarella, chopped

24 fresh basil leaves

Extra-virgin olive oil for drizzling

Salt to taste

Preheat the oven to 400 degrees F and lightly oil two 8-inch pizza pans.

Divide the dough into two balls and place them in the prepared pans. With oiled hands, stretch the dough the size of the pan and as thin as possible. Shape a wall of dough all around the edges to better contain the toppings.

Place the tomato slices at regular intervals on the dough. Scatter the mozzarella over the tomatoes and place 8 leaves of the basil on each pizza. Drizzle with a little olive oil and sprinkle with some salt.

Bake for 15 to 20 minutes, or until the edges of the dough start to brown. Garnish with the remaining fresh basil. Cut into wedges and serve.

Pizza with Vegetables and Meats | **PIZZA DEGLI AVANZI**

Believe me, you can create delicious dishes with leftover food. My mother made this pizza mostly with the leftovers of the *bollito misto* (mixed cooked meats), which is one of the glories of Italian cuisine. In America, for reasons I do not know, this dish has not flourished. I call this "The Kitchen Sink Pizza" for obvious reasons. The filling can be whatever you have in the refrigerator—meat, fish, or vegetables. This pizza is also really easy because you don't even need to make a crust, since it is covered with a layer of mashed potatoes.

6 servings

Extra-virgin olive oil

Unflavored dry bread crumbs

½ onion, chopped

1 garlic clove, chopped

1 teaspoon chopped fresh Italian parsley

1½ cups cooked vegetables of any kind

1 cup cooked meat, chopped

2 or 3 slices of prosciutto, coarsely chopped

1 or 2 ripe tomatoes, chopped, or ½ cup tomato puree

2 eggs, separated

2 medium potatoes, boiled

Salt to taste

Freshly milled pepper

¼ teaspoon nutmeg

2 tablespoons freshly grated Parmesan cheese

1 to 2 tablespoons unsalted butter

Preheat the oven to 375 degrees F. Lightly oil a 9-inch pie plate. Sprinkle bottom and sides with bread crumbs. Set aside.

In a large skillet heat about 1 tablespoon olive oil. Add the onion, garlic, and parsley and sauté until the onion is soft and translucent. Add the vegetables, meat, prosciutto, and tomatoes. Cook at a simmer for 10 minutes. Cool.

Mix in the egg yolks and transfer the mixture to the prepared pan. Smooth the top so it is even.

Peel the potatoes and mash them. Add salt, pepper, nutmeg, and Parmesan and mix well. Whip the egg whites until stiff and fold into the potato mixture. Spread evenly on the pie. Sprinkle top with some bread crumbs and dot with butter. Bake for 30 to 40 minutes, or until top is golden brown.

NOTE *You can also make this pie with leftover grilled or poached fish or seafood, especially shrimp. Add 1 cup cooked mushrooms, ¼ cup heavy cream, but no tomatoes or prosciutto.*

Easter Monday Pizza | **PIZZA DEL LUNEDI DI PASQUA**

Easter Monday is the traditional day for picnics in Italy, similar to the Fourth of July in the United States. This pizza was especially conceived just for such occasions. The recipe comes from the kitchen of my cousin Gianna Amore who lives in Campania.

Makes 30 to 40 squares

DOUGH

3½ cups all-purpose flour

½ teaspoon salt

6 tablespoons lard, chilled and cut into pieces, plus 2 tablespoons softened

1 egg, lightly beaten

½ cup white wine

FILLING

1 pound whole-milk ricotta, drained

½ cup freshly grated Parmesan cheese

½ cup freshly grated Pecorino Romano cheese

2 eggs, beaten

8 ounces Italian *salamino* (see note), or any sweet salami, finely chopped

Freshly milled pepper to taste

FOR THE DOUGH Combine 3 cups of the flour and the salt in a food processor. Add the chilled lard and the egg, pulsing until mixture resembles coarse meal. Start pouring in the wine. Stop as soon as a ball forms on the blades. Place the dough on a floured pastry board and knead for a few minutes, until the dough is soft. Shape the dough into a ball and wrap in plastic wrap. Chill for 20 minutes.

Roll out the dough into a rectangle. Brush with 1 tablespoon softened lard. Fold in thirds and roll out into a rectangle again. Repeat the folding and rolling, then fold the dough into thirds and wrap in plastic wrap. Chill for 20 minutes. Repeat the rolling, folding, and chilling 3 more times. Set aside.

FOR THE FILLING Combine the ricotta, grated cheeses, and eggs in a mixing bowl and beat until smooth and creamy. Add the salamino and season with pepper. Set aside.

Preheat the oven to 350 degrees F. Brush a 17 × 12-inch baking sheet with the remaining 1 tablespoon softened lard. Set aside.

Divide the chilled dough into 2 parts. Roll out one part into a rectangle slightly larger than the prepared baking sheet. Pierce the dough in several places with a fork. Pour the filling on it and smooth evenly.

Roll out the remaining dough into a rectangle large enough to cover the entire filling. Place over the filling and pinch all around to seal the pizza.

Bake for 45 minutes or until top is golden. Cool on a rack. Cut into squares and serve at room temperature.

NOTE Salamino *is a small salami the size of an Italian sausage. Any good quality salami will do, but* salamino alIa cacciatore *is the best. It can be found in Italian specialty stores and in some supermarkets.*

Pizza with Broccoli Rabe and Sausage | **PIZZA POVERA**

This is another dish that we appreciated during the wartime in Naples. We used to call this "the poor man's pizza." It is made with inexpensive ingredients such as broccoli rabe, which is cheap and abundant in Italy. With the fresh, succulent sweet sausages, also an inexpensive item, the pungent bite of the hot pepper and the garlic, this combination is an addictive and wonderful topping for pizzas.

Makes 2 (9-inch) pizzas

12 ounces sweet Italian sausages

1 batch broccoli rabe (about 1 pound) trimmed, washed and cut into 2-inch pieces

3 garlic cloves, sliced

1 small hot red pepper (optional)

1 batch Whole-Wheat Pizza Dough (recipe on page 60)

Pierce the sausages in several places and place them in a skillet. Cover with water and cook over high heat for 15 minutes, turning them once. Add the broccoli rabe, garlic, and hot pepper, if using, cover skillet and cook until the broccoli rabe is tender, stirring once in a while. If there is too much liquid, remove the lid and continue cooking until the sausages are quite brown. Remove from the heat, remove the hot pepper if used, and cool.

Preheat the oven to 400 degrees F.

Lightly oil two 9-inch pizza pans. Divide the dough in two parts and place each in a pizza pan. With oiled fingers, stretch the dough as thin as possible into the pans. Shape a little wall of dough all around the edges to better contain the topping.

Cut the sausages into ¼-inch-thick slices, and mix them back into the broccoli rabe. Spoon the mixture on top of the pizzas. Bake for 15 to 20 minutes, or until the edge of the dough starts to brown. Serve hot, cut into wedges.

Seafood Pizza

PIZZA MARINARA

This pizza has the succulent flavors of seafood and fresh tomatoes. I do not recommend using fresh clams because they will overcook.

4 servings

½ batch fresh pizza dough (recipe on page 59)

8 ounces small cooked shrimp or crabmeat

1 (6-ounce) can clams

1 small garlic clove, chopped

2 teaspoons chopped fresh Italian parsley

2 or 3 ripe tomatoes, diced

½ teaspoon dried basil, crumbled

Freshly milled black pepper, to taste

3 tablespoons extra virgin olive oil

Preheat the oven to 500 degrees F.

Oil a 15-inch pizza pan. Put the dough in the pan and with your oiled hands stretch the dough to cover the entire pan. Place the dough in the oven and bake for 20 minutes.

In a mixing bowl combine the shrimp (or crabmeat), the clams with their juices, garlic, parsley, tomatoes, basil, and pepper. Add the olive oil and mix well.

Remove the dough from the oven and spread the topping evenly over it. Return the pizza to the oven and continue baking just long enough to heat the topping, about 5 to 7 minutes. Cut into wedges and serve.

Pizza with Sausage, Spinach and Ricotta | **PIZZA RUSTICA NUDA**

The Neapolitans can make pizza on the spur of the moment with anything edible. This recipe is a good example, and it is quite delicious. You can use your imagination and use any leftovers you have in the house, but you must have ricotta.

8 servings or more

3 tablespoons dry unflavored bread crumbs or more

4 ounces *soppressata* (an Italian sausage)

1 cup or more cooked spinach (about 1 bunch fresh spinach)

3 pounds whole-milk ricotta, drained

½ cup freshly grated Parmesan cheese

4 eggs, beaten

Preheat the oven to 375 degrees F.

Butter a 10-inch pie dish and sprinkle it with 2 tablespoons bread crumbs.

Place the *soppressata*, spinach and remaining bread crumbs in the bowl of a food processor. Chop very finely and remove the mixture to another bowl.

Put half of the ricotta, half of the Parmesan and 1 egg in the food processor and mix well. Add the mixture to the bowl with the spinach. Process the remaining ricotta, Parmesan, and eggs and add to the bowl. Mix well and pour into the prepared pan.

Bake for 45 minutes, or until a tester inserted in the middle of the pie comes out clean. Cool a little and serve in slices.

Escarole Pizza "Neapolitan Style"

PIZZA DI SCAROLA ALLA NAPOLETANA

Neapolitans rave over this pizza, which is actually a pie. For an everyday meal, the escarole and condiments are enveloped in pizza dough. But at Christmas, among the many traditional dishes, this pizza becomes an elegant *torta rustica* whose delicate crust is made with puff pastry. The following recipe comes from the kitchen of my cousin Gianna who lives in the picturesque town of Frasso Telesino in the province of Benevento.

DOUGH

2 cups all-purpose flour

Salt to taste

1 egg

1 tablespoon extra-virgin olive oil

¼ cup white wine

FILLING

2 heads escarole, about 2 pounds

3 tablespoons extra-virgin olive oil

1 tablespoon unsalted butter

1 garlic clove, chopped

2 anchovies packed in oil, chopped, or ½ teaspoon anchovy paste

12 black olives, pitted and chopped

1 tablespoon capers, drained

2 tablespoons pine nuts

2 tablespoons raisins

FOR THE DOUGH Combine the flour and salt in a mixing bowl. Make a well in the center and add the egg, olive oil, and wine. Beat the mixture into a soft but firm dough. Shape into a ball, cover with a bowl, and set aside.

FOR THE FILLING Trim and wash the escarole. Blanch it in boiling water and drain. In a skillet, heat the olive oil and butter. Add the garlic and escarole. Cook over medium heat, stirring often, until the escarole is tender and most of the moisture has evaporated. Add all other ingredients and cook stirring for 5 more minutes.

Preheat the oven to 375 degrees F. Oil a 9-inch springform pan.

Roll out two-thirds of the dough into a circle large enough to line the bottom and sides of the prepared pan. Fit the dough into the pan leaving a little of the dough hanging over the rim. Fill with the escarole mixture.

Roll out the remaining dough into a second circle, place it over the filling and trim the excess dough with scissors. Pinch the edges together to seal the pizza well. Pierce top in several places with the point of a knife. Bake for 30 to 40 minutes, or until top is nicely golden.

Puff Pastry with Cheese | **MILLEFOGLIE AI FORMAGGI**

This is an elegant and unusual dish which probably comes from the *cucina aristocratica* imported by the French chefs. To make it easier I use commercial frozen puff pastry, which works well. The dough and the filling can be prepared in advance and assembled just before baking.

6 servings

3 tablespoons unsalted butter

½ package (8 ounces) frozen puff pastry, defrosted

2 tablespoons flour, plus more for dusting

2 eggs

1 cup plus 1 tablespoon milk

¼ teaspoon salt

Freshly ground white pepper to taste

½ teaspoon nutmeg

4 ounces Swiss cheese, shredded

8 ounces smoked whole-milk mozzarella, shredded

3 tablespoons freshly grated Parmesan cheese

Preheat the oven to 375 degrees F. Line a baking sheet with aluminum foil and lightly butter the foil with 1 tablespoon butter.

On a floured board stretch the dough as thin as possible (about ½ inch thick). Cut into 4 rectangles of equal size. Place them on the baking sheet.

Separate 1 of the eggs. Reserve the white. Combine the yolk with 1 tablespoon of the milk and brush the rectangles of dough. Pierce them all over with a fork and bake until the tops of the dough are golden and puffed. Remove from the oven and set aside.

In a saucepan, melt the remaining 2 tablespoons butter, add the 2 tablespoons flour, stir and cook for about 30 seconds. Remove the pan from the heat and slowly add the 1 cup milk while stirring constantly with a wire whisk. Return the pan to the heat and cook over medium to low heat, stirring constantly, until the mixture starts to boil. Remove from the heat and add the salt, pepper, nutmeg, Swiss cheese, and smoked mozzarella.

Beat the remaining egg and the reserved white lightly and add to the cheese mixture. Add 2 tablespoons of the Parmesan and mix well. Divide the cheese mixture into 3 parts and spread one part on 1 rectangle of dough. Sprinkle with some of the remaining Parmesan and top with another rectangle of dough. Continue layering the rectangles with the filling ending with the last rectangle. Sprinkle a little Parmesan on top and bake for 10 to 15 minutes or until the cheese mixture starts to ooze out of the dough. Cool a little and cut with a serrated knife.

sauces

Each year at the end of August, my family would leave the Tyrrhenian shore to end the summer at my grandmother's house in the Abruzzo mountains, spending the days on joyous picnics in the nearby woods or climbing the surrounding mountains. These were also the days of the *fare le bottiglie* (making bottles). In Italy, this means first and foremost one thing: bottling tomato sauce and tomato paste.

I remember the frantic activities during those days. The scent of tomato and basil mingled with the smell of burnt sugar spilling from the cauldrons of jams my mother was making. There were also vegetables to preserve. Many of them, such as baby artichokes, tender zucchini, and string beans, had already been canned during the summer, resting in order on the shelves of the pantry. By late summer, the peppers, eggplants, and pumpkins were awaiting their turn. Distant cousins and former housekeepers would be summoned to help. We children, too, were given assignments, which we loved and made us feel important.

My father had his hands in everything, and Uncle Filippo serenely organized the traffic. In the middle of the afternoon, there was always a generous *merenda* (snack). Later, when the men came to pick up their wives, the gathering turned into a party. The evening would end with a lovely *passeggiata fuori le mura* (walk outside the city walls) and a stop at a *caffè*. There was espresso and a *digestivo*, usually Cognac or grappa, for the men, a *bibita* (soft drink) or an espresso for the ladies, and ice cream for the children.

When I go back to Italy today, I can sometimes smell the scent of *le bottiglie*. It is not my imagination—farmers and many people with modest incomes still follow the tradition of canning fruits, vegetables, and sauces. They set up working tables outside, and anyone who walks by stops to chat. It is a heartwarming scene that always brings tears to my eyes and makes me cherish my memories of similar activities even more.

SALSE, SUGHI AND RAGÙ

Fortunately today excellent canned tomatoes are available in America. I make my students laugh when they ask me which brand of tomatoes they should buy. I always say, "those on sale in the supermarket. But if you see canned tomatoes from San Marzano, a town near Naples where the best tomatoes are grown, stock up on them!"

Many people wonder what Italy would do without tomatoes. True, true, we Italians have undoubtedly taken the use of tomatoes to glorious heights and deserve credit for it. But our sauces are not consistently red, not even our pasta sauces.

The reason why Italian food is so easy to prepare and full of natural flavors is because you do not need to make a separate sauce all the time. Mostly the sauce is an integral part of the dish, extracted from the ingredients being cooked, and not an additional entity like in French cuisine. Usually wine is added to the sauce that evaporates in the cooking process. Sometimes it is enriched with cream, but this is an innovation due to French influence prevailing in the northwest of Italy.

Salsa, *sugo*, and *ragù* all mean sauce in Italian, although there is a subtle difference between the last two. *Salsa* is usually served separately, for example *salsa verde*, a green sauce that usually accompanies fish or boiled meat. *Sugo*, on the other hand, is the sauce that dresses something or is incorporated into it, most often used with pasta. This is why *ragù* (from the French *ragout*), made with a variety of meats, also goes under the name of *sugo*. The meat is either chopped, like in *ragù alla Bolognese*, or kept in large pieces, like in *ragù all'Italiana* or *ragù alla Napoletana*. *Ragù* is the quintessential sauce for pasta.

For me, the scent of a *ragù* wafting in the air is the announcement of a Sunday dinner, especially in Naples. The city literally smells of *ragù*. The Sunday *ragù* used to be a real test. Luigi Braccili, a noted Italian food writer, said that its perfume indicated "status, economic condition and even culture." This is, of course, a thing of the past, but although I do not expect a *ragù* all the time, I still get worried when I am invited to dinner and smell nothing.

In Italy, and especially in the south, the favorite sauces for pasta are called *ragù della festa* (festive sauces). They are rich and almost always made with meat. The simple *sugo finto* (fake sauce), made with the basic ingredients onion, carrot, celery, parsley, tomato, and an aromatic herb bouquet, is the sauce that dresses the everyday pasta. It is the base of the recently popular Mediterranean cuisine, which has a long tradition in Italy.

Not too long ago matching a sauce with a certain kind of pasta was important. But things have changed. When I was growing up, nobody would dress homemade pasta or commercial short pasta with a fish sauce, which was limited to spaghetti or linguine. Today it is the individual taste that reigns, and I approve of this.

If the amount of sauce I suggest to dress a pound of pasta does not seem enough, remember that we Italians abhor pasta drowned in sauce. The sauce should complement the pasta, not obliterate it.

Basic Tomato Sauce | **SUGO FINTO**

This simple and flavorful tomato sauce tastes as if it was made with meat—hence its name *sugo finto*, "fake" sauce. Sometimes my mother cheated by adding a little bit of chopped prosciutto to the vegetables, as well as a touch of butter at the end. It was good!

Sugo finto and *marinara* are the most popular sauces that Italians, and especially Neapolitans, use to dress our daily pasta. The chopping of the vegetables—with the exception of the tomatoes—can be done in a food processor.

Dresses 1 pound of pasta

3 tablespoons extra-virgin olive oil

1 onion, chopped

1 carrot, chopped

1 rib celery, chopped

1 sprig Italian parsley

¾ teaspoon chopped fresh sage, or ¼ teaspoon dried

1 teaspoon tomato paste

1 (28-ounce) can peeled tomatoes, strained through a food mill (see note)

1½ teaspoons chopped fresh basil, or ½ teaspoon dried

Salt to taste

Freshly milled pepper to taste

In a saucepan, heat 2 tablespoons olive oil, add the chopped vegetables, parsley, and sage. Sauté over medium heat for 5 to 8 minutes.

Add the tomato paste, cook for 2 to 3 minutes stirring often, then add the strained tomatoes.

Bring to a boil, add the basil, and simmer for 30 minutes. Season with salt and pepper. Remove from the heat and stir in 1 tablespoon olive oil.

NOTE   *Never puree unseeded tomatoes in a food processor. It will crush the seeds and make the sauce bitter.*

Marinara Sauce | **SUGO ALLA MARINARA**

Although the word *marinara* comes from the Latin *mare* (the sea), it does not mean that the sauce contains fish. It is named *marinara* because it is often used as a base for fish dishes. The legend goes that Italian fishermen used to take this simple sauce with them when going out in their boats to dress their spaghetti and cook some fish in. It is the base for the classic *brodetto* or *zuppa di pesce*, the Italian equivalent of a *bouillabaisse*.

Dresses 1 pound of pasta

1 (8-ounce) can tomato puree

1 teaspoon tomato paste

2 tablespoons extra-virgin olive oil

2 garlic cloves, crushed

2 sprigs Italian parsley

1½ teaspoons chopped fresh basil, or ½ teaspoon dried

Place all the ingredients in a saucepan. Bring to a boil, reduce the heat and simmer, covered, for about 20 minutes, stirring once in a while. If the sauce seems too watery remove the lid and cook a little longer.

Remove the garlic and parsley, or strain through a food mill.

NOTE *Instead of basil you can use oregano. This sauce freezes well.*

Tomato and Basil Sauce

SUGHETTO AL FILETTO DI POMODORO E BASILICO

Quick and simple, this is a rustic sauce with a tangy, luscious summer taste. It is better when made with fresh, ripe tomatoes, but cherry tomatoes are a nice alternative since they seem to retain a good flavor year-round. I remember when traveling in Campania, all the farmhouses were festively decorated with vines of cherry tomatoes drying in the sun. They were used all through the winter to enhance the flavor of certain dishes.

Dresses 1 pound of pasta

¼ cup extra-virgin olive oil

2 garlic cloves, crushed

1 sprig Italian parsley plus 1 teaspoon chopped

1½ pounds fresh ripe tomatoes, peeled, seeded and cut into strips (see above)

½ cup loosely packed fresh basil leaves, chopped

Salt to taste

Freshly milled pepper to taste

In a saucepan heat 3 tablespoons olive oil, add 1 garlic clove and the sprig of parsley. Cook for 2 to 3 minutes, then remove both and discard. Add the tomatoes and cook uncovered, stirring often, for about 10 minutes.

Chop the remaining garlic clove. Add the chopped garlic, basil, salt, and pepper to the sauce. Cook for 5 minutes longer, stirring often.

Add the chopped parsley and remaining olive oil and stir.

Tomato Sauce with Capers and Basil | **SUGHETTO DI SALVATORE**

Salvatore, a Neapolitan nephew of mine by adoption, invented this sauce when he was a student away from home. It is quick and simple, but utterly delicious and ideal for spaghetti or linguine. This is a summer sauce, thus it is best made with fresh, ripe tomatoes, like the Neapolitans do. But when not available, you can use canned tomatoes.

Dresses 1 pound of pasta

1 pound fresh tomatoes, chopped or 1 (28-ounce) can peeled tomatoes

2 garlic cloves, chopped

5 or 6 basil leaves, chopped

1 heaping tablespoon capers, drained

2 tablespoons toasted unflavored bread crumbs

3 tablespoons extra-virgin olive oil

Preheat the oven to 375 degrees F.

Combine all the ingredients and place the mixture in a baking dish. Bake for 20 to 25 minutes. Serve on spaghetti or linguine.

Béchamel Sauce | **SALSA BALSAMELLA**

This is a basic sauce used for many dishes, especially for timbales and lasagne.

Dresses 1 pound of pasta

1 tablespoon unsalted butter

1 heaping tablespoon flour

1 cup cold milk

Pinch of salt

Freshly ground white pepper to taste

¼ teaspoon nutmeg

In a heavy saucepan, preferably an enameled one, melt the butter. Add the flour and cook, stirring, for a few minutes until creamy.

Remove the pan from the heat and slowly add the milk, a little at a time, whisking constantly until the mixture is smooth. Return the pan to the heat and cook the sauce, whisking constantly until it thickens and begins to puff. Let the sauce puff up once or twice and remove from the heat. Season with salt, pepper, and nutmeg.

NOTE *If a recipe calls for a thicker béchamel, add more flour at the beginning. For a thinner one, add more milk at the end.*

Tomato and Meat Sauce for Pasta | **IL RAGÙ**

A Neapolitan will say that there is nothing better then a dish of pasta dressed with a good *ragù*. Because of their fondness for it, this sauce is also known in Italy as *ragù alla Napoletana*, Neapolitan sauce. Neapolitans also add the famous *braciole* to it—thin slices of beef covered with a mixture of parsley and garlic and rolled and tied with kitchen twine. Other people of southern Italy do the same, but they add a slice of cheese, usually Caciocavallo, to their *braciole*.

Only at family dinners would my mother serve the *ragù* meats as a second course after the pasta. When we had guests, she didn't think it was right, or elegant, to have it following the *maccheroni* because the two dishes would have the same flavor. But I do serve the succulent *ragù* meats as a second course, and nobody has ever complained. However, if you want to keep the *ragù* meat for another use, make sure you also have some of the sauce to reheat it with.

Volumes have been written about the *ragù* by famous authors, including Eduardo de Filippo, the Neapolitan playwright. The sauce has also starred in movies. In *Marriage Italian Style* with Marcello Mastroianni and Sophia Loren, Mastroianni tries to teach Sophia how to make the *ragù*. Her reaction would not have pleased my mother—Sophia silently mouths curses behind his back and it brings the house down. This is why I always say, when I go to a movie in which profanity is spoken out loud to no end, that it is not necessary to use such words . . . leave it to the imagination!

Dresses 1 pound of pasta

¼ cup extra-virgin olive oil

2 onions, peeled and with a crisscross cut at the root end (see note)

1 celery stalk, cut in half

1 carrot, cut in half

1 sprig Italian parsley

1 pound beef chuck or rump

In a large heavy pot, heat the olive oil. Add the onions, celery, carrot, and parsley. Sauté briefly and add the beef, pork, and veal.

Pierce the sausages in several places with a pointed knife, which will prevent them from cracking. Add them to the pot. Cook until all meats are well browned, turning often and scraping the bottom of the pot.

Season with salt and pepper and add the wine. Let the wine evaporate.

Add the tomato paste, strained fresh tomatoes (or tomato puree), ½ cup water, and basil. Stir well, cover and reduce the heat to very low. Cook at a simmer until the meats are very tender, about 3 hours, stirring often.

1 pound pork shoulder, preferably with bone

1 pound veal shoulder, preferably with bone

1 pound sweet Italian sausages

Salt to taste

Fresh ground pepper

1 cup dry red wine

¼ cup tomato paste

6 pounds fresh, ripe tomatoes, cut into pieces and strained through a food mill, or 2 (28-ounce) cans tomato puree

¾ teaspoon chopped fresh basil, or ¼ teaspoon dried

Remove the meats from the sauce and put aside for another use. Serve the sauce over pasta.

NOTE *The crisscross at the bottom of an onion prevents it from falling apart.*

Leftover sauce can be frozen.

Bolognese Meat Sauce | **RAGÙ ALLA BOLOGNESE**

This is the most Italian of all sauces, made from Bologna to Naples and from Milan to Palermo. It is the essential sauce to dress homemade noodles, such as tagliatelle or fettuccine. There are several variations of it. In fact, if you put three Italians together to discuss the Bolognese, each one will have a different version. We are such individualists!

Dresses 1 pound of pasta

1 (¼-inch thick) prosciutto slice, cubed

1 sprig Italian parsley

1 onion, quartered

1 celery stalk, quartered

1 carrot, quartered

2 tablespoons olive oil

2 tablespoons unsalted butter

1 pound ground meat, a mixture of beef, veal, and pork

¾ teaspoon chopped fresh sage, or ¼ teaspoon dried

Salt to taste

Freshly milled pepper to taste

½ cup dry wine, preferably red

3 tablespoons tomato paste

2 cups chicken broth, homemade or a good quality canned broth

¼ cup heavy cream (optional)

In a food processor combine the prosciutto, parsley, onion, celery, and carrot. Process to a fine consistency.

In a saucepan, heat the olive oil and butter. Add the prosciutto-vegetable mixture and cook stirring until lightly browned. Add the meat and sage, and cook stirring frequently until brown. Season with salt and pepper. Add the wine and let evaporate.

Blend the tomato paste with the chicken broth and stir into the meat. Cover, bring to a boil, reduce the heat and let the ragù simmer for 1 hour. Add the cream (if using), stir and remove from the heat.

NOTE   *In Naples this sauce is also served on short pasta such as* rigatoni, penne, fusilli, *or* conchiglie.

Genovese Meat Sauce | **LA GENOVESE**

Despite a name attributing it to the city of Genoa, this is one of the most well-known Neapolitan pasta sauces. Vittorio Gleijeses, an author of many historical books on Naples and Campania, called *La Genovese* "the sacred monster that is not known in Genoa." Arthur Schwartz, in *Naples at the Table*, calls it "a Neapolitan mystery." It is believed that the sauce was imported in the 15th century by Genovese chefs who lived in Naples with their Genovese masters. No matter what the true story is, *La Genovese* is a most delicious sauce. The base is a large amount of onions and the usual *odori di cucina* (perfumes of the kitchen), which are cooked together with a nice piece of chunky meat, usually beef. It can also be made with veal or pork, or even without any meat at all, in which case it is called *falsa Genovese*, a "fake Genovese."

Dresses 1 pound of pasta or more

¼ cup extra-virgin olive oil

2 pounds beef chuck roast, tied

8 onions, cut into pieces

1 carrot, cut into pieces

1 celery stalk, trimmed and cut into pieces

1 sprig Italian parsley

1½ teaspoons chopped fresh marjoram, or ½ teaspoon dried

2 tablespoons chopped prosciutto

Salt to taste

Freshly milled pepper to taste

1 cup white wine

Freshly grated Parmesan cheese

Put the olive oil in a large pot with a wide bottom, add the meat and roll it in the oil. Set aside.

In the bowl of a food processor, chop all the vegetables and herbs to a coarse consistency. Add this mixture to the pot to cover the meat. Add the prosciutto and 2 cups water. Add salt and pepper. Cover the pot and bring to a boil, then immediately reduce to a simmer. Simmer for about one hour, once in a while turning the meat and stirring the vegetables.

When the meat starts to brown, reduce the heat to low and start adding the wine, a little at a time. Simmer for two more hours, adding more water if necessary. At the end, the sauce should have a nice brown color.

NOTE *The best pastas for this sauce are* penne, rigatoni *or* fusilli *but any kind can be used. Let the meat cool which makes it easier to slice.*

Veal and Mushroom Sauce | **SUGO DI VITELLO AI FUNGHI**

This uncomplicated and flavorful sauce was a Sunday dish for the Neapolitans, but nowadays it is made more frequently. Ideal for dressing homemade pasta, it is also good on short tubular pasta, such as *penne* or *rigatoni*.

Makes 2 cups

3 tablespoons unsalted butter

1 tablespoon extra-virgin olive oil

1 onion, cut in half

1 carrot, quartered

1 celery stalk, quartered

8 ounces shoulder or rump of veal in one piece

¼ cup dry white wine

½ cup dried porcini mushrooms, soaked in ¾ cup lukewarm water

1 teaspoon tomato paste

1 (28-ounce) can peeled tomatoes

4 ounces chicken livers, cut into small pieces

Salt to taste

Freshly milled pepper to taste

In a saucepan heat 2 tablespoons of the butter and the olive oil. Add the onion, carrot, and celery. Sauté briefly and add the veal. Brown on all sides, then add the wine. Let evaporate.

Gently remove the mushrooms from the water, reserving the water. Add the mushrooms to the veal. Strain the mushroom water through a paper towel or a coffee filter and add to the veal. Reduce the heat and cook at a simmer, covered, for 10 to 15 minutes. Add the tomato paste and tomatoes. Stir, crushing the tomatoes with a wooden spoon. Bring to a boil and simmer for 40 to 45 minutes, or until veal is tender, stirring often.

Strain the sauce through a food mill. Do not use a food processor, it will crush the seeds of the tomatoes and make the sauce bitter. Return the sauce to the saucepan.

In a small skillet, sauté the chicken livers with the remaining butter. Add to the sauce during the last 5 minutes of cooking. Remove the veal and reserve for another use (see note). Reheat the sauce before using.

NOTE   *The reserved veal can be chopped and added to the sauce.*

Sauce with Giblets and Mushrooms

SUGO CON FRATTAGLIE DI POLLO E FUNGHI

When we lived in Naples during World War II, food was scarce. My father used to take my brother and me to the butcher to buy the little meat we were allowed. He hoped that the butcher would feel sorry for these two growing children and give him a little more meat. Well, it usually worked because he would give us a bundle of *frattaglie* (a mixture of chicken organs) for free but without livers. They were too precious and reserved for special preparations. This sauce, which is excellent on *tagliatelle* or *fettuccine*, is the result of the butcher's generosity.

Dresses 1 pound of pasta or more

1 pound mixture of chicken gizzards and hearts (giblets)

1 tablespoon kosher salt

1 pound mushrooms, trimmed and washed

¼ cup extra-virgin olive oil

¼ cup dried porcini mushrooms, soaked, coarsely chopped, liquid drained and reserved

4 slices turkey bacon, each cut into 4 pieces

1 large carrot, quartered

1 stalk celery, trimmed and cut into pieces

2 sprigs Italian parsley

1 large onion, quartered

1 clove garlic

1 cup dry red wine

1 (16-ounce) can peeled tomatoes, chopped and liquid reserved

1 dry bay leaf

Place the gizzards and hearts in a bowl, add the kosher salt, fill with water and let stand for 15 to 20 minutes. This will remove any bacteria from the giblets. Do the same with the fresh mushrooms but do not leave them in the salted water for more than 5 minutes, then quickly rinse them under running water. Chop the mushrooms coarsely and wrap in paper towels to dry until ready to cook them.

In a large skillet heat 2 tablespoons olive oil and add the fresh and dried mushrooms. Cook until the water released by the mushrooms has evaporated. With a slotted spoon remove the mushrooms to a bowl and set aside. Reserve the skillet.

Meanwhile, drain the giblets and chop them coarsely.

In a food processor, place the bacon, carrot, celery, parsley, onion, and garlic. Chop very finely.

Place 2 tablespoons olive oil in the skillet, heat and add the chopped vegetable mixture and the giblets. Cook 5 to 8 minutes, stirring. Add the wine and simmer until it evaporates. Add the tomatoes with their liquid and the bay leaf, bring to a boil, and reduce the heat to low. Simmer for about 1 hour, or until the giblets are tender. Add the reserved porcini mushroom liquid and sautéed mushrooms during the last 5 minutes. Remove the bay leaf and serve over pasta.

Quick Hot Pepper and Garlic Sauce "Neapolitan Style"

AGLIO, OLIO E PEPERONCINO ALLA NAPOLETANA

This sauce is also called the "five minute sauce" because it takes no time to prepare. It is one of the sauces Italians make when they get together for an impromptu *spaghettata*—a get-together at someone's home, usually after an evening at the theater or the movies, to cook and eat spaghetti.

Use a large skillet to make the sauce, so you can toss the pasta directly with the sauce. Do not overdrain the pasta; remember that the Neapolitans, masters of pasta cooking, say, "*lo paghetto con la goccia*" ("spaghetti with the drop"), which means the pasta has to be moist. Before starting the sauce, have your linguine or spaghetti cooking and almost done.

Dresses 1 pound of spaghetti or linguine

¼ cup extra-virgin olive oil

3 large garlic cloves, crushed

1 small hot red pepper

2 tablespoons chopped fresh Italian parsley

Freshly milled pepper to taste

In a large skillet heat the olive oil, add the garlic and hot pepper. As soon as the garlic starts to color, add the parsley, remove from the heat (you may remove the hot pepper) and add the drained pasta. Toss and serve immediately.

Green Sauce | **SALSA VERDE**

When we saw my mother making this green sauce, we would not even ask for which dish. We didn't mind what it went with, we loved it so much. And indeed, this sauce, a must for a *bollito misto*, is so versatile that it can be used for many other dishes. It accompanies grilled or poached fish beautifully; it dresses seafood salads perfectly; and doubles as a zesty dip for vegetables, cold lobster, shrimp, delicate oysters, clams, or mussels. And it is a cinch to make. It also keeps for a week in the refrigerator, but must be covered with oil.

Makes 2 cups

2 garlic cloves

¼ cup dry unflavored bread crumbs

1 hard-boiled egg, quartered

3 anchovies packed in oil, or 1½ teaspoons anchovy paste

1 cup fresh Italian parsley leaves

2 tender celery stalks, with as many leaves as possible, cut into pieces

1 tablespoon red wine vinegar

Juice of 1 lemon

¾ cup extra-virgin olive oil

2 tablespoons small capers, drained

In a food processor place the garlic, bread crumbs, hard-boiled egg, anchovies, parsley, celery stalks, vinegar, and lemon juice.

Start the machine and pour the olive oil in slowly. Process until the mixture is pureed. Transfer to a mixing bowl and stir in the capers.

NOTE *If the mixture is too thick, add a little more lemon juice or vinegar. You can also add some of the cooking liquid from the food you plan to serve with the sauce.*

pasta, gnocchi, polenta & rice

ABOUT PASTA

There is evidence that pasta was made in Italy as far back as the 4th century B.C. In a tomb in the town of Cerveteri near Rome, a stronghold of the Etruscans who reigned in Italy from the 7th to the 4th centuries B.C., two walls are decorated with drawings of all the tools needed to make pasta: a wooden board, a rolling pin, a cutting wheel—just like the ones used today all over Italy. So let us please forget about Marco Polo introducing pasta to Italy from China in the 13th century, as some history books would have us believe. This is simply not true. Marco Polo recounts in his travel book *Il milione* that he tasted in "these extreme lands . . . foods similar to those we make." He was referring to thin Chinese noodles, which he calls *laganum*—they are the *laganelle* of the Neapolitan cuisine.

Also, the Roman poet Horace, in the 1st century, calls them *laganae* and talks of taverns in Naples where *laganae* were eaten. In one of his satires he expresses compassion for the Roman Emperor Tiberius, who, being so important, cannot go to the market with all his servants in tow without being noticed. Horace, however, an unknown poet, can roam from stall to stall, ask the price of wheat or salad without being recognized, and choose his own food. Afterwards he can go home to enjoy, undisturbed, his "bowl of leeks, chickpeas and *laganae*." Apparently, this was his favorite food.

There is nothing the Neapolitans love more than pasta. It is filling, nourishing, inexpensive and can be flavored in many ways. Imagination is all that's needed. However, exercising the imagination has to be a serious business. Let me explain. I cannot accept the silly combinations that modern chefs invent just to be different—I call them "pasta follies." For example, hand-rolled lasagna noodles, layered with roasted asparagus, bell pepper, ricotta, béchamel, fresh mozzarella, cherry tomatoes, basil, and shiitake mushrooms. Pasta dressed with one or two ingredients at a time that do not obliterate its natural flavor and the taste of the sauce is perfect. I have nothing against inventing new recipes; I do that all the time. But the result must be harmonious, not a messy concoction of ingredients that do not marry well. Americans have adopted pasta with a passion. But, as with many passionate love affairs in which love can become suffocating, pasta is in danger of being smothered. Tomato sauce, boiled in a pot with a pinch of salt and a few basil leaves, has been used since the early 19th century by open-air vendors in the south of Italy for seasoning macaroni. Neapolitans consider three sauces to be the most important for their *pastasciutta*: the simple *marinara*, based on tomatoes; the *ragù* with its variety of meats; and the *Genovese* with plenty of onions. In this chapter are the basics for making wonderful homemade pastas and more recipes for how best to serve and enjoy them. *Buon appetito*!

Basic Homemade Pasta and Variations

Homemade egg pasta used to be a luxury, prepared only for special occasions—Christmas, Easter, or birthdays. Dry pasta was what the Neapolitans used. In the old days, the narrow alleys of Naples, where an alluring display of macaroni and spaghetti hung from ropes stretched from wall to wall, or undulated from balconies and trellises, were a sight! You can still see this on the streets of some old *paese* like Gragnano, which is famous for its pasta.

When it comes to pasta, preferences vary from place to place. For instance, along the coast of Salerno, and in certain neighborhoods of Naples, people prefer homemade pasta with eggs. In the countryside and the mountains, on the other hand, pasta is often made by hand but without eggs, just with water. The preferred sauces for homemade pasta are those with meat. Since homemade pasta is viewed as something special, people would not "sacrifice" it to a simple tomato sauce.

Basic Pasta Dough with Eggs

The rule of thumb for the basic pasta dough is that the flour-egg ratio is always 1:1, so for a four-egg dough, measure 4 cups all-purpose flour and 4 eggs, etc.

MIXING THE DOUGH BY HAND

1 Put the flour in a mound in the middle of a wooden board or other adequate work surface. Make a well in the center and break the eggs into it. Beat the eggs with a fork for a few minutes.

2 Using the fork, gradually blend the flour into the eggs, adding as much of it as the eggs can absorb to gather the dough into a cohesive ball. You may not need all the flour. Knead until smooth and elastic, adding more flour if the dough gets sticky. The dough should be firm to the touch but not hard.

3 Place the dough under an inverted bowl and let it rest for about 20 minutes before using.

MIXING THE DOUGH WITH A FOOD PROCESSOR

1 Put the eggs in a food processor. Process until the eggs are mixed.

2 Add 1 cup flour and process gradually, adding more flour until a ball forms on the blades. Too much flour will make the dough crumbly. If this happens transfer the mixture to a wooden board, gather it into a ball, and add a little water. If the dough should come out too soft, knead it on the board, adding more flour.

3 Place the dough under an inverted bowl and let it rest for about 20 minutes before using.

NOTE *If necessary, the dough can be prepared up to this point the day before. Keep it well wrapped in plastic wrap, and refrigerate. Before using the dough, let it come to room temperature. The dough can also be frozen. Defrost at the bottom of the refrigerator the night before.*

STRETCHING AND CUTTING THE DOUGH

Cut the dough into 5 or 6 wedges. Start working with one piece at a time, and keep the unused parts under a bowl. Flatten the first piece of dough with your hands. Position the rollers of a pasta machine at their widest opening. Insert the dough between the 2 rollers, turn the handle and roll the dough through. Sprinkle the dough with flour, fold the dough into 3 parts, and roll again. Do this 2 or 3 times until the dough is smooth and not sticky.

Position the rollers of the pasta machine at the #1 setting. Roll the piece of dough without folding it, gradually setting the rollers at a narrower number, and flouring the dough when necessary. Roll until you reach the narrowest setting, or until the dough has the desired thinness.

Place the sheet of dough on kitchen towels. Do not use paper towels. Repeat the operation with the remaining dough. It is advisable to keep the sheets of dough covered with kitchen towels. Dry the sheets of dough for 10 minutes. If left to dry longer, the dough will become brittle and difficult to cut.

To cut pasta, feed the sheets of dough, one at a time, through the cutting rollers for the desired width. Place the noodles on kitchen towels to dry until ready to cook.

NOTE *The noodles can be kept in a cool place for a week or stored in the refrigerator. They can also be frozen.*

FOUR VARIATIONS OF HOMEMADE PASTA

NOTE *All variations are based on using 4 cups all-purpose flour and 4 eggs except where indicated.*

GREEN PASTA DOUGH

Add ¼ cup cooked, well-squeezed, finely chopped spinach to the eggs, mix and process the same way as with regular pasta. If you are using a food processor, start processing the spinach before adding the eggs and flour. Proceed as described on page 92.

RED PASTA DOUGH

Boil 1 unpeeled but trimmed small beet until soft. Peel and puree the beet and add it to the eggs. Proceed as described on page 92.

BLACK PASTA DOUGH

Add 2 pouches squid ink to the eggs. Fish stores sell little pouches of fresh or frozen ink. Each pouch is 0.05 ounces. Proceed as described on page 92.

CHOCOLATE PASTA DOUGH

For chocolate pasta, I use 2 eggs and 2 cups of flour, since I always mix it with other noodles. Mix 1½ tablespoons unsweetened cocoa with the eggs. Proceed as described on page 92. Remember that this is not a dessert, but a whimsical variation of regular pasta. I use it for tagliatelle Arlecchino, which is a mixture of colored tagliatelle.

Whole-Wheat Pasta Dough

PASTA DI FARINA INTEGRALE

This type of rustic pasta is used mostly for *pappardelle*. It can be dressed with various sauces.

6 servings

2 cups whole-wheat flour

1½ cups all-purpose flour plus more for kneading

4 eggs

1 tablespoon extra-virgin olive oil

BY HAND Combine the whole-wheat flour and 1 cup of the all-purpose flour on a pastry board and make a well in the center. Break the eggs into it, add the olive oil and beat the eggs briefly with a fork.

Blend in the flour, a little at a time, letting the eggs absorb only the amount of flour necessary to gather the dough into a ball. Knead the ball until smooth and elastic, adding more flour if the dough feels sticky. The dough should be firm to the touch but not hard.

Place the dough under an inverted bowl and let it rest for about 10 to 15 minutes.

IN THE FOOD PROCESSOR Place the eggs and the oil in a food processor. Process a few seconds and gradually add the flour, stopping as soon as a ball forms on the blades. Too much flour will make the dough crumbly. If this happens transfer the mixture to a pastry board and gather it into a ball. You may need a bit of water. If the dough should come out too soft, knead it on the board adding more flour. In either case knead the dough for about 10 minutes, or until smooth and elastic.

Place the dough under an inverted bowl and let it rest for about 20 minutes.

Stretch and cut dough as described on page 93.

NOTE *If necessary, the dough can be prepared the day before and refrigerated, well wrapped in plastic wrap. Let it come to room temperature before using. The dough can also be frozen. Defrost at the bottom of the refrigerator the night before using.*

Basic Lasagna Dough

This is a homemade pasta without eggs. It is the pasta used for dishes of the *cucina povera*, such as *pasta e fagioli* (recipe on page 51). If you want to make these recipes with homemade pasta, this would be the dough to use.

2 cups all-purpose flour plus more for kneading

½ teaspoon salt

1 cup or more water

BY HAND On a wooden board place the flour in a mound. Open a well in the center, add the salt and approximately ¾ cup water. Mix flour and water with a fork adding more water as needed. With both hands, start kneading the dough into a ball, using more flour if necessary to obtain a smooth, pliable ball. Cover the ball with an inverted bowl and let it rest for 15 minutes before using.

IN THE FOOD PROCESSOR Place the flour and salt in a food processor. With the machine running, start adding the water. Stop as soon as a ball forms on the blades. Remove the dough from the machine and knead for 10 minutes. Cover the ball with an inverted bowl and let it rest for 15 minutes before using.

Stretch the dough with a rolling pin to the required thinness or use a pasta machine. Cut the dough according to your recipe.

NOTE *Some recipes call for egg whites in this dough. Start by mixing the flour, salt and egg whites. You may not need water, but if the dough seems dry, add a little.*

SOME NOTES ABOUT COOKING PASTA

When cooking pasta, the rule is to bring the water to a boil in a covered pot. After it is boiling, add the salt. The addition of salt often halts the boiling process, so cover the pot again until the water is truly boiling before adding the pasta. Once the pasta is added, stir it and cover the pot again to allow the water to come back to a boil as soon as possible. Then cook the pasta according to package instructions.

Vermicelli with Tomatoes | **VERMICELLI CU' 'A PUMMAROLA 'NCOPPA**

Pummarola 'ncoppa is an expression used by the people of Campania to express their passion for everything served with tomatoes, not only vermicelli or spaghetti. But keep in mind that the food is never inundated by the tomato sauce but complemented by it. Fresh tomatoes, often the small pomodorini, are preferred, especially in this dish.

Prepare this fresh-tasting sauce while the pasta is cooking.

6 servings

1 pound vermicelli

3 tablespoons extra-virgin olive oil

½ onion, chopped

2 pounds fresh tomatoes, chopped, or 3 (1-pint) boxes cherry tomatoes, halved

8 to 10 fresh basil leaves

Freshly grated Parmesan cheese

Bring a large pot of salted water to a boil and cook the pasta according to the instructions on the package. Drain, but reserve some of the cooking water. Transfer the pasta to a warm serving bowl.

While the pasta cooks, heat the olive oil in a large saucepan, add the onion and cook for 5 or 6 minutes. Add the tomatoes. Cook at a simmer, stirring often, for about 15 minutes. Reserve one or two basil leaves for garnish and add the remaining to the sauce during the last minutes.

Pour the sauce over the pasta and stir well. If it is too dry, add some of the reserved water. Garnish with the basil leaves and serve with the Parmesan cheese.

Spaghetti with Tomatoes, Olives and Anchovies

SPAGHETTI ALLA PUTTANESCA

The Neapolitans say that they invented this dish. However, it is as popular in Rome and many other cities of Italy as it is in Naples, not only for its salacious name but because it is good. Well, this is a speedy dish that would allow the "good lady of the night" to return to her assignment as soon as possible!

3 tablespoons extra-virgin olive oil

2 anchovies packed in oil, chopped

2 garlic cloves, chopped

5 or 6 fresh tomatoes, peeled, seeded, and coarsely chopped

10 to 12 olives, pitted and coarsely chopped

1 tablespoon capers, drained

1 pound spaghetti

1 tablespoon finely chopped fresh Italian parsley

In a skillet heat the olive oil, add the anchovies and garlic and cook for 1 to 2 minutes. Add the tomatoes and cook at a simmer for 10 minutes, then add the olives and capers. Continue cooking for 5 more minutes.

Meanwhile cook the spaghetti in a large pot of salted boiling water until al dente. Drain, add the sauce, sprinkle the parsley over all and serve.

Spaghetti with White Clam Sauce

SPAGHETTI O LINGUINE ALLE VONGOLE IN BIANCO

For this dish the Neapolitans use *telline*, the nice little clams which are so abundant along the coasts of Italy. Unfortunately they are not available in the United States, so try to choose the smallest clams you can find. They are more tender and flavorful.

6 servings

2 dozen clams

1 tablespoon all-purpose flour

1½ pounds spaghetti

¼ cup extra-virgin olive oil

4 garlic cloves, chopped

1 small hot red pepper (optional)

1 sprig fresh Italian parsley, plus 1 tablespoon chopped

Place the clams in a large bowl of water, add the flour and toss. Let stand 15 to 20 minutes. (This will make the clams release any residual sand.)

Cook the spaghetti in salted boiling water according to the instructions on the package.

While the spaghetti cooks, heat the olive oil in a large skillet. Remove the clams from the water and add them to the skillet with the garlic, hot pepper, and sprig of parsley. Cover and cook, shaking the skillet once or twice, until the clams open, about 5 minutes.

Remove the skillet from the heat and discard the hot pepper and the clams that have remained closed. Add the chopped parsley and stir. Pour the sauce over the pasta and serve.

NOTE *In this very Neapolitan dish, the shells of the clams are not removed. Therefore, make sure to have a little bowl next to each person in which the shells can be discarded.*

Spaghetti with Mussels | **SPAGHETTI CON COZZE**

This was such a favorite in my home! We had it often, since it was so easy to prepare. In the United States, mussels come from cultivated beds, therefore they are quite clean and safe to eat.

6 servings

1½ pounds mussels, scrubbed and beards removed

1 tablespoon all-purpose flour or cornmeal

¼ cup extra-virgin olive oil

2 sprigs Italian parsley, plus 2 tablespoons chopped for garnish

2 garlic cloves, crushed

1 teaspoon tomato paste

1 (14.5-ounce) can peeled or pureed tomatoes

1 pound linguine or spaghetti

Place the mussels in a bowl, cover with water, add the flour and toss. Let stand for 15 to 20 minutes. (This will make the mussels release any residual sand.)

Rinse the mussels. Place them in a large skillet, add ¼ cup water and set over medium heat. As soon as they start to open, transfer them to a bowl. Discard the mussels that have not opened.

Working over the bowl to collect all the juices, remove the mollusks from the shells and place them in a clean bowl. Discard the shells. Strain the juices accumulated in the first bowl through a paper towel and set aside.

Heat the olive oil in the skillet. Add the sprigs of parsley and garlic cloves. As soon as the garlic starts to fry add the mussels, and cook, stirring for a few minutes. Set aside.

In a saucepan, combine the tomato paste and tomatoes from the can with the reserved liquid from the mussels. Bring to a boil, reduce the heat and simmer for about 15 to 20 minutes. Add the mussels, stir, and simmer for 5 minutes. Remove from the heat.

Cook the pasta in salted boiling water according to the instructions on the package. Drain and transfer to a serving bowl. Dress with the sauce, sprinkle the chopped parsley over all and serve.

Spaghetti with Clams, Mussels and Octopus

SPAGHETTI O LINGUINE ALLA POSILLIPO

Posillipo is one of the most enchanting quarters of Naples. Jettisoning out on the west of the city, its promontory forms the last embracing arm of the gulf. It has a long panoramic road that climbs up its hill, along beautiful villas and ending with a woods of immense sea pines. I go back to Posillipo every time I travel to Italy. I am lucky to have my cousin Franca, who married a Neapolitan, living there. In fact, this recipe comes from her repertoire. Every time I make this dish it is like filling the kitchen with the scent of the sea.

6 servings

1 pound clams

1 pound mussels,
scrubbed and beards removed

1 tablespoon all-purpose flour
or cornmeal

8 ounces small shrimp

1 tablespoon kosher salt

¼ cup extra-virgin olive oil

2 sprigs Italian parsley

4 garlic cloves, crushed

1 teaspoon tomato paste

1 (28-ounce) can peeled tomatoes

Salt to taste

Freshly milled pepper to taste

2 octopus, cut into small pieces,
or 2 squids, cut into thin rings

1 pound spaghetti or linguine

2 tablespoons chopped fresh
Italian parsley

Place the clams and mussels in a bowl, cover with cold water and add the flour. Stir and set aside for about 15 to 20 minutes. Place the shrimp in cold water, add the kosher salt, stir and let stand for 15 minutes.

When ready to cook, rinse the clams and mussels, place in a large pot with ½ cup water and set over low heat. As soon as they start to open remove the open ones to a bowl. Discard those which have not opened and the water.

Working over a bowl to collect the juices, remove the mollusks from the shells and place in a clean bowl. Discard the shells. Strain the juices accumulated in the first bowl through a paper towel and reserve.

Drain the shrimp, shell and devein them, but reserve the shells.

Heat the olive oil in the pot. Add the parsley and garlic and cook until garlic starts to color. Stir the tomato paste into the reserved juices of the mollusks and add to the pot. Add the tomatoes with their juices, stir and crush the tomatoes with a wooden spoon. Add salt and pepper.

Tie the shells of the shrimp in a cheesecloth and place in the middle of the pot. Add the octopus, cover and cook at a simmer for 15 to 20 minutes, and then add the shrimp. Cook 5 minutes, then add the clams and mussels, stir and remove from the heat.

Cook the pasta in salted boiling water. When ready, drain and place into a serving bowl. Remove the bundle with the shells from the sauce, squeezing out as much sauce as possible. Add the chopped parsley, dress the pasta with the sauce and serve.

Spaghetti with Zucchini

SPAGHETTI O LINGUINE CON ZUCCHINE ALLA SORRENTINA

This is a delicious and simple dish from the enchanting coast of Sorrento.

6 servings

3 tablespoons extra-virgin olive oil

3 medium zucchini, cut into thin slices

1 egg

1 tablespoon unsalted butter, melted

2 tablespoons kosher salt

1 pound spaghetti or linguini

4 ounces Caciocavallo cheese or Asiago, coarsely grated

Freshly grated Parmesan cheese

In a large skillet, heat the olive oil and add the zucchini. Cook stirring often until golden. Remove from the heat and set aside.

In a large bowl, beat the egg. Remove the zucchini from the skillet with a slotted spoon leaving the cooking juices at the bottom. Add the zucchini to the bowl along with the butter and mix well.

In a large pasta pot, bring water to a boil. Add the salt, and cook the pasta until it is al dente. Drain the pasta but reserve 1 cup of its cooking water.

Transfer the pasta to the skillet along with the zucchini mixture and reheat over low heat. Stir and add some of the reserved water from the pasta. Continue stirring and add the Caciocavallo cheese. Serve immediately with the Parmesan cheese passed around.

Seafood Spaghetti | **SPAGHETTI AI FRUTTI DI MARE**

This is a dish we ate at least once a week in my home. While our friends would consider Fridays when Catholics were forbidden to eat meat a day of punishment, in my house it was almost a feast. We knew that Papa (the specialty cook) was making one of his favorite dishes, *spaghetti ai frutti di mare*, spaghetti with "the fruits of the sea." Friends would often request this dish ahead of time when they were invited to dinner.

A necessary ingredient in this sauce, squid should be cooked very little when poached or sautéed. But when used in a sauce or a *brodetto* (fish stew), the cooking time should be from 45 minutes to 1 hour. What happens is that after a few minutes of cooking, the squid toughen. To make them tender again, you must cook them longer until they soften again. And in this recipe and similar ones, you want as much flavor as possible from the little beasts, another good reason to cook them longer.

Don't be put off by the length of this recipe. Yes, it requires a little patience but the result is well worth it. As you can see, many steps can be done in advance. Think of the blue Tyrrhenian Sea and go to work!

Dresses 1 pound of spaghetti

4 ounces medium shrimp

1 sprig Italian parsley plus chopped parsley for garnish

1 small hot red pepper (optional)

2 garlic cloves, peeled

12 small clams, scrubbed and rinsed

18 mussels, debearded, scrubbed, and rinsed

1 dry bay leaf

¼ cup plus 2 tablespoons extra-virgin olive oil

8 ounces squid, cleaned and cut into circles

Shell the shrimp but do not discard the shells. Tie the shells in cheesecloth together with the sprig of parsley, the hot pepper if using, and 1 garlic clove. Devein the shrimp and cut in half lengthwise.

In a large pot, place the clams and mussels, add the bay leaf and ¼ cup water. Cover and set on the heat. Steam for about 4 to 5 minutes, shaking the pot once or twice. Remove the lid and start transferring to a bowl all the clams and mussels that have opened. Discard any unopened ones. Remove the clams and mussels from their shells over the pot to collect all their juices. Discard the shells but keep a few to garnish the pasta. Strain the liquid accumulated in the pot through a paper towel and reserve.

Heat ¼ cup of olive oil in the pot. Chop the remaining garlic clove and add. Cook a few seconds stirring, then add the bundle with the shell mixture. Sauté for 2 to 3 minutes, stirring, then add the squid. Cook stirring for 2 to 3 more minutes, then add the wine. Let it reduce by half.

¾ cup dry white wine

1 teaspoon tomato paste

1 (28-ounce) can peeled tomatoes

2 small whitings, about 8 ounces, gutted with heads on if possible, or 1 monkfish tail

1 pound spaghetti

Salt to taste

Freshly milled pepper to taste

Add the tomato paste and tomatoes with their juice. Crush the tomatoes with a wooden spoon. Cover the pot, bring to a boil, lower the heat, and simmer over very low heat for about 40 minutes, stirring often. If the liquid tends to diminish, add some or all of the liquid collected from the clams and mussels. Push the bundle with the shrimp shells to one side of the pot and place the whitings or monkfish in the middle, cover and continue simmering until the fish is cooked: 8 minutes for the whiting, and 15 minutes for the monkfish. Transfer the fish to a plate. When cool, discard the skin and bones and flake the fish.

Meanwhile cook the spaghetti in boiling, salted water. Drain the pasta and place in a serving bowl.

Remove the pot from the heat. Remove the bundle with the shells, squeezing out as much juice as possible, and discard. Add the remaining juice from the clams and mussels, if any. Add the shrimp and simmer until they turn pink. Return the flaked fish to the pot. Season with salt and pepper. Remove from the heat.

Add the remaining 2 tablespoons olive oil to the sauce, stir, pour over the spaghetti and sprinkle the whole with parsley.

NOTE   *Sometimes I add scallops, which are not really found in Italy, to the sauce and cook them for a few minutes until done. If the scallops are too big, cut them into quarters.*

Spaghetti with Sun-Dried Tomatoes

SPAGHETTI RUSTICI

Here is a typical peasant dish with the scent of autumn. Before sun-dried tomatoes became the rage in America, you would find them only in rural places of Italy. They were indeed the sign of fall. Sun-dried tomatoes were not, by any means, considered gourmet food. They were essential to add flavor to a tomato sauce, and they were used sparingly.

Today sun-dried tomatoes are readily available. There is no need to buy those in olive oil, which are quite expensive. I do the olive oil part myself. Just soak the sun-dried tomatoes in lukewarm water for half an hour, drain and dry them well with paper towels. Place in jars and pour a good extra-virgin olive oil to cover. If you wish, you can add either a bunch of rosemary or a few basil leaves. They keep for a long time if stored in a cool, dark place or in the refrigerator. When you need the tomatoes, simply drain the olive oil and use. The olive oil is excellent for cooking.

6 servings

4 ounces sun-dried tomatoes packed in oil

2 red onions, chopped

1 garlic clove

¼ cup extra-virgin olive oil

1 teaspoon tomato paste

¼ cup dry red wine

½ cup chicken broth, homemade or canned, plus more as needed

A few hot red pepper flakes, crushed (optional)

1 pound spaghetti or linguine

2 teaspoons finely chopped fresh Italian parsley

In a large saucepan, combine the sun-dried tomatoes, onions, garlic, and 2 tablespoons of the olive oil. Cover and cook over low heat for 20 minutes, stirring often.

Combine the tomato paste with the wine and add to the pan.

Cook briefly and then add ½ cup of broth and the pepper flakes if using. Cook at a simmer, covered, until the tomatoes and onions are tender, about 20 to 30 minutes. If necessary add more broth. When finished pour this sauce in a food processor and puree. Return it to the pan.

Cook the pasta in salted boiling water according to the instructions on the package. Drain but reserve some of the cooking water.

Reheat the sauce if necessary. Remove from the heat, stir in the remaining olive oil, pour on the pasta and toss. If the pasta is a little dry, add some of the reserved pasta water. Add the chopped parsley and serve.

Fusilli with Tuna, Olives and Capers

FUSILLI ALLA NAPOLETANA

An erudite Italian writer, Carlo Bernardi, in an amusing article entitled *Il Paese dei Fusilli* describes a festive event in the town of Giovi, in the Cilento area of Campania. This delightful little town, perched on top of a hill overlooking the Gulf of Salerno on one side and that of Policastro on the other, stages a festival dedicated to the *fusillo*! The festival, called *sagra* in Italian, takes place in the middle of August for seven days and attracts a great number of visitors. But Mr. Bernardi points out that the *fusillo* of this festival is not the short, twisted pasta that we all know. No, the *fusillo* of Giovi is homemade with eggs, flour, a little water, and shaped into a long, straight narrow tube (*fuso* in Italian, hence *fusillo*) with a hole through the whole length of it. During the festival, the local women congregate in the kitchen of the ancient San Francis Convent and for seven days make and cook *fusilli*, which are then dressed with a succulent *ragù*.

In this quick and delicious recipe, tuna packed in olive oil is the crucial ingredient which gives the uncooked sauce its special taste.

6 servings

1 (6-ounce) can tuna packed in oil

4 ripe tomatoes, peeled, seeded and cut into chunks

20 black olives, pitted and cut into circlets

1½ tablespoons capers, drained

1 garlic clove, finely chopped

½ cup loosely packed fresh basil, finely chopped

2 sprigs Italian parsley, finely chopped

2 tablespoons kosher salt

1 pound fusilli

In a pasta bowl, place the tuna and its oil. Crumble the tuna, but not much, it should still keep some texture. Add the tomatoes, olives, and capers and mix well.

Add the garlic, basil, and parsley to the bowl. Toss to mix well.

In a large pasta pot, bring water to a boil, add the salt. As soon as the water comes back to a boil, add the pasta, stir, and cover the pot. Cook until pasta is tender. Drain and toss the pasta with the tuna and tomato mixture. Serve immediately.

Fusilli with Tuna Sauce | **FUSILLI DEL PESCATORE**

My cousin Franca extracted this recipe from a fisherman of Massa Lubrense, a charming town on the Amalfi Drive were she and her family spend the summer. She made this sauce when my husband and I were visiting with our friends from New York. They declared the fusilli "delicious and savory." It is essential to use good canned tuna packed in olive oil.

6 servings

1 (6-ounce) can tuna packed in olive oil

1 garlic clove, crushed

1 (8-ounce) can tomato sauce

20 black olives, pitted and sliced

1 tablespoon capers, drained

1 pound fusilli

1 tablespoon chopped fresh Italian parsley

Bring a large pot of water to a boil.

Drain the oil from the tuna into a saucepan. Heat and add the garlic. As soon as the garlic starts to sizzle, add the tuna. Cook, over medium heat, stirring and breaking the tuna into small pieces, about 3 to 5 minutes. Add the tomato sauce. Rinse the can with half a can of water and add. Stir, cover the pan, bring to a boil, reduce the heat to low, and simmer for 20 minutes, stirring often. Add the olives and capers. Cook just to heat through.

Bring water to a boil, add some salt and cover the pot. As soon as the water comes back to a boil, add the fusilli and stir. Cover the pot and let the pasta cook at a constant boil according to the package directions, stirring occasionally. Drain the pasta, dress with the prepared sauce, sprinkle with the chopped parsley and serve.

Spaghetti with Squid Sauce

SPAGHETTI O LINGUINE AL SUGO DI SEPPIA

If you are ever on the Amalfi Drive be sure to go fishing. You will surely have this tasty pasta cooked by one of the fishermen.

6 servings

3 tablespoons extra-virgin olive oil

2 garlic cloves, crushed

1 sprig Italian parsley

12 ounces squid, cleaned and cut into round strips, tentacles divided

¼ cup white dry wine

2 anchovies packed in oil, or 1 teaspoon anchovy paste

1 (16-ounce) can peeled tomatoes

1 pound linguine or spaghetti

1 tablespoon chopped fresh Italian parsley

Heat the olive oil in a large skillet, and add the garlic and parsley. As soon as the garlic starts to sizzle, add the squids. Cook stirring for about 5 minutes.

Add the wine. Let it evaporate, and add the anchovies and tomatoes with their juices. Crush the tomatoes with a wooden spoon while stirring. Cover, reduce the heat and cook at a simmer for 30 to 40 minutes, or until the squids are tender. Discard the garlic and the sprig of parsley if you wish.

Bring water to a boil, add some salt and cover the pot. As soon as the water comes back to a boil, add the spaghetti and stir. Cover the pot and let the pasta cook at a constant boil according to the package directions, stirring occasionally. Drain and dress the pasta with the sauce. Sprinkle with the chopped parsley and serve.

Pasta with Smoked Mozzarella | **PASTA AFFUMICATA**

You must have a good smoked mozzarella for this pasta. Its flavor enhances the pasta sauce, which is a delicate fusion of mozzarella and ricotta. It is a satisfying little dish, a meal in itself, which I usually end with only a good, juicy pear. Sometimes I am even tempted to slice the pear into the pasta. Well, you can try it!

6 servings

1 pound penne, rigatoni, fusilli or shells

2 cups whole-milk ricotta, drained

4 ounces fresh whole-milk mozzarella, diced

4 ounces smoked whole-milk mozzarella, diced

Bring water to a boil in a large pot, add some salt and cover the pot. As soon as the water comes back to a boil, add the pasta and stir. Cover the pot and let the pasta cook at a constant boil according to the package directions, stirring occasionally.

Place the ricotta in a heated shallow pasta bowl.

Drain the pasta but reserve 1 cup of its cooking water. Combine ¼ cup of the water with the ricotta. Add the pasta and toss. If the mixture becomes too dry, add a little more of the reserved water. Sprinkle the pasta with the mozzarellas. Toss once and serve. The mozzarellas should melt at the table.

Pasta with Zucchini Mozzarella Sauce

Nerano is one of the gems along the Amalfi Drive. This pasta is one of the specialties for which this town is famous.

6 servings

6 tablespoons (¾ stick) unsalted butter

1 tablespoon extra-virgin olive oil

1 pound zucchini, sliced in the round

1 pound penne or fusilli

1 egg yolk

¼ to ⅓ cup heavy cream

1 to 2 tablespoons chopped fresh basil, or 1½ teaspoons dried

4 ounces whole-milk mozzarella, diced

Freshly grated Parmesan cheese

Heat 3 tablespoons of the butter and the olive oil in a large skillet. Add the zucchini and cook stirring often until tender, 10 to 15 minutes. Transfer them to a serving bowl and keep warm.

Bring water to a boil, add some salt and cover the pot. As soon as the water comes back to a boil, add the penne and stir. Cover the pot and let the pasta cook at a constant boil according to the package directions, stirring occasionally.

While the pasta cooks, beat the egg yolk and cream. Add the basil, toss, add to the zucchini and toss again.

When the pasta is ready, drain it but reserve 1 cup of its cooking water. Add the pasta to the zucchini mixture, add the mozzarella and, if necessary, some of the reserved water (this pasta should be a little wet). Add the remaining 3 tablespoons of butter, toss well and serve with the Parmesan cheese.

Pasta with Zucchini and Ricotta

PASTA CON ZUCCHINE E RICOTTA ALLA FRASSO

We call this recipe *alla Frasso* after the place where my cousin Gianna and her husband Pasquale live. Frasso Telesino is a charming little town on a hill in the province of Benevento in Campania. Gianna, who is an excellent cook, made this dish for my husband Harold and me when we were visiting. Naturally I asked for the recipe.

6 to 8 servings

2 tablespoons extra-virgin olive oil

1 large onion, sliced

3 small zucchini, cut into small cubes

1 tablespoon cornstarch

¼ cup milk

½ cup heavy cream

1 tablespoon unsalted butter

1 pound short pasta, such as rigatoni, penne or fusilli

1 pound whole-milk ricotta, drained

Freshly grated Parmesan cheese

In a large skillet, heat the olive oil, add the onion and cook over low heat stirring often until soft and translucent, about 10 minutes.

Add the zucchini, stir and cover the skillet. Cook for 8 to 10 minutes.

In a small bowl, combine the cornstarch and milk, and add to the zucchini. Cook briefly and add the cream. Simmer over low heat until the zucchini are tender, about 5 to 8 minutes. Remove from the heat and add the butter. Mix and keep warm.

Bring water to a boil, add some salt and cover the pot. As soon as the water comes back to a boil, add the pasta and stir. Cover the pot and let the pasta cook at a constant boil according to the package directions, stirring occasionally. Drain, but reserve 1 cup of its cooking water.

In a serving pasta bowl, place the ricotta and soften it with some of the reserved water. Add the pasta and zucchini sauce and toss well. If the mixture is too dry, add some of the reserved water. Serve the pasta with Parmesan cheese.

NOTE *When available, my cousin adds 1 cup of meat* ragù *to the sauce.*

Seafood and Zucchini Penne

PENNE O FUSILLI AI FRUTTI DI MARE E ZUCCHINE

This is another favorite Neapolitan recipe combining *mare e terra*, the flavors of the sea and the land.

6 servings

24 mussels, debearded and scrubbed

12 clams, scrubbed

1 tablespoon all-purpose flour

2 tablespoons extra-virgin olive oil

1 onion, sliced

2 or 3 medium zucchini, cut into thin slices

8 ounces small shrimp, shelled, deveined and cut lengthwise in half

1 pound penne or fusilli

2 garlic cloves, crushed

1 or 2 sprigs Italian parsley

¾ cup dry white wine

1 tablespoon chopped fresh Italian parsley

Place the mussels and clams in a bowl, cover with water and add 1 tablespoon of flour. Let stand 15 to 20 minutes. (This will make the mollusks release any residual sand.)

In a large skillet, heat 1 tablespoon of the olive oil and add the onion. Reduce the heat and cook over low heat until the onion is soft and translucent. Add the zucchini and ¼ cup water. Cover and cook the zucchini, stirring often, until softened, about 8 to 10 minutes. Add the shrimp, cook over medium heat until they start to turn red, about 5 minutes. Remove to a bowl and keep warm.

Bring water to a boil, add some salt and cover the pot. As soon as the water comes back to a boil, add the pasta and stir. Cover the pot and let the pasta cook at a constant boil according to the package directions, stirring occasionally.

Heat the remaining tablespoon of olive oil, the garlic and sprig of parsley in the skillet. Drain the mussels and clams and add to the skillet. Add the wine and stir. Cook, shaking the skillet, until the mussels and clams have opened. Discard any that do not open. Remove the opened ones from their shells and place in a bowl; discard the shells and the sprig of parsley.

Pick up the mussels and clams with a slotted spoon and add them to the bowl with the zucchini. Strain the broth from the bowl and the skillet through a paper towel. Wipe the skillet clean and return the broth to it. Set the skillet over medium heat and add the zucchini mixture. Heat through.

Drain the pasta, place it in a serving bowl and dress it with the zucchini mixture. Sprinkle with the chopped parsley and serve.

Rigatoni with Fish Sauce | PACCHERI AL RAGÙ DI PESCE

Neapolitans have a great sense of humor and a funny way with words. *Paccheri* means "big slaps on the face." It is a typical Neapolitan pasta and not easy to find here, but *rigatoni* are a perfect substitute. Also, the ideal fish for this dish is the *scorfano*, "scorpion fish" in English. This is not easy to find either, so I suggest using a red mullet or a monkfish, which are quite flavorful.

6 servings

1 carrot

1 celery stalk

1 small onion

1 sprig Italian parsley

1/3 cup extra-virgin olive oil

2 red mullets, 1 1/2 pounds total, filleted and skinned but heads and bones reserved, or monkfish (see note)

1/4 cup red wine

1 (8-ounce) can tomato puree

1 tablespoon tomato paste

1 1/2 cups fish broth or water

1 tablespoon chopped fresh rosemary, or 1 1/2 teaspoons dried

1 cup black olives, pitted and halved

1 pound rigatoni

1 tablespoon chopped fresh Italian parsley

Chop the carrot, celery, onion, and parsley coarsely in a food processor.

In a large skillet heat 2 tablespoons of the olive oil. Add the chopped vegetables and sauté for a few minutes.

Cut the fish into 1/2-inch strips and set aside. Make sure the gills have been removed from the heads of the fish (if not it will make the sauce bitter). Break the bones into pieces and add these and the heads to the vegetables in the skillet. Sauté for a few minutes and then add the wine. Let simmer until evaporated. Add the tomato puree and cook covered over low heat for 5 minutes,.

Dilute the tomato paste in the broth and add to the sauce. Cover and simmer very gently for about 45 minutes, stirring every once in a while.

In a skillet heat 3 tablespoons of the olive oil, add the rosemary and fish strips. Sauté for 3 to 5 minutes over medium heat and then add the olives. Cook until fish is done, about 5 to 8 minutes. Keep warm.

Bring water in a large pot to a boil, add some salt and cover the pot. As soon as the water comes back to a boil, add the pasta and stir. Cover the pot and let the pasta cook at a constant boil according to the package directions, stirring occasionally. Drain and transfer to a mixing bowl.

Strain the sauce pushing the solids down to extract all the juices and flavor, reheat if necessary and pour half of it on the pasta. Toss.

To serve: Divide the remaining sauce among 6 plates, put pasta on them, top with the fish mixture and sprinkle with chopped parsley.

NOTE *If using monkfish, ask the fishmonger to give you some heads and bones of any white fish for your sauce. Monkfish, after being boned, should be cut into thin slices. It needs a little more cooking than the other fish.*

Two green peppers are sometimes added to this dish. The peppers are roasted, skinned and cut into strips (see recipe for Roasted Bell Peppers, page 262).

Penne with Whiting and Clams | **MACCHERONI MARECHIARO**

Marechiaro is a charming district of Naples, widely known because one of the most romantic Neapolitan songs is named after it. This dish is a typical specialty served in its local restaurants. Like so many of the sauces from the south of Italy, the tomato, which is the main element, does not cook long. The idea is to retain its fruity taste.

6 servings

1 pound grooved penne

¼ cup extra-virgin olive oil

2 garlic cloves, chopped

1 (28-ounce) can tomato puree

½ teaspoon dried oregano

2 fillets of whiting or flounder

12 ounces small clams or mussels, scrubbed and mussels debearded

1 tablespoon chopped fresh Italian parsley

Basil leaves for garnish

Bring water to a boil, add some salt and cover the pot. As soon as the water comes back to a boil, add the pasta and stir. Cover the pot and let the pasta cook at a constant boil according to the package directions, stirring occasionally. Drain but reserve 1 cup of its cooking water. Place the pasta in a serving bowl. Add 2 tablespoons of the olive oil, toss and keep warm.

In the same pot in which the pasta cooked, heat 2 tablespoons of the olive oil, add the garlic, cook a few seconds, then add the tomato puree and oregano. Cover and cook over medium heat for 10 minutes. Add the fish fillets, cook until the fish starts to flake, about 5 to 8 minutes. Flake the fish with a wooden spoon and add the clams. Cook until they start to open. Remove and discard any that don't open.

Return the pasta to the pot and continue cooking for a few more minutes while tossing, or until the pasta mixture is quite hot. If necessary add some of the reserved water.

Transfer the pasta to a serving bowl. Sprinkle with parsley and garnish with basil leaves and serve.

NOTE *Make sure to have little bowls on the table to discard the shells.*

Pasta with Broccoli and Fried Garlic

PASTA E BROCCOLI CON L'AGLIO FRITTO

Fast and savory, this pasta is pleasingly tangy with the scent of garlic and good olive oil.

4 to 6 servings

2 tablespoons kosher salt

1 pound bowtie or *rotelle* pasta

1 bunch fresh broccoli, trimmed and cut into small florets

2 carrots, diced

3 tablespoons extra-virgin olive oil

5 garlic cloves, chopped

1 tablespoon chopped fresh Italian parsley

2 or 3 ripe tomatoes, coarsely chopped

4 or 5 fresh basil leaves, chopped

In a large pasta pot, bring water to boil. Add salt and wait for the water to return to a boil, then add the pasta, broccoli and carrots. Stir and cook for 12 to 15 minutes. Taste for doneness. Reserve 1 cup of the cooking water and drain pasta and vegetables in a colander. Set aside.

Return the pot in which the pasta cooked to the heat. Add the olive oil, garlic, parsley, and tomatoes, and cook for 5 minutes stirring, then add the pasta and vegetables. Stir again and cook just to heat through. Stir in the basil. If the pasta is too dry, add a little of the reserved water and serve.

NOTE *This pasta is really a summer dish because it should be made with fresh tomatoes. It is also good served at room temperature.*

Rigatoni with Eggs and Prosciutto

RIGATONI CON UOVA E PROSCIUTTO

This festive dish can be served as a main dish. Of course the Neapolitans would not approve—pasta is always a first course for them. Decide for yourself, but in any case serve a light course afterwards, such as chicken or veal cutlets.

6 servings

1 pound rigatoni

3 eggs

4 ounces prosciutto in one slice, fat removed and diced (see note)

¼ cup heavy cream

½ teaspoon nutmeg

Freshly milled pepper to taste

4 ounces Gruyere cheese, coarsely chopped

Unsalted butter for dotting

Butter an ovenproof 9 × 13-inch casserole from which you can serve.

Preheat the oven to 375 degrees F.

In a large pot bring water to a boil, add some salt and cover the pot. As soon as the water comes back to a boil, add the rigatoni and stir. Cover the pot and let the pasta cook at a constant boil according to the package directions, but keep the pasta quite al dente.

In a large mixing bowl, beat the eggs, then add the prosciutto, cream, nutmeg, and pepper. Set aside.

Drain the pasta well and add to the mixing bowl. Toss thoroughly. Add the Gruyere, toss again and transfer the pasta to the prepared casserole. Dot with the butter and bake for 30 to 40 minutes, or until the top is nicely golden. Cool for 10 minutes before serving.

NOTE   *I buy the end pieces of the prosciutto, and when I need some, I cut it off myself. However you must ask your butcher or grocery store to set aside an end piece for you.*

Angel Hair Timbale with Mushrooms

TIMBALLO DI CAPELLI D'ANGELO

I make this elegant dish from the Neapolitan aristocratic table often when I have guests. With a light antipasto and salad it makes the most satisfying meal. However, do not forget dessert . . .

8 servings

2 tablespoons unsalted butter

Unflavored dry bread crumbs

1¼ pounds angel hair or capellini pasta

2 cups Veal and Mushroom Sauce (recipe on page 84)

8 ounces whole-milk ricotta, drained

2 eggs, lightly beaten

Freshly grated Parmesan cheese

1 pound whole-milk mozzarella, thinly sliced

Unsalted butter for dotting

Butter a 2-quart oval baking dish from which you can serve. Sprinkle with bread crumbs and set aside. Heat the oven to 375 degrees F.

In a large pot, bring water to a boil, add some salt and cover the pot. As soon as the water comes back to a boil, add the pasta and stir. Cover the pot and let the pasta cook at a constant boil according to the package directions, stirring occasionally. Drain and toss with half of the veal-mushroom sauce. Add the ricotta and beaten eggs, mix well.

Place one thin layer of the pasta in the prepared baking dish, sprinkle with Parmesan and top with a layer of mozzarella slices. Add a few spoonfuls of the sauce. Repeat layers until all ingredients are used, finishing with a layer of pasta.

Dot with butter and bake for 40 to 45 minutes. Cool 10 minutes before serving.

NOTE *As a first course for an important meal, I layer the ingredients in 3-inch ramekins and bake them for 30 to 40 minutes. Cool for 10 minutes, then unmold on individual plates. It looks elegant and appetizing.*

Spring Vegetable Timbale | **TIMBALLO DI MACCHERONI PRIMAVERA**

A simple *timballo* with a flavorful vegetable sauce made with broccoli and mushrooms, this is a convenient dish for a get-together since it can be prepared in advance. I always add some dried mushrooms to the fresh ones. It really adds an earthy element to the flavors.

6 to 8 servings

2 tablespoons dried porcini mushrooms

Unsalted butter for pan

¼ cup unflavored dry bread crumbs plus more for the pan

3 tablespoons extra-virgin olive oil

1 garlic clove, crushed

8 ounces mushrooms, sliced

1 bunch broccoli, trimmed, cut into florets, stems peeled and diced

3 or 4 ripe tomatoes, peeled, seeded, and diced

½ cup homemade pesto sauce

1 pound penne or ziti

2 eggs, beaten

8 ounces whole-milk mozzarella, thinly sliced

½ cup freshly grated Parmesan or Grana Padano cheese

Unsalted butter for dotting

In a bowl, soak the dried porcini mushrooms in 1½ cups lukewarm water and set aside.

Butter a 9-inch or 10-inch springform pan with unsalted butter and dust it with some bread crumbs. Set aside. Preheat oven to 375° F.

Heat the olive oil in a large skillet. Add the garlic and fresh mushrooms and cook until the liquid released by the mushrooms has been absorbed.

Gently lift the porcini mushrooms from their soaking liquid in order not to disturb the sediments at the bottom of the bowl, and add them to the skillet. Filter the soaking liquid through a paper towel and set aside.

Add the broccoli to the skillet and sauté for 2 to 3 minutes. Add the strained soaking liquid from the porcini and cook for 5 minutes, then add the tomatoes. Cook over medium heat for 8 to 10 minutes. Stir in 2 tablespoons of bread crumbs.

Add the pesto and cook 2 to 3 minutes, until the pesto is thoroughly heated. Discard the garlic.

Bring water to a boil in a large pot, add some salt and cover the pot. As soon as the water comes back to a boil, add the pasta and stir. Cover the pot and let the pasta cook at a constant boil according to the package directions, stirring occasionally, but keep it rather al dente. Drain and return the pasta to its pot. Add the eggs and mix well. Reserve a few broccoli florets for garnish before adding the remaining vegetable mixture to the pasta. Mix well.

Spread one-third of the pasta mixture in the prepared springform pan, add half of the mozzarella and sprinkle some of the Parmesan over. Repeat with another layer of pasta, the remaining mozzarella and some Parmesan. Top with the remaining pasta, sprinkle with the remaining Parmesan and 2 tablespoons bread crumbs and dot with butter.

Bake for 30 to 40 minutes, or until the top is golden. Cool for 10 minutes before removing the sides of the pan to place the timbale on a serving dish. Garnish with the reserved broccoli florets, slice, and serve.

Wheel Pasta with Meat Sauce | **ANELLETTI DEL MONZÙ**

This ring-shaped pasta, *anelletti*, got its name from the French chefs who were employed by the aristocratic Neapolitan and Sicilian families during the time of the Bourbon kings. The best sauce for this dish is Genovese Meat Sauce (recipe on page 83). However, any good *ragù* sauce will be appropriate.

6 servings

3 tablespoons unsalted butter

Unflavored dry bread crumbs

1 pound anelletti or wheel pasta

2 cups Genovese Meat Sauce (recipe on page 83), or any other meat sauce

¼ cup freshly grated Caciocavallo cheese

½ cup lard, vegetable, shortening, or olive oil

2 onions, chopped

¾ pound ground veal

½ cup dry red wine

1 tablespoon tomato paste

¾ cup chicken or beef broth

2 cups shelled fresh peas, or frozen and defrosted

1 pound Pecorino Romano or Sardo cheese, thinly sliced

Preheat the oven to 375 degrees F.

Butter a 10-inch springform pan with 2 tablespoons unsalted butter. Sprinkle with bread crumbs.

Bring water to a boil in a large pot, add some salt and cover. As soon as the water comes back to a boil, add the pasta and stir. Cover the pot and let the pasta cook at a constant boil according to the package directions, stirring occasionally. When done, drain the pasta and place it into a mixing bowl. Add 1 cup of the sauce and sprinkle the Caciocavallo over the pasta. Toss and mix well. Set aside.

In a large skillet heat the lard and sauté the onions. Add the ground veal and cook until it looses its red color. Add the wine and let evaporate. Add the tomato paste, stir well, add the broth, cover the pan and cook at a simmer for about 20 to 30 minutes, stirring every once in a while.

If using fresh peas, add them 8 minutes before the sauce is cooked. If using frozen peas, add at the last minute. Set aside.

Cover the bottom and sides of the prepared pan with some of the pasta. Fill the pan with the veal and peas mixture, top with the slices of cheese and cover with the remaining pasta. Spoon remaining meat sauce over the pasta. Sprinkle with bread crumbs and dot with the remaining 1 tablespoon of butter.

Bake for 30 to 40 minutes. Let rest for 15 minutes before removing the side of the pan. Place timbale on a dish and serve.

Tagliatelle with Lemon Sauce | **TAGLIATELLE AL LIMONE**

A delightful, simple sauce with the clean fragrance of fresh lemons; be sure to choose lemons with unblemished skins to use for the zest.

6 servings

1 batch Basic Pasta Dough (recipe on page 92)

Zest of 1 large or 2 small lemons, very finely chopped

3 tablespoons unsalted butter

2 cups heavy cream, slightly heated

Freshly grated Parmesan cheese

Stretch the dough according to the pasta recipe and cut into tagliatelle or fettucine. Spread the pasta on kitchen towels.

Place the lemon zest and butter in a pasta serving bowl. Keep in a warm place.

Cook the tagliatelle in plenty of salted boiling water for 2 to 3 minutes, then drain but reserve some of the cooking water.

Transfer the tagliatelle to the pasta bowl, toss and add the warm cream. Toss gently but thoroughly, and if the mixture is a little dry, add some of the reserved water. Serve with grated Parmesan cheese.

Whole-Wheat Pasta with Cooked Salami and Onion Sauce

PAPPARDELLE INTEGRALI AL COTTO E CIPOLLE

A rustic dish from the countryside of Campania. If you cannot find *salami cotto*, use a good American ham. The *pappardelle* are usually cut with a serrated wheel. They look great this way.

6 servings

3 ounces *salami cotto*,
each slice cut into thin strips
(see above)

3 tablespoons extra-virgin
olive oil

4 or 5 large onions, about 2
pounds, thinly sliced

½ teaspoon chopped
fresh rosemary

1 cup white dry wine

1 batch Whole-Wheat Pasta
Dough, made with 4 eggs (recipe
on page 94)

2 teaspoons chopped fresh
Italian parsley

Freshly grated Parmesan cheese

Chop one quarter of the salami very finely and place in a saucepan with the olive oil, onions, and rosemary. Cook over low heat, stirring often and adding the wine a little at a time until the onions are quite soft, about 30 to 40 minutes. Remove from the heat and add the strips of salami. Set aside.

Roll and cut the sheets of pasta into 6-inch long and ¾-inch wide noodles. Keep the noodles or *pappardelle* on trays covered with kitchen (not paper) towels until ready to cook. This can be done in advance, but keep the noodles in a cool place, not the refrigerator.

Cook the noodles in a large pot of salted boiling water until al dente, about 10 minutes. Drain but reserve 1 cup of the cooking water.

Reheat the sauce and toss with the noodles. If too dry, add a little bit of the reserved water. Sprinkle with the parsley and serve with the Parmesan cheese.

Black Fettuccine with Creamy Crab Sauce

FETTUCCINE NERE AL SUGO DI GRANCHIO E CREMA

This is a fancy and delicious dish served by fine restaurants along the Neapolitan coastline.

6 servings

1 batch Black Pasta Dough (recipe on page 93)

2 cups heavy cream

4 ripe pear tomatoes, peeled, seeded, and diced

1 pound fresh crabmeat

2 tablespoons freshly grated Parmesan or Grana Padano cheese, plus more for serving

1 heaping tablespoon chopped fresh Italian parsley

Cut the pasta dough for fettucine (¼-inch wide) according to the recipe on page 93. Set the pasta on trays lined with kitchen towels.

In a saucepan, bring the cream to a boil and simmer for 5 to 6 minutes. Add the tomatoes and cook at a simmer for 5 more minutes. Add the crabmeat and 2 tablespoons of the grated cheese. Cook just to heat through. Keep warm.

Cook the fettuccine in a large pot of salted boiling water, about 3 to 5 minutes. Drain, but reserve 1 cup of its cooking water.

Toss the fettuccine with the crabmeat sauce. If the mixture is too dry, add some of the reserved water. Sprinkle the pasta with the chopped parsley and serve with some grated cheese.

NOTE   *This recipe is an exception to the rule "no cheese on fish sauces" because of its cream base. If you prefer you can make this recipe with two-colored fettuccine: use a half batch of black and a half batch of green pasta (page 93).*

Seafood Ravioli | **RAVIOLI DI MARE**

In the past, homemade pasta was seldom dressed with fish sauces because their taste was considered too strong. But food tastes evolve, and people with imagination love to experiment. Lobster and other shellfish were found to complement a delicate homemade pasta very well.

My father the *buongustaio* (gourmand) would buy a lobster once in a while. They were sold only in some exclusive markets, and were expensive. My mother, with her innate sense of parsimony, used the lobster for more than one meal. This is how these ravioli were invented.

6 servings

RAVIOLI

2 tablespoons extra-virgin olive oil

1 garlic clove

1 sprig Italian parsley

½ cup lobster meat, or a mix of crabmeat, shrimp and scallops

½ cup white wine

2 egg whites, beaten

1 batch Basic Pasta Dough, prepared with 4 eggs (recipe on page 92)

PREPARE THE RAVIOLI FILLING Place in a skillet the olive oil, garlic and parsley. Heat and add the lobster meat or shellfish. Cook for 2 to 3 minutes. Add the wine, and let it evaporate, then remove from the heat and cool. Place the mixture into a food processor and add the egg whites. Chop finely.

PREPARE THE RAVIOLI Divide the dough into 2 parts and each part into 4 wedges. Roll one wedge at a time into thin sheets. (I use the last notch of my pasta machine because I like my stuffed pasta very thin.) Set the stretched pasta on kitchen towels (do not use paper towels). Keep the sheets covered with kitchen towels to prevent them from drying.

TO STUFF AND CUT THE RAVIOLI If using a ravioli tray (see note), place one sheet of dough over the tray and press the dough gently into its depressions. Place a small amount of the filling, no more than a teaspoon, into each depression. Dip your finger in a glass of water and run it along the lines where the ravioli will be cut. Cover the filled tray with another sheet of dough pressing down along the dampened edges to make sure the two sheets stick. Using a rolling pin, go over the tray. This will seal and cut the ravioli. Turn the tray over and gently separate the ravioli. Keep the ravioli on baking sheets or trays lined with kitchen towels (not paper) until ready to cook. Be sure to reassemble all the scraps of dough before they get too dry to be rolled out again for additional ravioli. Repeat this process until all the dough has been used.

If using a ravioli cutter, place a sheet of dough on a work surface and place 1 teaspoon of filling at appropriate distances on it. Dip your finger into water and dampen the dough alongside and in between the filling where the pasta will be cut. Cover with an equal size sheet of dough, press along the wet part to make the

SAUCE

1/3 cup extra-virgin olive oil

1 small onion, chopped

1 garlic clove, chopped

1/2 cup white wine

12 ounces small shrimp, peeled and deveined (reserve shells)

1/2 tablespoon all-purpose flour

1 1/2 tablespoons tomato paste

1 1/2 cups or more fish or chicken broth

Kosher salt

pasta adhere, and cut with a ravioli cutter. Keep the ravioli on baking sheets or trays lined with kitchen towels (not paper) until ready to cook. Repeat this process until all the dough has been used.

Reserve any unused filling.

PREPARE THE SAUCE In a skillet, put 1/4 cup of the olive oil, the onion and garlic. Cook over low heat until the onion is very soft but not brown, stirring often. Add a little bit of the wine to prevent the onion from coloring. Add the shrimp and cook until they turn red, stirring often. Remove to a mixing bowl and set aside. Wipe the skillet clean.

Add remaining oil and the shells of the shrimp to the skillet and sauté for 3 to 5 minutes. In a small bowl, combine the flour and tomato paste, soften with the remaining wine and add to the skillet. Simmer for 5 minutes. Add 1 cup of broth, bring to a boil and cook for 5 more minutes, stirring often. Place the mixture into a strainer over a bowl and push down to extract as much liquid as possible. Discard the solids and return the liquid to the skillet. If you have leftover filling from the ravioli, add it to the sauce. Dice the shrimp and add them to the sauce. If sauce is too thick, add a little more broth. Keep warm.

To cook the ravioli, bring a large pot of water to a boil. Add 2 to 3 tablespoons of kosher salt, cover the pot. Wait until the water comes back to a boil and add half of the ravioli, stir gently, cover the pot and let the water come back to a boil. Boil ravioli for 5 to 7 minutes and then taste one for doneness. If tender remove the ravioli with a slotted spoon to a colander. Bring the water back to a boil and cook the remaining ravioli.

Reheat the sauce, if necessary. Pour half of the sauce into a shallow pasta bowl and add the ravioli. Toss gently, add remaining sauce and serve.

NOTE *Ravioli trays and cutters are available in kitchen stores.*

Sometimes I find the edges of ravioli to be undercooked and hard. To avoid this, after cutting the ravioli, press all around each raviolo with your fingers. This will make the edges thinner, so that each one will cook evenly. This will not be necessary if using a ravioli tray.

Homemade Pasta with Seafood Sauce | **SCIALIATELLI CON SUGO DI PESCE**

It was our darling maid Maria who used to make this pasta for us, with a sauce of tomato, zucchini and sometimes fish when her brother, who was a fisherman, would give her some of his catch. Since I could not find the recipe among my mother's recipes, and I did not remember it very well, I turned to Arthur Schwarz and his superb book *Naples at the Table*. So it is with Arthur's kind permission that I use his recipe with a few variations to make it similar to Maria's version. The *scialiatelli* (pasta) can be prepared in advance.

6 servings

PASTA

3 cups plus ⅓ cup all-purpose flour

1 egg

1 egg yolk

¾ cup plus 3 tablespoons whole milk

½ cup freshly grated Parmesan cheese

¼ cup finely chopped fresh Italian parsley or basil

SAUCE

3 tablespoons extra-virgin olive oil

1 garlic clove, crushed

1 sprig Italian parsley

1 (28-ounce) can peeled tomatoes

8 ounces monkfish, cut into ½-inch cubes

8 ounces small shrimp, peeled and deveined

½ pound squid, cut into rings, tentacles divided

TO MAKE THE PASTA In a bowl of a food processor, place the flour, egg, egg yolk, milk, Parmesan, and parsley. Process until a ball forms on the blade. Knead a little on a floured board and add more flour if necessary. Cover with a bowl and let rest 5 to 10 minutes.

Cut a piece off the dough the size of a baseball. Keep the remaining dough covered. Flatten the piece with your hands. Insert the dough between the rolls of a pasta machine set at the widest setting (#1). Roll the pasta, then fold the sheet of dough in half and repeat the rolling. Do this a couple of times, sprinkling some flour on the sheet of dough to prevent sticking. Continue the rolling through the next settings until you reach #5. This dough should not be too thick. Place the sheets of dough flat on a baking sheet or a wooden board and cover them with kitchen towels. When you have finished stretching all the dough, place one sheet on a cutting board. With a sharp knife, cut it horizontally into ¼-inch wide strips. Place on a baking sheet covered with kitchen towels. Repeat the process until you have cut all the dough into *scialiatelli*. Cover with kitchen towels and place in a cool place.

TO PREPARE THE SAUCE Put the olive oil and garlic in a large skillet. Cook over medium heat, stirring the garlic around until it starts to color. Add the parsley and tomatoes with their juices. Cook for 5 to 10 minutes stirring and crushing the tomatoes with a wooden spoon. Cover and let the sauce simmer for 10 minutes.

Add the monkfish and cook stirring for 3 to 4 minutes. Add the shrimp, cook for a few minutes until they turn pink, and then add the squid. Cook for 3 to 5 more minutes (the squid will toughen if cooked too long).

Cook the pasta in a large pot of salted boiling water. Stir and cook until the pasta is al dente, about 3 minutes. Drain in a colander and transfer to a pasta bowl, add the sauce, toss and serve.

Homemade Green Noodles with Green Ricotta

SAGNARIELLI CON LA RICOTTA VERDE

With this simple pasta, the Neapolitans create a delicious and almost elegant dish.

6 servings

1 recipe Green Pasta Dough
(recipe on page 93)

1 pound spinach, washed,
trimmed, and blanched

1 pound whole-milk ricotta,
drained

¼ cup grated Pecorino Romano,
plus more for serving

¼ teaspoon nutmeg

1 tablespoon unsalted butter

1 carrot, boiled and diced

Prepare and stretch the Green Pasta Dough according to the recipe for lasagna dough (page 95). With a sharp knife or a cutting wheel, cut the sheets of dough into large noodles, about 1 inch wide. Set on trays lined with kitchen towels.

Place the spinach in a food processor. Chop very finely, add the ricotta, ¼ cup of the grated cheese, and the nutmeg. Process until the mixture is creamy and smooth. Transfer to a pasta serving bowl. Keep in a warm place, such as the corner of the stove.

In a small skillet, heat the butter and lightly sauté the carrot. Keep warm.

Cook the noodles in a large pot of salted boiling water, about 3 minutes. Reserve 1 cup of the cooking water and drain the pasta but keep it rather wet.

Pour ½ cup of the water into the bowl with the ricotta mixture. Stir well and add the noodles, tossing gently. If the mixture is too dry, add some more of the reserved water. Top with the diced carrot and serve with additional grated Pecorino Romano.

NOTE *To keep the bowl with the ricotta mixture hot, place the bowl on top of the pot in which you are boiling the water for the pasta. You can also put the bowl in an oven set at 300 degrees F for about 10 minutes.*

Lasagna with Sausage and Meatballs

LASAGNA DI CARNEVALE ALLA NAPOLETANA

Carnival is celebrated all over Italy. The abundance of food eaten on this occasion symbolizes the end of the forty days of *Quaresima* (Lent). Those are days of penitence imposed by the Christian calendar to purge believers from sins committed during the year. What better punishment for a good Italian, and especially a Neapolitan, than being deprived of a good meal with succulent meats and juicy *ragù*? But on the day of Carnival, all restrictions are cast to the winds.

I remember, as a child, going to Via Toledo with my parents to see the pageantry of the *passeggiata*—people strolling in fancy costumes, wearing funny masks and hats—for Carnival at the end of Lent. It was for this occasion that the famous *lasagna di Carnevale alla Napoletana* was served to the hungry crowd, rich or poor. "*Semel in anno licet insenire*" ("Once a year one is allowed to go crazy") is what the ancient Romans said to justify this extravaganza. Don't be scared by the length of this recipe; many steps can be prepared in advance.

6 to 8 servings

1 batch Basic Pasta Dough, prepared with 3 eggs (recipe on page 92)

MEATBALLS

8 ounces ground veal

2 tablespoons unflavored dry bread crumbs

1 egg

1 tablespoon freshly grated Parmesan cheese

Salt to taste

Freshly milled pepper to taste

1 to 2 teaspoons chopped fresh Italian parsley

3 tablespoons extra-virgin olive oil, plus more as needed

MEATBALLS Combine the veal, bread crumbs, egg, Parmesan, salt, pepper, and parsley in a bowl and mix well.

Shape marble-sized meatballs by rolling little amounts of the meat between the palms of your hands. Set aside on a plate, but do not let them touch.

In a skillet, place 3 tablespoons of the olive oil and sauté the meatballs in batches. You may need a little more oil during the process. Place the cooked meatballs on paper towels to drain.

FILLING Combine the ricotta, egg, mozzarella, and Parmesan in a mixing bowl. Mix well and refrigerate.

SAUCE Put the prosciutto, onion, and carrot in the food processor and chop very finely.

In a saucepan heat the olive oil and butter. Add the prosciutto mixture. Sauté for 5 to 10 minutes, then add the pork and sausages and brown on all sides. Add the wine and let evaporate. Add the tomato paste, tomatoes with juice, tomato sauce, basil, salt, and pepper. Cover the pan, bring to a boil, then reduce the heat and

12 ounces whole-milk ricotta, drained

1 egg, slightly beaten

8 ounces whole-milk mozzarella, coarsely chopped

2 tablespoons freshly grated Parmesan cheese

SAUCE

1 thick slice prosciutto (about 2 ounces), cut into cubes

1 onion, quartered

1 carrot, cut into 4 or 5 pieces

¼ cup extra-virgin olive oil

1 tablespoon unsalted butter

2 pounds lean pork shoulder, in 1 piece

8 ounces sweet Italian sausages

½ cup red wine

2 tablespoons tomato paste

1 (28-ounce) can peeled tomatoes

1 (8-ounce) can tomato sauce

1½ teaspoons chopped fresh basil, or ½ teaspoon dried

Salt to taste

Freshly milled pepper to taste

2 tablespoons unsalted butter

Freshly grated Parmesan cheese

let simmer until the meat is tender, about 2 hours, stirring once in a while, and if necessary, adding a little water.

LASAGNA NOODLES Divide the pasta dough into six wedges and roll each wedge through the rolls of a pasta machine up to the #4 or #5 setting. The sheets of the lasagna dough should not be too thin.

Using a paring knife or a pastry wheel, cut the sheets of dough the length of the pan you plan to use and about 2½ inches wide. Let the strips dry for a while on kitchen towels, uncovered.

ASSEMBLY Butter a lasagna dish.

Remove the sausages from the sauce and cut them into thin slices. Set aside. Remove the pork from the sauce and reserve for another use. Reheat the sauce.

Place a layer of lasagna noodles in the prepared dish, letting the noodles overlap a little. Top with a thin layer of the ricotta filling. Add a few of the meatballs. Cover with another layer of lasagna noodles. Scatter some of the sliced sausage on it. Top with some sauce, sprinkle with some of the Parmesan and cover with another layer of lasagna noodles. Repeat these steps until you have used all of the prepared ingredients, finishing with a layer of noodles.

Preheat the oven to 375 degrees F.

Dot the lasagna with butter and sprinkle with Parmesan. Bake 45 minutes, or until a knife inserted in the middle of the lasagna comes out very hot. If the top of the lasagna gets too brown, cover lightly with aluminum foil. Cool the lasagna for 10 minutes before cutting with a spatula.

NOTE *The finished uncooked lasagna can be prepared a day ahead and kept in the refrigerator overnight. It can also be frozen before baking it. Defrost the lasagna at the bottom of the refrigerator before baking.*

Basic Potato Gnocchi | **GNOCCHI DI PATATE**

After many experiments in the U.S., I found Yukon Gold potatoes to be the best for making gnocchi. The best sauces for gnocchi are simple ones. My favorite is the basic tomato sauce or *sugo finto*, or just butter with a hint of sage or saffron and a good sprinkling of Parmesan cheese. But there are many ways to dress gnocchi. Just remember that gnocchi should "sit" in their sauce for 10 minutes before serving.

6 servings

2 pounds Yukon Gold potatoes

1 egg

½ teaspoon salt

2 cups all-purpose flour, plus more as needed

Wash the potatoes but do not peel them. Put the potatoes in a pot, cover with cold water and bring them to a boil. The cooking time depends on the size of the potatoes. Check by piercing one or two potatoes with a fork. If it enters easily the potatoes are done. Cool the potatoes. Peel and rice them with a potato ricer or a food mill over a large mixing bowl. Do not use a food processor; it makes the potatoes gluey.

Add the egg and salt to the potatoes, mix and transfer to a pastry board dusted with flour. Add 1½ cups of the flour and start kneading the dough, adding more flour if necessary to prevent sticking. As soon as the dough holds together in a soft, smooth ball, stop kneading. This dough should not be handled too much and it does not need to rest.

TO FORM THE GNOCCHI Take a small amount of dough and shape it into a thin tubular roll (about ½ inch in diameter). Do this on the pastry board lightly dusted with flour. Cut the roll into 1-inch pieces. Gently press and roll each piece on the tine of a fork or on a cheese grater. Line the gnocchi on trays covered with kitchen towels. Do not use paper towels; they absorb humidity and might stick to the gnocchi. Keep the gnocchi in a cool place until ready to cook, but no longer than 40 to 45 minutes.

NOTE   *Fresh gnocchi, frozen in a single layer and then bagged, keep for 2 months or more in the freezer.*

Tricolored Gnocchi | **GNOCCHI DI PATATE TRICOLORE**

A festive dish in all of Campania, the sauce for these gnocchi should always be simple and clear to fully display the colors of the gnocchi.

6 servings

2 pounds Yukon Gold potatoes

1 egg

½ teaspoon salt

2 cups all-purpose flour, plus more as needed

1 small beet, boiled, peeled and pureed

½ cup cooked spinach, squeezed and pureed

1 stick (8 tablespoons) unsalted butter, cut into slices

8 ounces whole-milk mozzarella, diced

½ cup heavy cream

2 to 3 tablespoons freshly grated Parmesan cheese, plus more for serving

Wash the potatoes but do not peel them. Place the potatoes in a pot, cover with water and bring to a boil. The cooking time depends on the size of the potatoes. Check by piercing one or two potatoes with a fork, if it enters easily the potatoes are ready. Cool the potatoes. Peel and rice with a potato ricer or a food mill (never use a food processor) over a large mixing bowl. Add the egg and salt and mix well.

Dust a pastry board with flour and turn the mixture onto it. Knead the flour into the dough, starting with 1 cup and gradually adding more until the dough is not sticky any more. Divide the dough into 3 equal parts. Continue kneading, one at a time, until the dough holds together into a soft ball. Set the balls aside and cover them with a bowl.

Knead the pureed beet into one of the balls and the spinach into another. Use as much flour as necessary to prevent sticking but handle the dough as little as possible, just enough to incorporate the vegetable.

Make the gnocchi using one ball at a time, following the steps in "To form the gnocchi" of Basic Potato Gnocchi (recipe on page 128).

Cook the gnocchi in a large pot of salted boiling water until they float to the surface, about 2 to 3 minutes, then taste for doneness. They should be soft but not mushy. Drain, reserving half a cup of the cooking water.

In a pre-heated serving bowl, place the butter and gnocchi and toss. Add the mozzarella, cream, and 2 to 3 tablespoons of the Parmesan cheese. Toss gently. If the gnocchi seem too dry, add a little of the reserved water. Serve with additional Parmesan.

Gnocchi with Mushrooms

GNOCCHI DI PATATE ALLA CONTADINA

I prefer my gnocchi dressed with a simple sauce, and this one is just right. But the intriguing flavor of the dried porcini mushrooms and the butter gives this dish a rich, strong, rustic flavor. If one doesn't want to use butter, the same amount of olive oil will work well.

6 servings

½ cup dried porcini mushrooms

3 tablespoons unsalted butter

1 tablespoon extra-virgin olive oil

1 onion, chopped

1 (28-ounce) can peeled tomatoes

2 tablespoons chopped fresh Italian parsley

1 cup chicken or beef broth

Salt to taste

Freshly milled pepper

1 recipe Basic Potato Gnocchi (recipe on page 128)

Freshly grated Parmesan or Grana Padano cheese

Soak the mushrooms for 30 minutes in 1 cup of lukewarm water. Set aside.

In a large skillet, heat 2 tablespoons of the butter and the olive oil. Add the onion and cook over medium to high heat until soft and translucent, stirring often.

With a slotted spoon, gently lift the mushrooms from the water to a cutting board so as not to disturb the sediment of grit which might have accumulated at the bottom. Strain the mushroom water through a paper towel or a coffee filter. Set aside.

Chop the mushrooms coarsely and add to the onion. Cook stirring and adding the water from the mushrooms a little at a time. Let the sauce reduce and add the tomatoes with their juices. Crush the tomatoes with a wooden spoon while stirring them. Bring the sauce to a boil and add 1 tablespoon of the parsley. Reduce the heat and simmer for 30 minutes. Add some of the broth if sauce becomes too thick. (You may not need all the broth.) Add salt if needed and pepper. Remove from heat and add remaining parsley.

Cook the gnocchi in a large pot of boiling, salted water until they float to the surface. Let them boil for 2 to 3 minutes, but taste for doneness; they should be soft but not mushy. Drain and transfer the gnocchi to a pre-warmed bowl. Add the remaining tablespoon of butter and the sauce. Toss and keep warm for about 10 minutes before serving with the grated cheese.

Spinach and Ricotta Gnocchi | **GNOCCHI NUDI**

In Naples, these most delicate gnocchi are viewed as a refined variation. Made with a spinach and ricotta mixture, they are dressed only with butter and Parmesan cheese, and called *nudi* (naked) because they resemble the filling for ravioli. My brother and I loved these gnocchi, but it had to be a very special occasion for my mother to prepare them because the gnocchi are a little tricky to make. If you do not use the right amount of flour, the gnocchi might fall apart in the boiling water and become a "polenta" (we Italians call everything mushy and unappetizing a polenta). My gnocchi did became a "polenta" once so I drained the whole thing in a fine mesh colander, placed it in a buttered pie pan, baked it, and bluntly called it a "flan." My guests found my "flan" delicious.

6 servings

1 pound fresh spinach, trimmed, washed, cooked and squeezed dry

15 ounces whole-milk ricotta, drained

3 eggs, lightly beaten

1/3 cup freshly grated Parmesan or Grana Padano cheese, plus additional for topping

1/2 teaspoon nutmeg

1/4 teaspoon salt

1 1/4 teaspoons freshly milled pepper

4 to 5 tablespoons all-purpose flour, plus more for dusting

3 tablespoons unsalted butter

1 tablespoon kosher salt

Chop the spinach very finely by hand. Do not use a machine as it will become too liquid. Put the spinach in a mixing bowl. Add the ricotta, eggs, 1/3 cup of the grated cheese, the nutmeg, salt, and pepper. Mix well. Gradually add the flour by tablespoons. The mixture should be soft, but not running, and if necessary add a little more flour.

Preheat the oven to 375 degrees F. Generously butter an ovenproof dish from which you can serve and in which the gnocchi will fit in one layer.

Dust a wooden board with flour. Form little croquette-shaped dumplings from the dough, about 2 inches long, and roll them in the flour. Set aside until all are finished. Do not handle too much.

Bring water to boil in a large pot and add the salt. When the water returns to a boil, drop 8 to 10 gnocchi at a time into the pot. Boil for 3 to 4 minutes and remove the gnocchi with a slotted spoon to a colander. When drained, place them in the buttered dish. Continue until you have cooked all the gnocchi. Sprinkle the gnocchi generously with grated cheese and dot with remaining butter. Place in the oven and bake for 15 minutes.

ABOUT POLENTA

The history of polenta is interesting. It is a well-known fact that corn is a native plant of the New World that was extensively cultivated when Christopher Columbus first reached its shores. He brought the first seeds of the plant to Spain when returning from his initial voyage. But like all new things, it took time for the plant to become known in Europe. In fact, the earliest recorded mention of corn in Italy was in the early 1500s. It arrived at the Venetian shore around 1530 and was widely appreciated. Its cultivation began in northern Italy and around the fertile Po Valley.

Corn has a strange name in Italy, due to a blunder of the Venetians. Since most of the shipments arriving at the port of Venice came from the East, they called corn *grano Turco*, Turkish grain, assuming that it had come from there. Corn eventually became quite accepted in Italy, mostly in the north and among the rural population, since it was filling and cheaper than wheat.

Italians, since Roman times, had been accustomed to eating a mushy mix of millet, sorghum, barley or buckwheat called *pultes*. Polenta (coarse cornmeal) arrived in Naples more or less at the same time it reached Venice. It didn't become immediately popular there, but the Neapolitans, with their usual imagination and penchant towards experimenting with new things (remember they were the first to taste the mysterious tomato) began to cook it. Dishes with polenta include *polenta pasticciata* or *maritata* ("married" polenta) with layers of polenta, meat sauce, and cheeses. Soon, similar regional concoctions started to appear everywhere, some of which are still popular today. In the Veneto, where polenta is eaten every day, there is the famous *polenta e osei* topped with small birds. The *polenta al maiale* (polenta with pork) is a dish from Calabria. The *pastuccia* from Abruzzo is polenta baked with sausages, raisins, and pork belly or cheeks; and there is also the ancient dish *migliaccio* from Campania, made with pork cracklings. With this variety of dishes, polenta reached widespread acceptance.

As corn became more popular, it was also picked up by the artists of the Renaissance. In a 1516 painting, Rafael included some ears of corn on the frieze of his painting *Cupid and Psyche*. Guiseppe Arcimboldi, the sixteenth-century painter of allegorical faces composed of vegetables, included ears of corn in five of his whimsical portraits. Also attesting to the early arrival and appreciation of corn is an adornment on a column in the Doge's Palace in Venice, built in 1550.

Basic Polenta | POLENTA MIA

Polenta is usually made with water, but my mother made it more flavorful. Most of the time she cooked the polenta in chicken broth, or dissolved a bouillon cube or two in the water. She also dressed it with sauce or layered it with cheese, sausages, and vegetables.

Usually polenta recipes tell you to boil the liquid first and pour the polenta in a steady stream while mixing. Do not listen. Go cold, follow my recipe, and you will never have a lumpy polenta. I learned this from the Italian chef and cookbook author Lidia Bastianich. She is a real *polentona*—that's what southerners call the polenta-eating people of the north.

6 to 8 servings

2 cups polenta flour (coarse cornmeal)

7 cups chicken broth or water (see note)

Salt to taste

Put the polenta flour in a heavy pot, preferably a copper one but any heavy pot will do. Start adding the broth, a little at a time, while stirring to prevent lumps.

Place over medium heat and cook, stirring constantly for about 35 minutes. Add the salt. The polenta is done when it starts to pull away from the sides of the pot. Add more broth while cooking if the polenta is too dense. The final consistency of the polenta, soft or hard, is to your taste or what the recipe calls for. I prefer mine a little soft.

NOTE *If using water, add a chicken or beef bouillon cube. For* polenta pasticciata, *you can dress the polenta by adding butter and cheeses such as Gorgonzola, Taleggio, or Stracchino. You can also buy instant polenta, which cooks in 5 minutes and is not bad.*

Polenta, cut into slices, can be reheated on a grill. This is very common in the Veneto.

Polenta Crostini
CROSTINI DI POLENTA

Polenta can also be used to make delicious crostini. You do not need a recipe, but following are a few suggestions to spur your imagination. The important thing is to have a polenta with a very solid consistency. Therefore cook it a little longer. Then spoon the polenta into a loaf pan and refrigerate it overnight. The next day, unmold the polenta, cut it into squares and then cut into triangles. The polenta pieces can be deep-fried or simply grilled and eaten as bread. Top them with your favorite ingredients.

My favorite toppings for crostini are:

Mozzarella with a bit of Parmesan, a few drops of tomato paste and a basil leaf

Fontina, Gruyere or Gorgonzola cheese

Smoked mozzarella

Sautéed mushrooms

Clam ragout (recipe on page 135)

Slices of cooked sausages, ham or prosciutto, with or without a little mozzarella

Fried zucchini or eggplant

Warm the crostini in a 300-degree oven for 8 to 10 minutes before serving.

NOTE Polenta also goes well topped with nuts, especially walnuts.

Polenta with Pork Ragout | **POLENTA AL RAGÚ DI MAIALE**

Makes 3 to 4 cups

1 onion

1 garlic clove

1 celery stalk

1 carrot

1 tablespoon extra-virgin olive oil

2 ounces pancetta, diced

1½ pounds pork chops, meat cut into 3 to 4 chunks, bones removed but set aside

½ cup dry wine

1 teaspoon tomato paste

1 (28-ounce) can peeled tomatoes

1½ pounds Italian sausages, cooked and crumbled

1 small *diavoletto* (dried Italian hot red pepper) (optional)

1 batch Basic Polenta (recipe on page 133)

In a food processor, place the onion, garlic, celery, and carrot. Chop finely.

In a heavy saucepan, heat the olive oil and add the pancetta. Cook briefly, then add the pork and bones and sauté until brown. Add the wine, let evaporate and then add the tomato paste and tomatoes with juices. Crush the tomatoes with a wooden spoon while stirring.

Cover the pan, bring to a boil and simmer for 1 hour, stirring once in a while. Add the sausages and *diavoletto* during the last 15 minutes. Remove the bones. Pour the ragout onto the hot polenta to serve.

NOTE *Mushrooms, fresh or dried, are often added to this sauce. Sauté the mushrooms separately and add them during the last 10 minutes. This sauce is also delicious on pasta.*

Polenta with Clam Ragout

POLENTA CON RAGÙ DI VONGOLE

The ragout is what makes this dish really Neapolitan. Since you will need 1 pound of shelled clams, I recommend using a container of frozen clams, which are less expensive. I sometimes combine some fresh mussels with the clams. It is better to use just water when making the polenta for this dish to keep the seafood flavor intact.

Makes 1½ cups sauce

½ cup extra-virgin olive oil

2 garlic cloves, chopped

2 sprigs Italian parsley, plus 2 teaspoons chopped

1 (28-ounce) can peeled tomatoes

1 pound frozen clams, defrosted

1 batch Basic Polenta (recipe on page 133)

In a skillet heat the olive oil, add the garlic and 2 sprigs of parsley. Cook briefly letting the flavor of the garlic and parsley explode into the oil, then remove and discard the parsley.

Add the tomatoes and their juices. Crush the tomatoes with a wooden spoon while stirring. Simmer for 20 to 25 minutes, covered, stirring once in a while.

When ready to serve add the clams and the chopped parsley and simmer for a few minutes to heat the clams.

Transfer the hot polenta to a bowl and top with the clam ragout.

Polenta Casserole with Sausage | IL MIGLIACCIO

This dish goes back to the times of the Romans. It was originally made with millet, since corn, which is the base for today's *migliaccio*, had not yet come from America. Similar versions of *migliaccio* appear in some Renaissance books, even some sweet variations. On the island of Ischia, the *migliaccio*, prepared with capellini, is still dressed with a rich custard and candied orange zest today. For the Neapolitans, this dish was—and is—a feast.

6 servings or more

1 pound sweet Italian sausages

1 pound polenta flour (coarse cornmeal)

5 cups lukewarm water

2 slices prosciutto, cut into strips (optional)

1 cup freshly grated Parmesan cheese

Unflavored dry bread crumbs for pan

Put the sausages in a skillet and pierce them with the point of a knife. Cover with water and simmer until the water has evaporated and only the juices remain, turning the sausages once or twice. Remove them to a cutting board, reserving the juices. Cool and slice in thin rounds.

Preheat the oven to 375 degrees F.

Place the polenta flour in a large pot and start adding 5 cups lukewarm water while stirring with a wire whisk. Place over medium heat and cook, stirring the polenta continuously for about 30 minutes. If the polenta gets too dry, add more warm water. Towards the end, add the juice from the sausages, the prosciutto, Parmesan, and sausages. Stir well.

Butter a pie dish and sprinkle with bread crumbs. Pour the polenta in and smooth the top. Sprinkle some more bread crumbs over and bake for about 30 minutes. Cool for 10 minutes before serving.

Polenta Gnocchi with Cheese | **CUPOLA DI POLENTA**

A friend of my mother, who lived next door to us in Naples, gave her a recipe similar to *gnocchi alla Romana* made with semolina. It was an inspiration for my mother, who then used polenta instead of semolina. It was delicious. In fact, mother started to make it when we had guests, and she didn't feel ashamed to serve "only" polenta because it looked quite impressive and tasted so good.

6 servings

2 cups polenta flour (coarse cornmeal)

1 teaspoon salt

¼ teaspoon nutmeg

3 to 4 cups milk

2 tablespoons unsalted butter, plus more for dotting

2 egg yolks

4 ounces Fontina cheese, grated

¼ cup freshly grated Parmesan or Grana Padano cheese, plus more for sprinkling

In a heavy pot, place the polenta flour, salt, and nutmeg. Slowly pour in the milk and 1 cup water, stirring constantly to prevent lumping. Put on the heat and cook stirring until the mixture starts to pull away from the sides of the pot, about 30 minutes. If the polenta is too dense, add a little more milk or water. However, this polenta should be rather solid.

Remove the polenta from the heat. Stir in 2 tablespoons of butter, the egg yolks, Fontina, and Parmesan.

Pour the polenta on a flat, wet surface. With wet hands, smooth the top and flatten it to an even ¼ inch thickness. Cool completely.

Butter a pie pan from which you can serve. Preheat the oven to 375 degrees F.

With a small round cookie or tortellini cutter, cut the polenta into 1-inch circles and arrange one layer in the prepared dish. Sprinkle with some grated cheese and dot with butter. Add a second layer of polenta, starting one inch away from the rim. Sprinkle with cheese and dot with butter. Continue layering bringing each layer in an inch more than the previous layer so that at the end the dish looks like a cupola. Finish with grated cheese and dot with butter. Bake for 15 to 20 minutes, or until top is golden.

ABOUT RICE

Rice is one of the most ancient foods in the world. The Chinese have been cultivating it since 2,800 B.C. A thousand years later, rice appeared in India. Alexander the Great introduced it to the Greeks. The Romans knew it as an exotic plant, and may have used it as food. However, the spread of rice in Italy was the work of the Arabs, who first introduced it to Sicily during the 9th and 10th centuries. It was in this region that rice was first grown. Rice reached the north of Italy during the 15th century. It was first cultivated in the fields that a member of the powerful Sforza family of Milan had donated to his mistress, Lucia de Mariano. In 1475, this same family sent a gift of two sacks of rice, then considered a rarity, to the Estense Court in Ferrara. As the result of this gift, rice began to be cultivated around the towns of Modena and Reggio Emilia. Today, Italy is the largest rice producer in Europe.

Despite the assumption that rice is a northern Italian prerogative, it is eaten all over the country, and every region has its own way of cooking it and its own specialties. The essayist and food writer Nello Oliviero, in his book *Storie e Curiosità del Mangiare Napoletano* (*History and Curiosities of Neapolitan Food*), says, "Take rice away from a China man and he will die, take it away from a Lombard, and he will become melancholic, take it away from a Neapolitan and he will never notice." Despite Mr. Oliviero's belief, rice and risotto have become quite popular in Naples today, especially in restaurants. When we lived in Padua near Venice, my mother, who had never been too fond of rice, fell in love with risotto, so we ate it often. Risotto has also become very popular in America.

Some of the most famous Italian rice dishes come from the south. Naples has its *sartù di riso* which is an elaborate rice timbale. From Palermo comes the delicious *arancini di riso* (rice balls stuffed with *ragù*). Modern Romans often eat *suppli al telefono*, which is similar to *arancini* but with the addition of mozzarella. The snack's name is associated with a telephone because when you bite into a *suppli*, the hot mozzarella threads like a telephone cord.

Risotto with Mushrooms | **RISOTTO CON FUNGHI**

At the arrival of autumn, the markets of Campania are full of their intoxicating aroma, and if you enter a Neapolitan restaurant, you smell them as well—porcini mushrooms. This is their season, and one is bound to feast on them. Unfortunately, when they arrive in America, that special aroma seems lost, and they are pricey on top of it. So to beat the odds, do as I do. Invest in a large bag of dried porcini mushrooms. Yes, I know, they are expensive too, but a handful goes a long way when combined with regular, inexpensive white mushrooms. The dried porcini will give your risotto that earthy touch that it needs to be authentically Italian.

6 servings

3 tablespoons unsalted butter

1 tablespoon extra-virgin olive oil

1 onion, sliced very thin

12 ounces fresh white mushrooms, coarsely chopped

1/2 cup dried porcini mushrooms, soaked for 20 minutes and chopped (reserve soaking water)

2 cups Arborio rice

1/2 cup white wine

6 or more cups warm chicken broth, preferably homemade

Salt to taste

Freshly milled pepper

Freshly grated Parmesan cheese

In a heavy pot, heat 2 tablespoons of the butter and the olive oil. Add the onion. Cook over low heat until soft and translucent. Add the fresh and dried mushrooms. Cook stirring often until they release all their moisture.

Add the rice, cook stirring for 3 to 5 minutes. Add the wine and let evaporate.

Strain the reserved mushroom soaking water through a paper towel and stir into the rice. Start adding the broth, ¼ cup at a time, stirring constantly over low heat until it is almost absorbed. Add more broth and continue stirring and adding broth until the rice is cooked, about 20 minutes. At this point the rice should be al dente. Taste it and, if needed, cook a little longer. Add salt, if you wish, and pepper.

Remove the risotto from the heat and stir in the remaining butter. Serve with the Parmesan.

NOTE *Do not be tempted to use only dried porcini for this risotto. Their flavor is too strong and will be overpowering.*

Baked Layered Rice | **SARTÙ DI RISO**

The name of this dish, *sartù*, is a reminder of foreign influence in the Kingdom of the Two Sicilys, of which Naples was one of the capitals. The word comes from the French *surtout*, which means "above all," and the dish was one of the specialties of the *Monzùs*, the cooks of the aristocracy. Today *sartù* is a famous dish not only in the region of Campania and Sicily, but all over Italy. It is an excellent, elegant dish, perfect for a dinner party. It takes time to prepare, but it can be made ahead.

8 servings or more

Unsalted butter for pan

1 cup dry unflavored bread crumbs

1 tablespoon kosher salt

1 pound Arborio rice

4 eggs

3 Italian pork sausages

1½ pounds ground beef

1 tablespoon chopped fresh Italian parsley

½ cup Parmesan cheese

1 tablespoon unsalted butter

1 tablespoon extra-virgin olive oil

1 thin slice pancetta, finely chopped

3 to 4 cups *ragù* (recipe on page 80)

2 cups frozen peas, defrosted

4 ounces prosciutto, chopped

Butter a 10-inch springform pan with unsalted butter. Sprinkle some of the bread crumbs on the bottom and sides of pan. Set aside in a cool place.

Bring 3 quarts of water to a boil. Add the kosher salt, and as soon as the water comes back to a boil, add the rice, stir and cook very al dente, about 15 minutes. Transfer the rice to a mixing bowl and add 3 eggs. Mix well and set aside.

Place the sausages in a skillet. Prick them in several places. Cover the sausages with water and bring to a boil. Cook over medium heat until the water has evaporated. Continue cooking the sausages, turning them often, until they brown. Remove from the skillet, allow to cool and then slice them.

Place the ground beef in a bowl. Add the remaining egg, 1 tablespoon of the bread crumbs, the chopped parsley and 1 tablespoon of Parmesan. Mix well. Shape the meat into cherry-size balls.

Heat the butter and olive oil in a skillet. Add the pancetta, cook stirring for a few minutes. Add the meatballs, and gently sauté until brown.

Coat bottom and sides of the prepared springform pan with some of the rice.

Add 2 cups of the ragù to the remaining rice, mix well, then add the peas and chopped prosciutto. Mix again.

To assemble the *sartù*, sprinkle the bottom layer of rice in the pan with Parmesan. Spoon ¾ cup of the *ragù* over it. Scatter 3 tablespoons of the chopped

¼ pound Caciocavallo or Provolone cheese, coarsely chopped

2 hard-boiled eggs, peeled and sliced

Caciocavallo, some of the sliced sausages, some meatballs, and a few slices of hardboiled eggs over the *ragù*. Cover with a thin layer of the rice mixture and evenly sprinkle with Parmesan. Repeat the layering as described until the rice is finished. Top with additional Parmesan and ragù. Cover with a good sprinkling of the bread crumbs and dot with butter. At this point the *sartù* can be refrigerated overnight.

When ready to cook, heat the oven to 400 degrees F. Bake the sartù for 30 minutes, then reduce to 375 degrees F and continue baking until the top is nicely browned, about 30 more minutes. Let the dish rest for 15 minutes before unmolding it. Serve on a round plate with additional Parmesan and the remaining ragù.

Seafood Risotto | **RISOTTO ALLA POSILLIPO**

Posillipo is one of the most beautiful and elegant districts of Naples, located on a hill overlooking the Gulf of Naples. It has many lovely restaurants, where mainly seafood is served. This is one of the typical dishes, but as you can see the rice is boiled and not simmered like a risotto, which must be stirred constantly until cooked.

6 servings

1 pound mussels

1 pound clams, preferably small

¼ cup extra-virgin olive oil

3 garlic cloves, crushed

8 ounces fresh, ripe tomatoes, peeled, seeded, and chopped

1 tablespoon kosher salt

2 cups Arborio rice

2 tablespoons chopped fresh Italian parsley

To clean the mussels and clams, place them in a bowl, cover with water and add 1 tablespoon of flour. Let them sit for 15 to 20 minutes before rinsing. This will make the mollusks release any residual sand. Also remove the beards from the shells of the mussels if there are any.

Heat the olive oil in a large saucepan. Add the garlic and cook until it starts to color, then add the tomatoes. Stir, cover, reduce the heat, and simmer for about 20 minutes.

Meanwhile place the mussels in a skillet and turn the heat on low. As soon as the mussels start to open, remove them with a slotted spoon to a bowl. Remove the mussels from their shells over another bowl to catch their juices. Discard the shells. Wipe the skillet clean and add the clams. Set them on the heat and proceed the same way as with the mussels, again saving the juices when opening. Discard any mussels or clams that do not open.

Combine the juice of the mussels and clams and strain through a coffee filter or paper towel. Add the juices, mussels, and clams to the tomato sauce and remove from the heat.

In a pot, bring 6 cups water to a boil. Add the salt and pour in the rice. Stir and then simmer until the rice is al dente, about 20 minutes. Drain the rice in a colander and put in a serving bowl.

Reheat the sauce. Add the sauce to the rice, mix well, sprinkle the parsley over the rice and serve.

Risotto with Herbs and Zucchini

RISOTTO IN BIANCO E VERDE CON ERBE E ZUCCHINE

This risotto goes well with our modern way of eating. Since it is a recipe from the south, it is made with olive oil, not butter. But if nobody is looking add a little butter at the end, although I think that the aroma of the herbs gives it enough taste.

6 servings

¼ cup extra-virgin olive oil

1 onion, finely chopped

1 celery stalk, preferably with a few leaves

1 sprig Italian parsley

2 or 3 sage leaves

4 or 5 sprigs dill or fennel greens

4 small zucchini (about 1 pound), diced

5 to 6 cups homemade chicken broth

2 cups Arborio rice

Salt to taste

Freshly grated Parmesan cheese

In a saucepan, heat 3 tablespoons of the olive oil, and add the onion. Cook over low heat until the onion is soft and translucent.

Place the celery, parsley, sage, and dill in a bowl of a food processor and chop finely. Reserve one tablespoon of this mixture and put the remaining into the saucepan with the onion. Stir, cook briefly, and then add the zucchini. Stir and cook for 5 to 7 minutes.

In another pan, bring the broth to a boil and reduce it to a simmer.

Add the rice to the zucchini mixture, stir until the rice absorbs all the juices. Start adding the broth ½ cup at a time while stirring constantly. Cook until liquid is absorbed before adding another ½ cup of broth. Continue cooking the rice, stirring and scraping the bottom and sides of the saucepan while adding more broth until the rice is almost tender, about 20 minutes. Add salt and the reserved herb mixture. Stir and remove from the heat. Add 1 tablespoon olive oil. Stir and serve with a generous amount of Parmesan cheese.

"Sea and Land" Risotto with Clams and Mushrooms

RISOTTO CON VONGOLE E FUNGHI MARE E TERRA

Naples is surrounded by sea and land—*mare e terra* in Italian. This enticing risotto combines some of the best elements of both. Tender cherrystone clams and savory seafood broth blend beautifully with the earthy flavors of the onion, garlic, and mushrooms. The porcini mushrooms and saffron elevate this risotto to a meal that will impress dinner guests.

6 servings

2 dozen cherrystone clams

1 tablespoon all-purpose flour

Bottled clam broth (optional)

3 cups fish broth or water

⅓ cup extra-virgin olive oil

1 onion, thinly sliced

2 garlic cloves

2 cups coarsely chopped mushrooms

¼ cup dried porcini mushrooms, soaked and chopped (optional)

2 cups Arborio rice

½ teaspoon powdered saffron, or 1 teaspoon saffron threads

2 teaspoons chopped fresh Italian parsley

1 tablespoon unsalted butter

Place the clams in a bowl, cover with water and add the flour. Stir and let stand for 15 to 20 minutes. (This will make the clams release any residual sand.)

Drain the clams and place them in a skillet over low heat until they start to open. Transfer the open clams to a bowl and continue until all the clams have opened. Discard any that don't open. Remove the clams from the shells over a bowl in order to save the juices. Set the shelled clams on a chopping board and chop them coarsely. Strain the clam juice through a paper towel and reserve.

Measure the clam juices to 1 cup liquid, adding some bottled clam broth to make 1 cup if necessary. Pour into a pot. Add 3 cups fish broth and bring to a boil, lower heat, and simmer.

Heat 3 tablespoons of the olive oil in a heavy skillet and add the onion. Add one whole garlic clove, then chop the remaining clove and add it. Cook until the onion is soft and translucent, stirring often.

Add all the mushrooms and cook stirring often until they release all their moisture. Add the rice and cook stirring until it is well coated with the juices in the skillet.

Start adding the simmering broth to the rice, ½ cup at a time, while stirring constantly. Cook until the liquid is almost absorbed before adding another ½ cup. Continue cooking the rice, stirring and scraping the bottom of the skillet while adding more liquid until the rice is almost tender, about 18 minutes. Add the saffron, stir to mix, and cook until the rice is al dente, about 5 minutes longer.

Remove the whole garlic clove and discard. Add the clams to the rice. Stir in the parsley, and remove from the heat. Stir in the butter and serve.

Risotto with Spring Vegetables | **RISOTTO VARIOPINTO**

Depending on the season, this risotto can be made *alla primavera* (with spring vegetables) such as asparagus, peas, zucchini, string beans; or *all' autunno* (with fall vegetables) such as peppers, sun-dried tomatoes, cauliflower, or pumpkin. As the Neapolitans do, just use your imagination!

6 servings

2 tablespoons unsalted butter

1 tablespoon extra-virgin olive oil

1 onion, chopped

1 garlic clove, chopped

1 celery stalk, diced

2 carrots, diced

1 bunch asparagus, about 12 stalks

1 or 2 firm tomatoes, cut into small cubes

2 cups Arborio rice

¼ cup dry white wine

6 cups homemade chicken broth, or broth made with 2 bouillon cubes

1 cup frozen peas, defrosted

Salt to taste

Freshly milled pepper to taste

1 tablespoon chopped fresh Italian parsley

2 to 3 tablespoons freshly grated Parmesan cheese

In a large skillet or a heavy saucepan, heat 1 tablespoon of the butter and the olive oil. Add the onion and cook over medium heat, stirring often, until the onion is soft and translucent. Add the garlic, celery, and carrots. Cook stirring for about 10 minutes.

Break off the tough ends of the asparagus and discard. Peel the stems and dice each stem, reserving the tips. Add the diced stems to the skillet with the onion and continue cooking for about 5 minutes. Add the tomatoes and stir. Add the rice and cook for 2 to 3 minutes, stirring. Add the wine and let evaporate.

Meanwhile, in a separate pot, bring 6 cups of broth to a simmer.

Add 2 ladles of the hot broth at a time to the rice, stirring constantly while the liquid is absorbed. Continue adding the broth and stirring until the rice is almost done, about 18 minutes. Stir in the peas and cook for a few minutes. Taste for doneness, season with salt and pepper and add the parsley. Stir and remove the risotto from the heat. Add the remaining tablespoon of butter and the Parmesan. Mix well.

While the risotto is cooking, blanch the remaining asparagus tips in the hot broth, remove with a slotted spoon and keep warm.

Garnish individual plates of risotto with the asparagus tips and serve with additional Parmesan.

Rice and Cabbage | **RISO E VERZE**

This is a dish of rural origins. Country people, when talking about this dish, will tell you to pick out a beautiful, big cabbage because they want a big dish to satisfy a good appetite. My mother learned to make it from our maid Maria when we were living in Naples. It became a staple in the wintertime when the winds from the north made even Naples a little chilly.

6 servings

2 tablespoons extra-virgin olive oil

1 thick slice bacon, diced

2 onions, coarsely chopped

1 head cabbage, preferably red

5 cups hot water

1 beef or chicken bouillon cube

2 cups Arborio rice

2 tablespoons freshly grated Parmesan cheese, plus more for serving

In a large pot, heat the olive oil, add the bacon, cook briefly and then add the onions. Cook over low heat, stirring often, for about 5 to 7 minutes.

Meanwhile, cut the cabbage into strips. Wash well but do not drain the strips too much. Add them to the pot. Stir well, cover the pot and simmer until the cabbage is almost cooked, about 15 minutes, stirring every once in a while. If mixture is dry, add some of the hot water.

Meanwhile, bring the hot water to a boil and add the bouillon cube.

Pour the broth over the cabbage and bring to a boil. Add the rice, stir and cook until the rice is tender, about 18 to 20 minutes. Stir in 2 tablespoons of the Parmesan. Serve with additional Parmesan.

Baked Rice with Eggplant | **RISO AL FORNO CON LE MELANZANE**

The people of Campania love eggplants. They use this vegetable in the most imaginative ways and this baked rice dish is a good example. It can be prepared in advance.

6 servings

2 small eggplants

½ cup plus 1 tablespoon extra-virgin olive oil

1 teaspoon dried basil, crumbled

2 ounces prosciutto

1 onion, quartered

3 tablespoons unsalted butter, plus more for dotting

Freshly milled pepper

2 cups tomato puree, fresh or canned

½ cup Arborio rice

3 cups chicken or beef broth, heated

Unflavored dry bread crumbs

Freshly grated Parmesan cheese

8 ounces whole-milk mozzarella, thinly sliced

Preheat the oven to 375 degrees F.

Peel the eggplants and cut crosswise into thin slices. Place the slices on a baking sheet. Combine ½ cup of the olive oil with half of the basil. Brush the eggplant slices on both sides with this mixture. (You may need more oil.) Bake for 10 minutes turning once. Set aside.

In a food processor chop the prosciutto and onion.

In a skillet heat 2 tablespoons butter and 1 tablespoon olive oil. Add the prosciutto mixture and sauté, stirring often, until the onion is soft, about 8 minutes. Sprinkle with pepper and add the tomato puree and remaining basil. Cover, bring to a boil and cook at a simmer for about 20 minutes.

Transfer half of the sauce to a bowl and set aside. Add the rice to the remaining sauce, cook stirring until the tomato sauce is reduced. Start adding the broth, a little at a time, cooking and stirring constantly. Do this for about 15 minutes. (You may not need all the broth, the rice should remain quite al dente.) Remove from the heat and stir in 1 tablespoon butter.

Butter a soufflé dish and sprinkle with bread crumbs. Spread a layer of rice on the bottom of the dish, top it with some Parmesan and a few eggplant and mozzarella slices. Spoon some of the reserved tomato sauce over. Repeat until all the ingredients are used, keeping ½ cup sauce for the final layer. Sprinkle with a little more Parmesan and dot with butter. Bake for 20 to 25 minutes. Cool 10 minutes before serving.

Rice with Squid | **RISO NERO**

This is an unusual rice dish, popular both in Campania and in the Veneto area. It demonstrates once again how the food of Italy is not southern, northern, western, or eastern but regional, and sometimes the north and the south meet. In the Veneto, this dish is called a risotto and is made with butter, whereas in Campania, its name is *riso nero* (black rice), and it is made with olive oil. In Italy, squids are sold with their ink sac, unlike in America, but you can ask your fishmonger to get ink sacs for you or you can buy the ink frozen.

6 servings

1 pound squid, skinned

3 tablespoons extra-virgin olive oil

2 garlic cloves, chopped

½ cup white dry wine

1½ cups Arborio rice

6 cups fish stock, heated

Ink from squid (3 to 5 sacs) (see note)

2 tablespoons finely chopped fresh Italian parsley

Wash the squid well and cut into ringlets. Chop the tentacles.

In a skillet, heat 3 tablespoons of the olive oil and add the garlic. Cook and stir for a few seconds, then add the squid. Cook briefly, add the wine, and allow to evaporate.

Add the rice and cook stirring until the rice has absorbed the liquid. Add one ladle of the stock and stir until absorbed. Continue adding more stock, a ladle at a time and stirring constantly until the rice is tender, about 20 minutes. Add the squid ink during the last 5 minutes. At the end the rice should be a little wet, but not soupy.

Serve with a sprinkling of parsley, which will contrast nicely with the black color of the rice.

NOTE *If you do not use the ink, you can add 8 ounces of tomato sauce to the dish after adding the squids and wine. Let it simmer for 10 minutes and continue as described in the recipe.*

fish

Since antiquity, fish in Italy has been sold in special markets, such as the *forum piscarium* of the ancient Romans. But this was not just a place to buy fish; it was also a place to gather where people discussed current events and the value of fish. This is described in detail in the writings of the Roman poet and satirist Juvenal. He makes fun of Roman vices and indulgences in the story of Emperor Domitian, who called a meeting of his counsel to decide how to—cook a turbot! Apicius, the famous gourmand of antiquity, sings the glories of blue fish such as mackerel, sardines, and anchovies. And let's not forget *garum*, a fish sauce that the Romans doused on almost every food they ate.

Although Italy is surrounded by the sea, Italians did not relish fish very much in the recent past. The dietary restriction of Catholicism, which prescribed *il mangiare di magro* (meatless eating on Fridays and other religious holidays) made the rebellious Italians think that it was an imposition. But now that the Church has erased these restrictions and fish has been anointed "healthy," Italians do eat fish, especially on Fridays. They believe that on that day the fish is really fresh, and perhaps they are right. I buy fish on Fridays because I find a wonderful variety in my open-air market in New York.

Buying fish today can be a bit difficult. I grew up with the dictum "Look your fish in the eye" to determine if the fish is fresh—when the eye is cloudy and not brilliant, the fish is not fresh. Well, when do you see a fish with the head on these days? The only thing you can do is rely on the vendor, or if he is not looking, and if the fish you want is within reach, lower your nose and smell it. Buy fish the day you intend to use it, and keep it in the refrigerator until ready to cook.

When we lived in Naples, I used to go to the *pescheria* (fish market) with my father and watch the vendors display their fish with pride. Their pushcarts where shining in different colors—red snappers, blue mackerels, gray soles, candid squid, black mussels, pink shrimp, and the local *pannocchia*, a crustacean whose flavor is similar to the lobster. It was impossible not to "look the fish in the eye!"

The recipes in this book will tell you how long to cook the fish. Overcooked fish is not worth eating, so be sure to follow the instructions. Perfectly cooked fish should flake easily, look opaque, be moist and flavorful. In Campania, the most valued is the *pesce di scoglio*, literally "fish from the rock." The natives insist that the fish must come from *il golfo* (the gulf), never mind whether it's the Gulf of Naples, Salerno, or Amalfi.

Poached Fish | **PESCE BOLLITO**

I have always loved poached fish. It can be served with a simple dressing of oil and lemon. In my house, the fish often came with some luscious sauce or a homemade mayonnaise. Salmon is my favorite fish for this recipe. I know it is not Neapolitan, but it is easily available in the United States. Sea bass, red snapper, and sturgeon also work well. If you cannot get a fish with the head on, ask your fishmonger to give you a head of the same type of fish you are cooking, which you can add to the boiling water.

6 to 8 servings

1 celery stalk, cut into several pieces

1 carrot, cut into several pieces

1 large onion, cut into 6 wedges

2 sprigs Italian parsley

2 dry bay leaves

¼ cup wine vinegar

1 heaping teaspoon kosher salt

10 peppercorns, crushed

1 (6- to 7-pound) whole fish, cleaned but with the head on (see above)

Green Sauce (recipe on page 87)

Place all the ingredients except the fish and sauce in a fish poacher. Add water to come up 2 inches above the solids. Bring to a boil and cook for 15 to 20 minutes. Place the fish rack in position, it should just touch the water. Add the fish. Cover and cook for 20 to 30 minutes depending on the size of the fish. Cool a little, remove the head and bones and serve with Green Sauce.

NOTE   *A nice way to serve this fish is on a platter surrounded by sprigs of parsley and cherry tomatoes. Serve the sauce on the side.*

Fish Fillets with Shellfish and Tomatoes

PESCE ALLA PIZZAIOLA

Alla pizzaiola means "cooked with tomatoes" which are chopped or sliced. This dish is easy, quick, and just right for a summer evening. After such a repast, we would go out for a *passeggiata* on our beautiful street overlooking the Bay of Naples, and then sit at a café to enjoy an ice cream *al fresco*. It was the perfect finish for a simple and light meal.

6 servings

2½ to 3 pounds white fish fillets (halibut, monkfish, bass, or sole)

Flour for dredging

24 scrubbed and debearded mussels or clams, or a mixture of the two

3 tablespoons extra-virgin olive oil

3 garlic cloves, crushed

1 small hot red pepper (optional)

1 sprig Italian parsley

1 tablespoon fresh rosemary, or 1 teaspoon dried

¼ cup dry white wine

Salt to taste

Freshly milled pepper to taste

2 cups chopped fresh tomatoes, or 1 (28-ounce) can whole, peeled tomatoes, drained and chopped or sliced

½ cup fish broth or water

1 tablespoon chopped fresh parsley

Cut the large fish fillets into serving size pieces. Dredge the pieces in flour.

To clean the mussels and clams, place them in a bowl, cover with water and add 1 tablespoon of flour. Let them sit for 15 to 20 minutes before rinsing. (This will make the mollusks release any residual sand.) Also remove the beards from the shells of the mussels if there are any.

In a skillet large enough to hold the fish in one layer, heat the olive oil. Add the garlic, hot pepper if using, parsley, and rosemary. As soon as the garlic starts to sizzle, add the fish. Cook for about 5 minutes over high heat, turning the fish once.

Add the wine and season with salt and pepper. Cook over high heat to let the wine reduce by half, about 5 minutes.

Spread the tomatoes over the fish and add the fish broth. Place the mussels or clams all around the skillet. Cover and simmer until the shells open, about 5 minutes. Discard any mussels or clams that haven't opened. Serve sprinkled with the chopped parsley.

Skate with Capers | **RAZZA AI CAPPERI**

Skate is a delicate fish that can now be found in most fish markets. My mother, who got this recipe from a Neapolitan friend living next to us, did not need to soak the fish in milk since Italian skates are not very big and therefore do not need to be tenderized. But since the skate in the United States is sold at an advanced age, I find that a milk bath restores its freshness. Skate, by the way, is a fish that will improve if kept one day in the refrigerator.

6 servings

6 boneless, skinned skate wings

¾ cup milk

Salt to taste

Freshly milled pepper to taste

Flour for dredging

¼ cup extra-virgin olive oil

2 garlic cloves, crushed

Juice of 1 lemon

2 to 3 tablespoons capers, drained

2 tablespoons chopped fresh parsley

Place the fish on a large platter, pour the milk on it and sprinkle with salt and pepper. Refrigerate for at least 30 minutes, turning once.

Drain the fish, dredge each piece in flour and shake off the excess.

Heat the olive oil in a large skillet in which the fish fits in one layer (you can also use two skillets, dividing the ingredients between them). Add the garlic and as soon as it starts to sizzle, add the fish. Cook over medium heat for 3 to 5 minutes on one side. Using a large spatula, turn the wings and cook for 2 to 3 minutes but do not overcook; the skate wings should have a nice golden color.

Squeeze the lemon juice on the skate, sprinkle with the capers and reduce the heat to low. Cook for about 2 minutes longer. Sprinkle with the parsley and serve.

Sole Fillets with Bay Scallops | **FILETTI DI SOGLIOLE ALLE PERLE**

This dish was my idea. The *perle* (pearls) were the tiny clams that came from the Tyrrhenian Sea. But when I saw the little bay scallops here in New York, I knew I had found my real "pearls."

6 servings

2 tablespoons unsalted butter

12 small sole fillets with skin (4 ounces each)

12 ounces bay scallops

Juice of half a lemon

¼ cup unflavored dry bread crumbs

2 to 3 teaspoons chopped fresh Italian parsley

Freshly milled pepper to taste

¼ cup dry white wine

Preheat the oven to 375 degrees F.

Lightly butter an ovenproof dish from which you can serve. Add 6 of the fillets, skin side down, in one layer. Scatter the bay scallops over the fish, sprinkle with half of the lemon juice, the bread crumbs, half of the parsley, and some pepper. Dot with half the butter. Place the remaining fillets on top. Pour the wine around the fish, dot with the remaining butter.

Bake for 20 to 30 minutes, or until the fish starts to flake when touched with a fork, basting a few times while cooking. Add the remaining lemon juice. Serve hot, sprinkled with the remaining parsley.

Breaded Trout | **TROTE ALLA MUGNAIA**

Alla mugnaia is a common way of cooking certain fish in Italy. The name means "in the style of the miller's wife" because she is usually covered with flour, just like the trout. I buy farm-raised trout, which tastes very much like those from Campania. If you can find wild trout, go for it! Sole, flounder, or mullet can also be used.

6 servings

6 trout (about 12 ounces each), gutted but preferably with heads on

Cornmeal flour

½ stick unsalted butter

1 tablespoon extra-virgin olive oil

2 lemons

2 teaspoons chopped fresh Italian parsley

Dredge each trout in cornmeal flour. Shake off the excess.

Use one large or two smaller skillets in which the fish can fit snugly. Heat 2 tablespoons of the butter and the olive oil (if you use two skillets, you may need a little more). Sauté the fish on both sides over medium heat until nicely golden, about 5 minutes on each side. Remove the fish to a serving plate and keep warm. Discard the cooking fat and wipe the skillet clean.

Return the skillet to the stove and melt the remaining butter. Add the juice of one lemon and the chopped parsley and pour it over the fish.

Cut the other lemon into wedges and place it around the fish. Serve immediately.

Oven-Poached Sea Bass

SPIGOLA ALL'ACQUA COTTA E ALLORO

The Italian name of the dish—*all'acqua cotta*—means "cooked water." A good description, however, would be "flavored water." Make sure that your fish is really fresh when you make this recipe. Remember, you must look the fish in the eye. I am not joking! This dish should be made with a large fish whose head, with sparkling and reflective eyes, is still on. However, when stuck, you can use fish fillets, but make sure they are thick, and ask the fishmonger to give you a fish head to add to the water.

6 servings

1 celery stalk, trimmed and cut into 4 pieces

1 onion, quartered

1 carrot, cut into 4 pieces

3 sprigs Italian parsley

1 teaspoon kosher salt

Freshly milled pepper to taste

1 sea bass (4 pounds), cleaned and gutted with its head on (see note)

1 garlic clove

½ cup white wine

3 dry bay leaves

2 tablespoons extra-virgin olive oil

1 tablespoon unsalted butter

In a large pot, place the celery, onion, carrot, 1 sprig of parsley, salt, and pepper. Add 2 cups water and bring to a boil. Cook for 20 minutes.

Strain the broth from the vegetable pot and cool. Reserve the broth. Puree the vegetables through a food mill. If puree is too thick, add some of the reserved broth.

Preheat the oven to 375 degrees F.

Place the fish in an oval baking dish. Stuff the head of the fish with the remaining parsley and the garlic. Add the wine.

Pour the remaining broth on the fish. Add the bay leaves and olive oil. Bake for 15 to 20 minutes, or until the eye of the fish has popped out.

Discard the bay leaves. Remove and discard the head of the fish. Bone the fish and serve it with the reserved vegetable puree, to which you may add the butter.

NOTE   *Any whole fish can be cooked this way, including a salmon.*

Striped Bass Baked in Foil | **PESCE IN CAMICIA**

The Italian name for this dish, *camicia* (shirt), refers to the aluminum foil in which the fish is wrapped and baked. In nicer restaurants along the Gulf of Naples, this dish is presented with great aplomb, brought to the table on an elegant cart. The waiter "undresses" the fish, portions it, and after removing the head, offers the cheeks to the most beautiful lady at the table. Hey, we are in Naples here. Did you know that the cheeks of the fish, any fish, are considered a delicacy? My brother Mimmo and I used to fight over them, but fortunately there were two!

6 servings

1 striped or sea bass (3 to 4 pounds), cleaned and scaled but head on (see note)

Salt to taste

Freshly milled pepper to taste

¾ teaspoon chopped fresh thyme, or ¼ teaspoon dried

¼ cup cognac

¼ cup white wine

3 tablespoons extra-virgin olive oil or spicy oil (see note)

8 ounces small shrimp, shelled, deveined, and sliced in half

1 small to medium tomato, sliced

Preheat the oven to 400 degrees F.

Sprinkle the fish inside and out with the salt and pepper. Insert the thyme into the cavity of the head.

Place the fish over a doubled layer of aluminum foil large enough to enclose the fish. Fold the edges of the foil up to contain the liquids.

Combine the cognac, wine, and oil. Pour this mixture over the fish and turn the fish over so that it is well-coated.

Scatter the shrimp all around the fish and arrange the tomato slices over it. Close the aluminum foil over the fish, but not too tight so that some of the steam can escape.

Bake for 20 minutes. Reduce the heat to 375 degrees F. Open the top of the pouch and bake for 6 to 10 more minutes.

NOTE *Since some people dislike looking a fish in the eye, fillets or steaks can be used.*

To make spicy oil, mix 1 cup extra-virgin olive oil with 1 hot red pepper and 1 crushed garlic clove in a jar. Shake and use when needed.

Fish in Wine Sauce | **PESCE UBRIACO**

In Naples we used to make this recipe mostly with swordfish or tuna. We called it "drunken fish" for obvious reasons, and it was delicious. I find that salmon works beautifully as a substitute.

6 servings

¼ cup extra-virgin olive oil

Juice of half a lemon

1 teaspoon fresh rosemary

2 teaspoons chopped fresh Italian parsley, plus 1 tablespoon for sprinkling

1 cup dry white wine

6 salmon steaks

2 garlic cloves, thinly sliced

¼ teaspoon fresh thyme

Salt to taste

Freshly milled pepper to taste

Lemon wedges

In a large shallow dish, combine the olive oil, lemon juice, rosemary, 2 teaspoons parsley, and wine. Toss the salmon steaks in it, turning several times to coat both sides well. Marinate for 1 hour or longer in the refrigerator.

Preheat the oven to 375 degrees F.

In a baking dish in which the fish can fit in one layer, place the fish and marinade. Add the garlic, thyme, salt, and pepper. Bake for 30 minutes, or until the sauce has reduced, and the fish flakes when pierced with a fork. Serve hot, sprinkled with the remaining tablespoon parsley and surrounded by lemon wedges.

NOTE *This recipe also works well with sturgeon, bluefish, or tuna.*

Sautéed Anchovies or Sardines

ALICI O SARDINE IN PADELLA

When I see fresh anchovies and sardines at the fish market, I immediately buy them. It is a little of a bother to clean them, but if you are a good customer, the fishmonger will do it for you. Anchovies and sardines can be grilled, sautéed, deep-fried with just a dusting of flour, or baked. Stuffed sardines, a dish that takes a lot of patience to prepare, are a specialty in some parts of Campania and southern Italy.

We Italians always like to cook our fish with the head on, and this is the way it is done in Naples. Some people, because the anchovies are so small, do not even bother removing the innards. The bone is tender and can be eaten. Especially when deep-fried, everything tastes delicious. Besides, the bones are a good source of calcium.

6 servings

2½ pounds fresh anchovies or sardines

¼ cup extra-virgin olive oil

Salt to taste

Freshly milled pepper to taste

2 tablespoons chopped Italian parsley

1 garlic clove, chopped

½ teaspoon chopped fresh oregano, or 1½ teaspoons dried

1 tablespoon capers, drained

½ cup dry white wine

4 ripe tomatoes, chopped

Gently scale the fish, if necessary. Remove the heads by pulling them off. This usually also removes the innards; if not, remove them with your fingers.

Wash the anchovies and place them in a skillet. Do not worry if they overlap a little. Add the olive oil and sprinkle with salt and pepper. Add 1 tablespoon of the parsley, the garlic, oregano, and capers.

Set on medium heat. As soon as the fish starts to sizzle, add the wine and let evaporate over high heat. Add the tomatoes and gently stir and shake the skillet. Cook for 5 to 10 minutes. Add the remaining chopped parsley and serve with the lemon wedges.

NOTE   *In Naples this dish is served with* crostini, *crunchy slices of bread brushed with olive oil and baked for a few minutes.*

**BRUSCHETTA WITH
RICOTTA AND HERBS**
page 19

TUNA-STUFFED TOMATOES
page 27

ESCAROLE SOUP page 46

**PIZZA WITH TOMATOES,
MOZZARELLA AND BASIL**
page 64

SPAGHETTI WITH MUSSELS
page 99

RIGATONI WITH EGGS AND PROSCIUTTO
page 115

POACHED FISH page 153
with GREEN SAUCE page 87

SPICY VESUVIUS CHICKEN
page 174

VEAL CUTLETS WITH
EGGPLANT, MOZZARELLA
AND TOMATOES page 197

ARTICHOKES AND FAVA BEANS
page 252

POTATO SALAD WITH
BELL PEPPERS AND ARUGULA
page 283

**SALAD WITH ROMAINE,
MARINATED ARTICHOKES,
AND BEETS**
page 285

RICOTTA WHEAT PIE
page 298

Baked and Breaded Sardines | **SARDINE O ALICI IN TORTIERA**

In Naples and Campania, this dish was usually made on Fridays or religious holidays, when Catholics weren't supposed to eat meat.

6 servings

¼ to ⅓ cup extra-virgin olive oil

1½ pounds fresh sardines or anchovies, cleaned and washed

Juice of half a lemon

½ cup fine dry unflavored bread crumbs

1 garlic clove, finely chopped

½ teaspoon dried oregano

Salt to taste

Freshly milled pepper to taste

Preheat the oven to 375 degrees F. Oil a baking dish from which you can serve.

Place the sardines in a mixing bowl, add 1 tablespoon of the olive oil and the lemon juice and toss.

Place the sardines in the baking dish, overlapping slightly. Smooth the top.

In a small bowl combine the bread crumbs, garlic, oregano, salt, and pepper. Spread this mixture on the fish and drizzle with the remaining olive oil. Bake for 10 minutes, or until the top is golden.

NOTE *Instead of oregano, you can use 1 tablespoon chopped fresh dill or fennel greens.*

Grilled Bluefish with Herbs

PESCE AZZURRO AI FERRI CON SALSA ALL'ALLORO

Any grilled fish can be dressed with this aromatic sauce. Years ago, we used to spend the summers in East Hampton. I would find excellent bluefish and mackerel there, just like the kind we used to buy in Naples. They were very fresh and went well with this savory herb mix.

6 servings

3 garlic cloves, cut in half, plus 1 garlic clove, chopped

2 or 3 sprigs Italian parsley

6 bluefish (about 8 ounces each), cleaned but with heads on

Extra-virgin olive oil

Juice of 1 lemon

1 large onion, sliced

2 dry bay leaves

5 or 6 fresh mint leaves

5 or 6 fresh basil leaves

Salt to taste

Freshly milled pepper

¼ cup fish broth or water

Lemon wedges

Place half a garlic clove and a few parsley leaves in the head or cavity of each fish. Smear some olive oil on the fish and drizzle with some of the lemon juice.

Put the chopped garlic, remaining lemon juice, onion, bay leaves, mint, basil, salt, pepper, and broth in a saucepan. Bring to a boil and simmer for 10 minutes over very low heat. Discard the bay leaves and puree the sauce in a food processor.

Lightly oil the rack of a broiler and place the fish on it. Broil for about 8 to 10 minutes on one side. Turn the fish and continue cooking for 8 minutes longer. The fish is done when the eye pops out, or if the flesh flakes easily when pierced with a fork.

Reheat the sauce and spoon it over the fish or serve it on the side. Surround the fish with lemon wedges.

Fish Fillets with Olives and Capers

PESCE ALL'OLIVE E CAPPERI

Any fish can be used in this recipe. It can be whole, filleted, or cut into slices. The tangy capers, a favorite condiment of the Neapolitans, give this dish its assertive flavor. Use chopped fresh tomatoes instead of puree, to obtain a lighter sauce. I also prefer sweet California olives to the Italian salted or sun-dried olives, which in my opinion make the sauce too harsh.

6 servings

SAUCE

3 tablespoons extra-virgin olive oil

1½ cups pureed fresh or canned tomatoes (see note)

1 teaspoon chopped fresh Italian parsley

¾ teaspoon chopped fresh basil, or ¼ teaspoon dried

1 garlic clove, chopped

1 whole small *diavoletto* (hot red pepper) (optional)

FISH

Flour for dredging

Salt to taste

Freshly milled pepper to taste

6 trout, or 5 to 6 pounds fish fillets or steaks

2 tablespoons extra-virgin olive oil

2 tablespoons unsalted butter

¼ cup dry white wine

20 black olives, pitted and cut into circlets

2 tablespoons capers, drained

TO PREPARE THE SAUCE   Place all sauce ingredients in a saucepan. Cover, bring to a boil, reduce the heat and simmer for 10 minutes. Remove the hot pepper.

TO PREPARE THE FISH   Combine flour, salt, and pepper. Dredge the fish and shake to remove excess flour.

In a large skillet in which the fish can fit snugly, heat the olive oil and butter. Sauté the fish for 3 to 5 minutes on each side, add the wine and let evaporate. Add the sauce and simmer for 10 minutes. Add the olives and capers and simmer for 5 more minutes. Serve immediately.

NOTE   *Never puree tomatoes in a food processor. Use a food mill.*

Baked Porgy with Sun-Dried Tomatoes

ORATA AL FORNO CON POMODORI SECCHI

This is a rather common fish in the Gulf of Naples and is readily available in the United States, however, a red snapper or bass will do as well. In Italy porgies are not very big—one fish can be served per person. In the United States, I have seen larger ones that can feed two to three people. Since the cooking method is the same, shop according to your need.

The sun-dried tomatoes give a truly Mediterranean flavor to this recipe.

6 servings

⅓ cup extra-virgin olive oil

6 porgies (10 to 12 ounces each), cleaned, preferably with the heads on

6 garlic cloves, crushed

6 sprigs Italian parsley, plus 1 tablespoon chopped

¾ cup dry white wine

Salt to taste

Freshly milled pepper to taste

Juice of 1 lemon

½ cup sun-dried tomatoes packed in oil, drained and chopped

Pour the olive oil into a baking dish in which the fish can fit snugly. Add the fish and turn several times to coat both sides with the oil. Place one garlic clove and one sprig of parsley in the head or cavity of each fish. Pour the wine over and sprinkle with salt and pepper. Refrigerate for at least 30 minutes.

Preheat the oven to 400 degrees F.

Place the fish in the oven and bake for 20 minutes. Reduce the heat to 375 degrees F. Add the lemon juice and tomatoes and continue baking for 10 more minutes, basting the fish with their juices a few times. The fish are done when they flake easily if touched with a fork. Sprinkle with parsley and serve.

Christmas Eve Fried Vegetables and Seafood

FRITTURA DELLA VIGILIA

This recipe is a traditional Christmas Eve dish and is another version of the famous *fritto misto all'italiana*, which also contains variety meats such as brains and sweetbreads. Since on Christmas Eve many Catholics do not eat meat, this *fritto* is composed mostly of fish and *baccalá* (salted dried cod), which in Naples is always included.

6 to 8 servings

1 head cauliflower, divided into florets

1 bunch broccoli, divided into florets

2 medium zucchini, cut into sticks

2 or 3 celery stalks, cut into 2-inch sticks

1 pound *baccalá* (salted dried cod), soaked and cubed

8 ounces squid, cleaned and bodies cut into circlets

8 ounces small shrimp, shelled and deveined

3 eggs, separated

3 tablespoons flour

Salt to taste

Freshly milled pepper to taste

Canola oil for frying

¼ cup extra-virgin olive oil

Lemon wedges

Blanch all the vegetables in boiling water. Drain and pat dry. Wash and pat dry all the fish.

Beat the egg yolks, add the flour and enough water to make a soft batter. Add salt and pepper. In a separate bowl, beat the egg whites until stiff, and then gently fold into the batter.

In a large skillet, combine some canola oil and olive oil so it comes up to 1 inch from the brim. Heat to the smoking point. As a test, drop in a piece of bread soaked in vinegar. If the bread floats on the surface, the oil is ready.

Dip the vegetable pieces into the batter and drop them into the oil. Do this in batches. Fry until golden and drain on paper towels. Keep warm until all pieces are cooked. Do the same with the *baccalá*, squid, and shrimp. Serve surrounded by lemon wedges.

Conger Eel on a Spit | **CAPITONE ALLO SPIEDO**

Il capitone, the conger eel, is a sacred part of the *cenone* (Christmas Eve dinner) in Campania, as well as other parts of Italy. My father used to buy the eels alive, and we kept them in the bathtub where the eels would swim happily, unaware of their destiny. A popular family story is that my Aunt Ela went into the bathroom unsuspecting, and then screamed at the top of her lungs, "There are snakes in the bathtub!"

We roasted the eels on a spit. In my opinion this is the best way because the natural fat of the fish, encased in the skin, releases its true flavor, and the skin itself becomes deliciously crunchy. Ideally the eel should be cooked on a wood fire, but it can also be cooked on a gas grill.

6 servings

3-pound conger eel, scrubbed clean and cut into 6 pieces

¼ cup plus 2 tablespoons white wine vinegar

½ cup dry white wine

3 tablespoons extra-virgin olive oil

Salt to taste

Freshly milled pepper to taste

7 fresh bay leaves

1 large sprig Italian parsley

Place the pieces of eel in a bowl, add the vinegar and cover with cold water. Let stand for 10 minutes, rinse well and set aside.

In a mixing bowl combine the wine, olive oil, salt, and pepper. Place the eel in this mixture and turn so that every piece is well coated. Chill for at least 1 hour.

When ready to cook, alternate on a spit 1 bay leaf and one piece of eel until all the eel and bay leaves are used. Reserve the marinade. Cook the eel over a wood fire or gas grill, turning it often if the spit is not automatic and you are using a gas grill. Cook for about 15 to 20 minutes, basting with the marinade, using the sprig of parsley as a brush. The cooking time varies according to the thickness of the eel. The skin, at this point, should be brown and crunchy.

NOTE *It is a good idea to put a piece of bread at each end of the spit—this will keep the pieces of eel in place.*

Skate and Mushroom Casserole

TORTIERA DI RAZZA E FUNGHI

My mother used to make several casseroles with fish, and this one with skate was inspired by Baked and Breaded Sardines (recipe on page 161).

6 servings

4 boneless skate wings, skinned (about 2½ pounds)

Fish broth (optional)

2 tablespoons extra-virgin olive oil, plus more for drizzling

Freshly milled pepper to taste

2 garlic cloves

1 sprig Italian parsley

12 ounces mushrooms, thinly sliced

¼ cup dried porcini mushrooms, soaked in ½ cup lukewarm water

¼ cup dry unflavored bread crumbs

1 teaspoon freshly grated Parmesan cheese

1 tablespoon chopped Italian parsley

Poach the wings in salted boiling water, or better yet in fish broth if you have it handy.

Preheat the oven to 350 degrees F. Oil a baking dish from which you can serve and add the wings in one layer. Season with pepper.

In a skillet heat 2 tablespoons of the olive oil and add 1 clove of the garlic and the sprig of parsley. Cook for 1 to 2 minutes, then add the fresh mushrooms.

With a slotted spoon, remove the dried porcini mushrooms from their water. Strain the water through a paper towel and reserve. Chop the mushrooms coarsely and add them to the skillet. Stir and cook until the liquid released by the mushrooms has evaporated. When done, remove the garlic and parsley and discard. Spoon the mushrooms over the skate.

Chop the remaining garlic clove very finely and combine it with the bread crumbs, Parmesan, and chopped parsley. Moisten with some of the remaining water from the porcini and sprinkle over the mushrooms. Drizzle with a little olive oil and bake for about 20 to 25 minutes. Serve hot.

NOTE *You can use baby artichokes instead of the mushrooms. Slice the artichokes very thinly and cook them exactly like the mushrooms.*

poultry and rabbit

I love chicken, and cook it often and in many ways. It is the most adaptable of all meats. The famous French gastronome Jean Anthelme Brillat-Savarin wrote: "Poultry is for the cook what a canvas is to a painter." How true!

Poultry's versatility knows no boundaries. Most of the time cooking it is easy, but it stirs the imagination. In this chapter you will find some classic, easy recipes, such as *pollo alla diavola* (Spicy Grilled Chicken), but also sophisticated ones that the *Monzù*, the chefs of Neapolitan nobility, originally made with capon. Also included are a turkey recipe and duck recipe.

Rabbit is as healthy, versatile, and delicious as chicken. Despite our contemporary preoccupation with healthy food, rabbit is not readily available in supermarkets and has not yet become popular on the American table. Hopefully these rabbit recipes will inspire you to give it a try!

Spicy Grilled Chicken | **POLLO ALLA DIAVOLA**

This is probably the easiest way of cooking a chicken. At one point in my life, though, *pollo alla diavola* was almost always eaten in a *trattoria*. It meant an outing to the country, or to a little cove on the Amalfi Drive overlooking Capri. The chicken was cooked over an open pit above a charcoal fire, and the scent was incredible. Given the festive mood, we were allowed to eat with our fingers, a no-no when we were at home.

Since I now live in New York, I cook my *pollo alla diavola* on a gas grill. You can also use the broiler of your oven—the scent wafting through the house is . . . almost Neapolitan. A little imagination is sometimes the best condiment.

6 to 8 servings

3 broiler chickens (2½ to 3 pounds each)

Extra-virgin olive oil as needed

Salt to taste

1 tablespoon freshly milled pepper or to taste

2 lemons

1 to 2 tablespoons chopped fresh Italian parsley

Split each chicken on its back from neck to tail. Turn the chickens and press hard with your hand over the breasts to flatten the bones. Cover with a piece of wax paper and pound with a mallet or a heavy skillet to make the chickens as flat as possible.

Place the chickens in a large roasting pan. Lightly coat both sides of the chickens with olive oil, sprinkle with salt and a good amount of pepper. Squeeze the juice of one lemon over the chickens and sprinkle them with parsley. Let stand at room temperature for one hour. If you aren't cooking them right away, refrigerate after that.

Prepare the barbecue or preheat the broiler. Cook the chickens turning them often and brushing them often with the pan juices, about 25 minutes each side.

Cut the remaining lemon in wedges and serve it with the chicken.

NOTE *For a less peppery taste, use a mixture of chopped herbs, such as oregano, sage, and thyme. My mother called this version* alla cherubino *for its "angelic" dressing.*

Chicken with Sour Pickles

POLLO ALLA FRANCESCHIELLO

The origin of this recipe is undoubtedly Neapolitan. What makes this dish so unusual is the addition of pickled vegetables called *sottaceti*. They are usually sold under the name *giardiniera*. The vibrant multicolored vegetables can be seen through the glass jars in which they are preserved. *Sottaceti* can also be served as a side dish with poached or roasted fish or meats. For this recipe, if you cannot find the *sottaceti*, use cornichons or small sour pickles.

6 servings

1 chicken (about 3 pounds), cut into serving pieces

3 tablespoons extra-virgin olive oil

Salt to taste

Freshly milled pepper to taste

½ cup white or red dry wine

2 garlic cloves, crushed

1½ teaspoons chopped fresh rosemary, or ½ teaspoon dried

1 small *diavoletto* (hot red pepper) (optional)

1 tablespoon chopped *sottaceti*, or same amount sour pickles (see above)

10 black olives, pitted and sliced

2 tablespoons chopped fresh Italian parsley

Wash the chicken pieces and pat them dry.

In a large skillet heat the olive oil, add the chicken and brown, turning the pieces often. Season with salt and pepper. Discard some of the fat. Add the wine and let evaporate. Add the garlic, rosemary, and *diavoletto* if using. Cover, reduce the heat, and simmer for about 45 minutes, stirring once in a while. If it becomes too dry, add some water (a few tablespoons at a time).

Remove the lid, add the *sottaceti* and olives and remove the red pepper if used, and cook uncovered, over high heat for a few minutes longer. Sprinkle with parsley and serve hot.

Chicken Cacciatore | **POLLO ALLA CACCIATORA**

This recipe is a classic, so of course opinions differ about its preparation. My *cacciatore* is a simple recipe made the way my mother used to prepare it. At times she would add ingredients on a whim according to season. Because the "hunter" (*cacciatore*) of the recipe name usually dwells in the woods, mushrooms were a favorite. But if you want to make it more *alla Napoletana*, fresh tomatoes are the best, together with red or green peppers and even olives.

4 to 6 servings

1 chicken (3 pounds), cut into small pieces (with bones)

¼ cup extra-virgin olive oil

2 garlic cloves, crushed

1 small onion, quartered

1 small carrot, cut in 4 pieces

1 stalk celery, trimmed and cut in 4 pieces

1 sprig of Italian parsley plus 1 tablespoon chopped

1 tablespoon prosciutto fat (optional)

1 small *diavoletto* (hot red pepper) (optional)

2 dry bay leaves

2 teaspoon tomato paste

¾ cup dry wine, white or red

Salt to taste

Freshly milled pepper to taste

½ cup chicken broth or water, if necessary

Wash and pat the chicken dry.

In a large skillet heat the olive oil. Add the garlic, and as soon as it starts to sizzle, add the chicken and brown.

In a food processor, finely chop the onion, carrot, celery, sprig of parsley and the prosciutto fat.

Add the chopped mixture to the skillet. Cook over medium-high heat stirring and turning the pieces of chicken often. Add the *diavoletto* if using, the bay leaves, and tomato paste. Stir and add the wine. Let evaporate and continue cooking until the chicken is done. If it gets too dry, add a little broth or water. Add salt and pepper. Remove the bay leaves and the hot pepper before serving. Serve sprinkled with the chopped parsley.

Spicy Vesuvius Chicken | **POLLO ALLA VESUVIO**

This is a rather "hot" dish—there is a lot of hot pepper in it. But if you prefer it milder, reduce the amount of hot pepper flakes and call it "non-active Vesuvius." After all, that beautiful mountain on the Gulf of Naples is not smoking anymore.

6 servings

1 (3 pound) chicken, cut into pieces

1 tablespoon kosher salt

3 small red potatoes, unpeeled and quartered

1 red onion, sliced into 6 sections through the root end

1 teaspoon oregano

1½ teaspoons hot red pepper flakes

½ cup olive oil

Salt to taste

Freshly milled pepper to taste

½ cup red wine

2 to 3 teaspoons chopped fresh Italian parsley

Preheat the oven to 425 degrees F.

Place the chicken in a bowl, add the kosher salt, cover with water and set aside.

Place the potatoes and onion in a large bowl. Add the oregano, pepper flakes, and half of the olive oil. Toss well.

Remove the chicken from the bowl, rinse and dry with paper towels. Add the chicken to the bowl with the vegetables. Add salt and pepper and toss well.

Oil a baking dish into which the chicken and vegetables will fit in one layer. Add the chicken mixture. Drizzle with the remaining olive oil and put the dish in the oven.

Reduce the heat to 375 degrees F. Bake until chicken starts to brown on the top, about 30 to 40 minutes. Add the wine. Continue cooking, basting frequently, until the vegetables are tender and the chicken is cooked through, about 30 minutes more.

Place the chicken and vegetables on a serving plate. Sprinkle with the parsley and serve with a good bottle of Aglianico, or another, equally good red wine.

Poussins with Cognac and Rosemary

POLLETTI AL COGNAC E ROSMARINO

In my house this simple and elegant recipe was made mostly during the summer with *polleti novelli* (very young chicken). My father's assistant would bring a couple of them from his farm as a present for the starving children of *il dottore*, my brother and me. In Naples we didn't use cream, which was precious and reserved to make butter. A bit of milk was enough. In the United States butchers sell these small chickens under the French term *poussins*. They weigh a little more then a pound. I have also used Cornish hens for this recipe with excellent results.

4 to 8 servings

4 poussins or Cornish game hens

Salt to taste

Freshly milled pepper to taste

4 sprigs rosemary, or ½ teaspoon dried for each bird

8 garlic cloves, crushed

3 tablespoons unsalted butter

2 tablespoons extra-virgin olive oil

4 ounces chopped prosciutto

½ cup cognac or brandy

½ cup heavy cream

Preheat the oven to 350 degrees F.

Wash and dry the birds and sprinkle with salt and pepper. Place one sprig of rosemary and two garlic cloves in the cavity of each bird. Truss them with twine.

Heat the butter and olive oil in a large skillet. Add two of the birds at a time and brown on all sides.

Spread the prosciutto at the bottom of a roasting pan into which the birds can fit side by side or use two smaller ovenproof dishes. Arrange the birds in the pan, breast side down. Roast for 15 minutes and then turn breast side up. Sprinkle with cognac and bake for one hour, or until their joints move easily, basting the birds every once in a while with their own juice.

Transfer the birds to a platter and keep them warm. Pour the fat off the roasting pan but keep the juices (see note). Whisk the juices with the heavy cream and warm over low heat.

Cut the birds in half or quarter them. Discard the rosemary sprigs and garlic. Arrange the pieces on a serving platter. Add all the bits of meat and juices that accumulated when cutting the birds and serve with the cream sauce.

NOTE *After I remove the meat I degrease the pan by lightly placing a paper towel over the juices. Then I gently remove the paper. You will see that the fat remains on the paper. I do this once or twice to obtain a leaner sauce.*

Stew of Chicken Legs with Sausage and Mushrooms

STUFATINO DI GAMBE DI POLLO E SALSICCE

This recipe comes from the town of Positano on the Amalfi Drive. It is another good example of the inventiveness and parsimony of the people of Campania.

6 servings

1 cup flour for dredging

Salt to taste

Freshly milled pepper

½ teaspoon dried rosemary or oregano

12 meaty chicken drumsticks, skinned

¼ cup extra-virgin olive oil

8 ounces sweet sausage meat, crumbled

1 cup red wine

1 teaspoon tomato paste

¼ cup dried porcini mushrooms, soaked in ½ cup lukewarm water

1 pound mushrooms, quartered or sliced

1 tablespoon chopped fresh Italian parsley

Combine the flour, salt, pepper, and herbs. Dredge the chicken legs in it and shake off excess flour.

In a skillet large enough to contain the chicken legs in one layer, heat the olive oil, add the chicken legs and sausage meat. Sauté for 7 to 8 minutes. Add ¾ cup of the wine and let evaporate.

Combine the tomato paste and remaining ¼ cup wine and add to the skillet. Cook for 5 minutes, stirring.

Remove the porcini from the water with a slotted spoon being careful not to disturb the sediment at the bottom of the water. Strain and reserve the water. Chop the porcini and add to the skillet, along with the fresh mushrooms. Cook stirring until the water released by the mushrooms has evaporated. Continue simmering until the chicken is cooked, about 30 to 40 minutes, adding the water from the porcini, a little at a time, to keep the *stufatino* moist. Serve sprinkled with the chopped parsley.

Rollatini with Chicken Liver | **ROLLATINE DI POLLO ALLA LUCULLO**

Lucullus, a Roman general, was famous for his high standard of living. Thus the word "Lucullian" was coined by the Romans for lavish and extravagant banquets. My father must have been an admirer of this general, because he was always telling stories about the Lucullian banquets he attended when he was a bachelor. One day my mother got a hold of some *pâté de foie gras* (pureed French goose liver) and a truffle, a real rarity in Naples. She included both in her *rollatine*, which were usually modestly stuffed with chicken livers and cockscombs (yes, we ate them!). My father liked the dish immensely and declared it worthy of Lucullus. So the name remained, and to this day we call it *alla Lucullo*. I find that sweet California olives work well as a substitution for the expensive truffles. You may call them "mock truffles."

6 servings

16 large chicken cutlets, pounded thin

¼ cup plus 2 tablespoons Marsala wine

4 ounces chicken livers, washed and picked over

1 sprig Italian parsley

¾ teaspoon chopped fresh sage, or ¼ teaspoon dried

1 egg

4 ounces canned *pâté de foie gras*

Small black truffle, chopped, or ½ cup black olives, chopped

Salt to taste

Freshly milled pepper to taste

2 tablespoons unsalted butter

1 tablespoon extra-virgin olive oil

Take 4 of the cutlets, the smallest of the bunch, cut these in pieces and place in a food processor. Add 2 tablespoons of the Marsala, the chicken livers, parsley, and sage. Chop very fine. Add the egg and *foie gras*. Process until well mixed. Transfer to a bowl, add the truffle or olives and mix with a fork. Season with salt and pepper.

Spread the liver mixture over the remaining cutlets, roll them up and tie with kitchen twine.

In a large skillet, heat the butter and olive oil. Add the *rollatine* and gently brown on all sides, turning them often, about 10 minutes. Add half of the remaining Marsala wine, cover and cook over low heat for 10 more minutes. Remove the cover and let the wine evaporate. Continue cooking the chicken for approximately 20 minutes.

Place the *rollatine* on a serving plate and keep warm. Deglaze the skillet with the remaining Marsala scraping with a wooden spoon to remove all the brown particles clinging at the bottom and the sides of the pan. Remove the twine from the *rollatine*, pour the wine sauce over them and serve hot.

Chicken Pot Pie with Mortadella

TEGAMINI DI POLLO ALLA MORTADELLA

The flavor of this simple dish, which my mother, always the parsimonious one, made with leftover chicken, is delicious. Nowadays I use fresh chicken breasts, and lo and behold, you can call it an elegant dish. The texture—complex and succulent—with the intricacy of ricotta and mozzarella, and the savory flavor of the mortadella is pleasantly surprising.

6 servings

6 boneless chicken breast halves, cubed

¾ cup dry Marsala wine

Extra-virgin olive oil

8 slices mortadella

2 sprigs Italian parsley

½ cup whole-milk ricotta, drained

½ cup freshly grated Parmesan or Grana Padano cheese

2 eggs

½ teaspoon nutmeg

Freshly milled pepper to taste

8 ounces fresh mozzarella, cut into 6 slices

Extra-virgin olive oil

Place the chicken in a shallow dish and add the Marsala. Marinate the chicken for at least 20 minutes.

Preheat the oven to 375 degrees F. Lightly oil 6 (1-cup) ramekins. Line each with a slice of mortadella.

Remove the chicken cubes from the marinade and drain, reserving the marinade. Process the chicken, the remaining 2 slices of mortadella and the parsley in the food processor until very fine. Put the mixture into a bowl and add the ricotta, Parmesan, eggs, nutmeg, and pepper. Mix well.

Fill the ramekins with the chicken mixture. Smooth the tops and put 1 slice of mozzarella on top of each and pour a little of the Marsala marinade over each.

Place the ramekins on a baking sheet and bake for 40 to 45 minutes, or until the tops are firm and browned. Cool for 10 minutes before unmolding.

NOTE *My mother used to place a lettuce leaf on each plate, then unmold the ramekins on top of them. I use a sprig of curly parsley for garnish.*

Chicken in Tuna Sauce | **POLLO TONNATO**

Leftover chicken again? Well, with this recipe you can make the leftover meat of a roasted or boiled chicken taste different and delicious. Canned tuna is a favorite in Campania, because it is an ingredient that makes a dish go a long way. This is a real example of the *cucina povera*—inexpensive ingredients and great flavor.

6 servings

1 (6-ounce) can tuna packed in olive oil

2 anchovies packed in oil, chopped, or 1 teaspoon anchovy paste

½ cup mayonnaise

Juice of half a lemon plus more as needed

2 sprigs Italian parsley

3 cups cooked chicken, boned, skinned and cut into chunks

2 tablespoons capers, drained

2 hard-boiled eggs, sliced

Lettuce for garnish

In a food processor combine the tuna and its oil, the anchovies, mayonnaise, lemon juice, and parsley. Process to a smooth cream.

Place the chicken on a serving platter and pour the tuna sauce over it. Sprinkle with capers and garnish with the eggs and lettuce. Serve at room temperature.

Spinach-Stuffed Turkey Breast

ROTOLO DI TACCHINO ALLA GIANNA

Turkey is considered such an American bird that people are surprised when they find out that many delectable and important dishes in Italy are prepared with turkey. This one is the invention of my cousin Gianna Amore who lives in Campania and is a fabulous cook. It is great for a party as it can be prepared in advance, it can also be served cold, and the presentation is very pretty.

8 servings

3 tablespoons extra-virgin olive oil

4 eggs, well beaten

2 tablespoons unsalted butter

1 pound spinach, trimmed and washed

4½-pound turkey breast, boned with skin

Salt to taste

Freshly milled pepper to taste

4 slices mortadella

2 tablespoons freshly grated Parmesan cheese

1½ teaspoons chopped fresh rosemary, or ½ teaspoon dried

¼ cup white wine

1 cup chicken broth

Heat 1 tablespoon of olive oil in a skillet. Add half of the beaten eggs. Spread out to make a flat, thin omelet, turning it once. Repeat with the remaining eggs. Set the omelets aside. Wipe the skillet.

In the same skillet in which you cooked the eggs place 1 tablespoon of the butter, add the spinach, cook stirring once or twice until water released by the spinach has evaporated, 5 to 8 minutes. Set aside.

Spread the breast of turkey, skin side down on the counter, remove the fillets and set them aside. Flatten the breast somewhat to give it an even shape, sprinkle with salt and pepper and place one of the omelets on top of the breast. Cover with the slices of mortadella.

Spread the spinach over the mortadella and sprinkle with the Parmesan cheese. Top with the remaining omelet. Place the fillets lengthwise in the center. Fold in the two sides of the breast to enclose the filling. Secure with kitchen twine, giving the meat the form of a big roll.

In a heavy pot or Dutch oven in which the roll can fit snugly, heat the remaining butter and olive oil. Add the rosemary and the turkey roll, browning it on all sides. Add the wine and let evaporate. Add half of the broth, cover, reduce heat and simmer for about 1½ hours, turning meat occasionally. If there is not enough liquid, add more broth. To check for doneness, pierce the meat with a skewer, the juice should run out clear, if not cook longer. Serve hot or cold.

NOTE   *This turkey can also be baked in a preheated oven at 375 degrees F, loosely covered with aluminum foil, for about 1 to 1½ hours. Baste it frequently.*

Duck with Pearl Onions | **ANATRA IN PENTOLA**

Roast duck is wonderful, but we tend to forget that there are other ways of cooking this bird. This hearty recipe, which comes from the countryside of Campania, is absolutely delicious. At one time, duck was considered a luxury in Italy; only the peasants who raised ducks and the aristocrats who could afford to buy them ate duck often. I remember as a child in Naples, how my brother Mimmo and I fought for the succulent neck—in Italy poultry is sold with every part attached. Fortunately my mother would arrive in time to break the desired tidbit in two pieces so we could happily nibble on it without breaking each other's necks.

4 servings

DUCK

1 duck (about 4 pounds), cleaned and ready to cook

3 cups homemade or canned chicken broth

1/2 cup white wine

2 sprigs Italian parsley

1 pound pearl onions

4 cloves

Salt to taste

Freshly milled pepper to taste

SAUCE

4 large onions, sliced

3 tablespoons unsalted butter

1 tablespoon extra-virgin olive oil

2 tablespoons all-purpose flour

1 cup reserved duck broth

1/2 cup white wine vinegar

1 teaspoon sugar

TO PREPARE THE DUCK Fill a large pot with enough water to cover the duck once it is placed in it. Bring to a boil and carefully plunge the duck in. Boil for about 10 minutes. (This will release some of the fat from the duck.) Drain the duck and discard the water. Return the duck to the pot, add the broth, wine, and parsley. Bring to a boil, reduce the heat, and simmer covered for about 1 hour. Remove the duck from the broth, cool, and refrigerate, covered with aluminum foil. Chill the broth for a few hours, and then skim the grease off the top.

Place the duck in a large pot. Peel the onions and make crisscross cuts at their root ends. Place the onions around the duck. Add the cloves, salt, pepper and half of the reserved broth. Cover and cook over medium-low heat until the duck is cooked, about 1 hour.

TO PREPARE THE SAUCE In a saucepan place the onions, butter, and olive oil. Heat, cover the pan and reduce the heat to a minimum. Cook for 10 to 15 minutes. Uncover the pan and cook stirring until the onions begin to color.

Place the flour in a small bowl and add enough broth, about 3/4 cup, to reach a liquid consistency. Add this mixture to the onions, cover and reduce the heat to a minimum. Cook stirring often until the onions are almost creamed. Add the vinegar and sugar, cook for a few more minutes.

Carve the duck and place the pieces, skin side up, in a roasting pan. Put it under the broiler for 5 to 8 minutes, or until nicely colored. Serve surrounded by the pearl onions with the sauce on the side.

Rabbit with Sour Pickles | **CONIGLIO AI SAPORI**

With the tangy flavor of pickles and capers, and a hint of spiciness, this dish tastes very Mediterranean.

8 servings

2 fresh rabbits (about 2½ pounds each), cut into serving pieces

¼ cup white wine vinegar

¼ cup extra-virgin olive oil

4 or 5 garlic cloves, crushed

1 small *diavoletto* (hot red pepper) (optional)

3 dry bay leaves

1½ teaspoons chopped fresh rosemary, or ½ teaspoon dried

1½ teaspoons chopped fresh sage, or ½ teaspoon dried

½ cup dry wine, red or white

Freshly milled pepper to taste

¾ cup coarsely chopped *sottaceti* or pickles

1 tablespoon capers, drained

1 tablespoon chopped fresh Italian parsley

Place the rabbit pieces in a noncorrosive bowl, add the vinegar and cover with water. Let stand at least 1 hour.

Drain the rabbit pieces and place in a heavy skillet. Add the olive oil, garlic, hot pepper if using, bay leaves, rosemary, sage, wine and sprinkle with pepper.

Cover the skillet and cook over medium heat for about 1 hour and 15 minutes. Add the pickles and capers and continue cooking until the rabbit is tender, about 10 to 15 minutes longer. If you have too much liquid reduce it to a minimum while stirring the meat and scraping the bottom of the skillet. Serve sprinkled with the chopped parsley.

Rabbit in Tomato Sauce | **CONIGLIO ALL'ISCHITANA**

I had to wait until the end of WWII before I could travel to Capri and Ischia. During the war, it was too dangerous because of frequent air raids. From Il Vomero, the hill on which we lived in Naples, we could see the two islands floating in the blue Mediterranean Sea. A few years after WWII, we went on vacation to Ischia, and it was wonderful to visit the villages, the quiet coves and little beaches we had seen from far away. We also had wonderful food, including one of the island's specialties: *coniglio all'Ischitana,* a rabbit dish that seemed to be cooked with all the aromas of the island.

But going back to my story once more, it wasn't until I was married that I visited Capri for the first time. It was my husband Harold who took me to Capri. As a good American he had been there before, and it gave him great pleasure to show the island to an Italian. We also went to Ischia, and notwithstanding the wariness of my American husband towards rabbit, we had *coniglio all'Ischitana.*

4 to 6 servings

1 (3- to 4-pound) rabbit, cut into serving pieces

1 tablespoon kosher salt

¼ cup extra-virgin olive oil plus more for drizzling

1 bunch fresh thyme or rosemary

1 cup red wine

1 (28-ounce) can peeled tomatoes

3 fresh basil leaves

Place the rabbit pieces in a noncorrosive bowl, add the kosher salt, cover with cool water, stir and set aside for 20 to 25 minutes. (This will clean the rabbit of possible impurities.)

When ready to cook, remove the rabbit pieces from the water, rinse and dry.

In a large skillet, heat 2 tablespoons of the olive oil and add the rabbit. Cook stirring for 5 to 10 minutes, then add the thyme or rosemary. Stir and continue cooking until the rabbit pieces start to brown. Add the wine, a little at a time and let it evaporate before adding more.

When the wine is completely evaporated, add the tomatoes with their juice. Crush them with a wooden spoon. Add the basil. Reduce the heat and cover. Let simmer for about 45 minutes to 1 hour, turning the rabbit pieces once in a while. If the sauce gets too thick, add some water. Drizzle some olive oil on the meat during the last minutes of cooking. Remove the herbs and serve.

NOTE *It is important to use fresh herbs for this dish to retain the fresh aroma of the sauce.*

This sauce is excellent to dress spaghetti.

Lemon Rabbit | **CONIGLIO AL LIMONE**

This recipe is adapted from Jo Bettoja's enthralling book *Southern Italian Cooking*. Jo is an American married to an Italian and lives in Italy. Every time we see each other, we talk of the fact that she has an Italian husband and I an American one! And, of course, we exchange recipes. The only problem with this *piatto solare* (sunny dish) from Amalfi is finding one of the ingredients for which the recipe is famous—lemon leaves. But I have used lettuce leaves with almost equal success.

6 servings

1 rabbit (2 to 3 pounds), cut into serving pieces

Juice of 2 lemons

¼ cup extra-virgin olive oil plus more for drizzling

2 tablespoons chopped fresh rosemary

½ cup fine dry unflavored bread crumbs

⅓ cup freshly grated Parmesan cheese

1 garlic clove, chopped

3 tablespoons chopped fresh Italian parsley

Freshly milled pepper to taste

Several large lemon or lettuce leaves

1 lemon, cut into wedges

Place the rabbit pieces in a noncorrosive bowl, add the juice of 1 lemon, cover with cold water and let stand for 1 hour. When ready to cook, drain and dry the pieces of rabbit with paper towels.

In a large skillet, heat the olive oil, add the rabbit pieces and half of the rosemary. Brown the rabbit quickly, adding more olive oil if necessary. Remove from the heat.

Preheat the oven to 375 degrees F. Oil a baking dish into which the pieces of rabbit will fit snugly.

In a bowl combine the bread crumbs, Parmesan, garlic, parsley, pepper, and remaining rosemary. Roll the pieces of rabbit in this mixture and set aside.

Oil the lettuce leaves and wrap one or two pieces of rabbit in each. Place the bundles in the dish, drizzle with olive oil and squeeze the juice of the other lemon over them. Bake for 50 minutes. Turn the pieces over and bake for 10 more minutes. Serve hot, passing the lemon wedges around.

Rabbit with Herbs and White Wine

CONIGLIO ALLA CACCIATORE

This is a simple and classic way of cooking rabbit. Of course, like many other dishes in the *cacciatore* (hunter) style, there is always a local or personal touch to it. This one does not include tomatoes.

6 to 8 servings

1 rabbit (3 pounds),
cut into serving pieces

¼ cup wine vinegar (red or white)

¼ cup extra-virgin olive oil

3 garlic cloves

4 sprigs rosemary,
torn into pieces

Salt to taste

Freshly milled pepper to taste

1 cup white wine

1 tablespoon chopped fresh
Italian parsley

Two hours before cooking, place the rabbit pieces in a noncorrosive bowl, cover with water and add the vinegar. Keep in a cool place for two hours. If you don't cook them right away, keep in the refrigerator.

When ready to cook, drain the rabbit pieces and dry with paper towels.

Heat the olive oil in a large skillet, add the whole garlic cloves and some of the rosemary. As soon as the garlic starts to color, add the rabbit pieces, the remaining rosemary, some salt and pepper. Cook for 5 to 10 minutes, adding a little wine at a time, and turning the pieces of rabbit often. When the wine has evaporated, cover the skillet, reduce the heat and cook for about 30 minutes. If the meat gets too dry, add a little water. The rabbit is cooked when the meat comes easily off the bone. Remove the garlic, sprinkle with parsley and serve.

veal

Varro, a prolific Roman scholar and writer, called Italy the "land of the veal." To this day, veal is the preferred meat of the Italians. Even in regions where lamb and pig reign supreme, veal is greatly appreciated and prepared in many delicious ways.

The meat of the Campanian veal is particularly flavorful, because the animals graze on pastures covering the region's slopes. Most of the veal sold in Italy is *vitellino da latte* (milk veal). It means that the animal has been fed only with milk. This meat is very expensive and usually reserved for *scaloppine*, cutlets, medallions, etc.—dishes that require only short cooking.

Conventional veal, which is what we eat in the United States, is the meat from young calves. It is still nice and flavorful, but not as tender as the Italian kind.

Veal, being delicate meat, lends itself to be prepared with a myriad of condiments and with wine, broth, vinegar, or vegetables. It is an ideal meat for stuffing, especially with prosciutto or sausage. Their assertive flavors enhance the delicacy of the veal, forming a pleasant contrast. Some cuts of veal take very swift cooking, others can withstand long, gentle simmering. Veal is nourishing meat, easily digestible, low in fat and therefore a bonus in terms of modern dietary standards.

Veal Roast with Dried Porcini and Sun-Dried Tomatoes

ARROSTO DI VITELLO CON FUNGHI E POMODORI SECCHI

This dish is flavored with dried porcini and the robust tang of sun-dried tomatoes. In Naples, our sun-dried tomatoes came from clusters of cherry tomatoes we left out in the sun. They were never too hard and still a bit moist, I don't know why. Perhaps my mother didn't let them shrivel too much, or the gentle breeze of the Neapolitan wind kept them moist.

6 servings

½ cup dried porcini mushrooms

1 tablespoon extra-virgin olive oil

1 tablespoon unsalted butter

1 small onion, or 1 leek, sliced

1 garlic clove

½ cup unflavored dry bread crumbs

1 cup sun-dried tomatoes packed in oil, coarsely chopped (see note)

¼ teaspoon dried rosemary

¼ teaspoon dried thyme

¼ teaspoon dried sage

Freshly milled pepper to taste

1 veal rump roast (4 pounds), boned

1 heaping teaspoon grainy mustard

Soak the mushrooms in lukewarm water for about 20 minutes.

In an ovenproof casserole, heat the olive oil and butter. Add the onion and garlic. Cover and cook over low heat until soft, stirring once in a while, about 15 minutes.

Gently lift the mushrooms from the water without disturbing the sediments at the bottom. Filter the water through a paper towel and set aside. Chop the mushrooms coarsely and add to the casserole. Cook for 5 to 8 minutes. With a slotted spoon, transfer the mixture to a mixing bowl. Either remove the garlic or mash it, then add the bread crumbs, sun-dried tomatoes, herbs, and pepper. Mix well.

Preheat the oven to 350 degrees F.

With a knife, open the veal lengthwise like a book. Sprinkle with pepper and spoon the stuffing evenly in the center. Close the roast and secure the veal with kitchen twine to keep in place, and rub it all over with the mustard.

Place the veal in the casserole and pour the mushroom liquid over it. Roast for 1½ to 2 hours, or until the juices run clear when the meat is pierced with a fork, turning the meat every once in a while.

NOTE *Sun-dried tomatoes packed in oil are quite expensive, but you can buy the dry ones for less money. Just soak the sun-dried tomatoes for 30 minutes in lukewarm water, drain and dry them. Place them in a jar, cover with extra-virgin olive oil and some herbs of your choice like basil, oregano, or fennel. Store in the refrigerator. They will keep for over a year.*

Veal Cutlets with Peas and Prosciutto

COTOLETTE DI VITELLO CON PISELLI E PROSCIUTTO

This is common fare in Italy today, but when I was growing up, cutlets were scarce, and my mother stretched them with subtle additions. Fortunately she was a good cook.

6 servings

3 pounds veal cutlets, pounded thin

All-purpose flour for dredging

1 tablespoon extra-virgin olive oil

2 tablespoons unsalted butter

1½ teaspoons chopped fresh sage, or ½ teaspoon dried, crumbled

Salt to taste

Freshly milled pepper to taste

Juice of 1 lemon

2 ounces prosciutto, shredded

¾ cup frozen peas, defrosted

Lightly dredge the veal cutlets in flour. Chill for 20 minutes.

In a large skillet heat the olive oil and 1 tablespoon butter. Add the sage. Cook the cutlets in batches, 5 minutes on one side, and 3 on the other. Season each batch with salt and pepper. Transfer the cutlets to a serving platter.

Pour the lemon juice in the skillet and cook for about 5 minutes scraping the brown particles at the bottom of the skillet. Pour this sauce on the cutlets and keep warm.

Add the remaining tablespoon butter to the skillet, heat, add the prosciutto, cook a few seconds and then add the peas. Cook just to heat through and serve with the cutlets.

Veal Loaf | **PASTICCIO DI VITELLO**

Of the many dishes we used to eat when I lived in Naples, some are classics, while others, such as this one, are the result of having to manage with what was available. Mother liked to serve this meatloaf for lunch when we had friends over. I have started to do the same since everybody seems to like it, and all admire its presentation.

The loaf is usually served sliced and surrounded by a spinach salad dressed with oil, a touch of vinegar and sprinkled with orange or tangerine segments.

6 or more servings

Unsalted butter for the pan

Unflavored dry bread crumbs

2 tablespoons unsalted butter

2 to 3 tablespoons extra-virgin olive oil

3 carrots, diced

3 tablespoons freshly grated Parmesan cheese

1½ pounds fresh spinach

1½ pounds ground veal

Salt to taste

Freshly milled pepper to taste

2 tablespoons Marsala wine

2 eggs, beaten

Preheat the oven to 350 degrees F. Butter a meatloaf pan and sprinkle it with bread crumbs.

In a saucepan heat 1 tablespoon butter and 1 tablespoon olive oil. Add the carrots and sauté over medium heat for 3 to 5 minutes, but do not let brown. Add a little water and cover the pan. Reduce the heat and cook until the carrots are tender. Puree the carrots, add 1 tablespoon Parmesan, and set aside.

Add the spinach to the saucepan and cook until wilted. Puree the spinach and add the remaining 2 tablespoons of Parmesan.

Wipe the pan clean and heat the remaining tablespoon butter and 1 tablespoon olive oil. Add the veal. Cook over high heat stirring for about 10 minutes, then season with salt and pepper. Add the Marsala and let evaporate. Combine the beaten eggs with the veal.

Place one layer of the veal at the bottom of the prepared pan, top with a layer of spinach, followed by a layer of veal and a layer of carrots. Repeat the layering and finish with the veal. Sprinkle the top with bread crumbs and bake the loaf for about 40 minutes. Cool for 5 minutes, then unmold. Let the loaf stand for 10 more minutes before slicing.

Veal Roast with Herbs | ARROSTO DI VITELLO ALLE ERBE

A classic roast, simple and easy to make, this is usually served on Sundays.

6 or more servings

3 tablespoons extra-virgin
olive oil

2 slices prosciutto

1 garlic clove, crushed

1 tablespoon fresh rosemary,
or 1 teaspoon dried

1½ teaspoons fresh thyme,
or ½ teaspoon dried

2 sprigs Italian parsley

4 pounds shoulder of veal,
boned and tied

Freshly milled pepper to taste

Salt to taste

¾ cup dry white wine
plus some for basting

Chicken or beef broth (optional)

Preheat the oven to 375 F. Oil a baking dish into which the veal fits snugly.

In a food processor place the prosciutto, garlic, and herbs. Chop very fine.

Pierce holes into the veal and insert some of the chopped mixture into the holes. Smear the veal with olive oil and place it in the prepared pan. Sprinkle with pepper. Roast the veal 1 hour, basting often with some wine and the juices accumulated at the bottom of the pan.

Sprinkle the roast with salt. Continue cooking for 30 to 45 minutes more. Check for doneness by piercing the meat with a skewer. If the juices run out clear, the veal is done; otherwise cook a little longer. Remove the roast from the pan and let rest for 10 minutes before slicing.

Spoon the fat off the juices in the pan. Add half of the wine to the dish and scrape the brown particles clinging to the bottom and sides. If you want more sauce you can add the remaining wine and also a little broth. Reheat and serve with the veal.

Veal Medallions in Marsala Sauce

MEDAGLIONI DI VITELLO AL MARSALA

Similar to scaloppine, these medallions have a more succulent sauce. It is an elegant dish. At my home it was served on a bed of spinach cooked in butter, or with a creamy potato puree.

6 or more servings

3 tablespoons unsalted butter

1 tablespoon extra-virgin olive oil

1 bunch fresh rosemary

12 boned veal medallions (about 3 pounds)

½ cup Marsala wine

1 cup homemade or canned chicken broth

½ cup heavy cream

1 tablespoon lemon juice (optional)

In a large skillet into which the medallions can fit in one layer, heat 2 tablespoons of the butter and the olive oil. Add the rosemary, let it develop its flavor, then add the medallions and sauté on both sides. Cook for about 3 to 4 minutes on each side, depending on their size. Transfer the medallions to a serving dish and keep warm.

Add the Marsala to the skillet and cook over high heat, scraping with a wooden spoon to remove the brown particles clinging at the bottom and sides of the pan. Reduce the wine by half and then add the broth and cream. Cook until the mixture starts to thicken.

Remove the sauce from the heat, discard the rosemary, and stir in the remaining tablespoon butter and the lemon juice if using. Pour the sauce over the medallions and serve.

Veal Chops with Arugula and Tomatoes

COSTOLETTE DI VITELLO ALL'ORTOLANA

A recipe which contains ingredients from the backyard garden (*orto*), like in this case tomatoes and arugula, is called *all'ortolana*. Choose rib chops that are not more than ½-inch thick. Have them "frenched" by your butcher, which means scraping the meat off the "handle" bone of the chop, up to where the solid part is attached. My brother used to call this type of chops *la cotoletta col manico*, the chop with the handle. He loved to brandish one and bite into it like a savage. I still remember how furious my mother would become, but we all laughed in the end.

6 servings

6 large veal chops from the rib, ½ inch thick, frenched

1 cup unflavored dry bread crumbs for dredging

1 teaspoon chopped fresh Italian parsley

1½ teaspoons chopped fresh sage, or ½ teaspoon dried, crumbled

Freshly milled pepper to taste

3 eggs

2 tablespoons milk

¼ cup extra-virgin olive oil

1 to 2 tablespoons balsamic vinegar (see note)

1 bunch arugula, trimmed, coarsely chopped

3 firm ripe tomatoes, diced

1 cup canola oil

Salt to taste

Place each chop between two pieces of wax paper. With a meat pounder, flatten the meat to ¼ inch thickness (this can also be done by the butcher).

On a platter combine 1 cup or more of the bread crumbs with the parsley, sage, and some pepper.

Beat the eggs with the milk and dip one chop at a time into the eggs and dredge in the breadcrumb mixture. Pat the chops to make the crumbs adhere. Chill for 1 hour.

Just before cooking the chops, combine 2 tablespoons of the olive oil and the balsamic vinegar in a bowl. Add the arugula and tomatoes, but do not toss.

Pour the canola oil in a skillet and add the remaining 2 tablespoons of olive oil. Heat to the smoking point and fry the chops, a few minutes on each side, or until nicely golden. Drain on paper towels. Sprinkle with salt.

Toss the arugula and tomato salad. Set chops on 6 individual plates, top with salad and serve.

NOTE *Balsamic vinegar, which came from the region of Emilia Romagna in the north, is a relatively new addition to Neapolitan cooking and was not available during the war. In fact, balsamic vinegar and canola oil had never been seen in Naples. To save olive oil, which was precious, we used* olio di semi, *a seed oil to which we added a little olive oil for flavor.*

Veal Chops with Porcini Mushrooms and Tomatoes
COSTOLETTE DI VITELLO ALLA CACCIATORA

Alla cacciatora is a style of cooking favored by many Neapolitans because its condiments are so basic. What you need are some of the *odori di cucina*, the "perfumes of the kitchen": onions, carrots, celery, garlic, and parsley. The *cacciatora* is considered a classic, although you cannot take this too literally since we often add our own personal touch. Perhaps this is the fun of cooking Italian. I quite often use red wine with veal and even with chicken. It gives the meat a better color.

6 servings

3 to 4 tablespoons all-purpose flour for dredging

1 teaspoon dried sage

6 veal chops from the shoulder

¼ cup extra-virgin olive oil

1 onion, thinly sliced

Salt to taste

Freshly milled pepper to taste

¾ cup dry red wine

1 strip lemon peel

½ cup dried porcini mushrooms, soaked in warm water

4 ripe tomatoes, peeled, seeded, and coarsely chopped

1 tablespoon chopped fresh Italian parsley

Combine the flour and sage. Dredge the chops in it and shake off the excess flour.

In a skillet large enough to contain the chops in one layer (or use two skillets), heat the olive oil and add the onion. Stir, cover, and cook over low heat until the onion is quite soft, but not colored, about 15 minutes.

Add the chops to the skillet and sauté on both sides until brown. Season with salt and pepper. Add the wine and lemon peel. Let the wine evaporate.

Carefully remove the mushrooms from the water so as not to disturb the sediment at the bottom. Strain the water and set aside. Chop the mushrooms coarsely. Add the mushrooms and chopped tomatoes to the skillet. Cover and cook over medium heat for about 20 to 25 minutes. Keep in mind that sometimes veal releases too much liquid. If this happens, uncover the skillet and let evaporate. On the other hand, if there is not enough liquid, add the reserved water from the mushrooms. At the end, the chops should not be dry, but have a rather thick sauce. Sprinkle with parsley and serve.

Breaded Veal Cutlets | **COTOLETTE ALLA MILANESE**

In Italy this *cotoletta* is ubiquitous from Milano, where it originated, to Palermo, Rome, and Naples. A staple at home, we loved them, and they were our school meal, our quick dinner, and an elegant second course for longer dinners. When we went for our summer outings to the hill of Posillipo, we always had them in a *panino*. The cutlets are good hot and cold, and can be prepared in advance and cooked at the last minute. By the way, the true *cotoletta alla milanese* is on the bone, but the more common cooking method is without bone.

6 servings

6 large veal cutlets, lightly pounded

All-purpose flour for dredging

3 eggs

2 tablespoons milk

Freshly milled pepper to taste

Unflavored dry bread crumbs for dredging

3 tablespoons unsalted butter

1 tablespoon extra-virgin olive oil

Salt to taste

Lemon wedges

Dredge the cutlets in flour. Set aside.

In a bowl beat the eggs with the milk and some pepper. Dip the cutlets, one at a time, into the egg mixture and dredge in bread crumbs. Pat the cutlets on each side to let the crumbs adhere. Refrigerate for 20 minutes. (This will prevent them from absorbing too much oil.)

In a skillet heat the butter and olive oil, and fry the cutlets on both sides until golden. Transfer to a serving platter, sprinkle with salt and serve surrounded by lemon wedges.

Veal Cutlets with Eggplant, Mozzarella and Tomatoes

COTOLETTE ALL'AMALFITANA

This is a delicious and simple recipe from the beautiful town of Amalfi. In Sorrento, this dish is made without eggplants; apparently the people of Sorrento are not so fond of this vegetable, whereas in Amalfi it is adored. In fact, there is a dish in which eggplants are combined with chocolate! To read more about this, I recommend Arthur Schwartz's book *Naples at the Table*.

6 servings

2 small eggplants

1 tablespoon extra-virgin olive oil, plus more for brushing the eggplants

2 tablespoons unsalted butter

All-purpose flour for dredging

6 veal cutlets, well pounded

8 ounces whole-milk mozzarella, cut into six slices

2 or 3 tomatoes, cut into 12 slices

1/2 cup freshly grated Parmesan cheese

2 tablespoons chopped fresh Italian parsley

Preheat the broiler or grill.

Cut each eggplant into 3 slices about the length of the cutlets. Brush the slices on both sides with olive oil and broil or grill for about 3 minutes per side.

Heat the butter and 1 tablespoon olive oil in a skillet. Lightly flour the cutlets and sauté 3 cutlets at a time on both sides for a few minutes. Place the cutlets on a baking sheet. Top each with 1 slice of eggplant, 1 slice of mozzarella, and 2 tomato slices. Sprinkle the cutlets with Parmesan. (The cutlets can be prepared in advance up to this point.)

Preheat the oven to 375 degrees F and bake the cutlets for 15 to 20 minutes, or until the cheese has melted. Sprinkle with parsley and serve.

NOTE *In the winter instead of fresh tomatoes, the locals use a marinara sauce and garnish the cutlets with fresh basil leaves.*

Veal Cutlets in Marsala | **SCALOPPINE AL MARSALA**

This is perhaps one of the most common and traditional ways of cooking veal *scaloppine*. The Neapolitans prefer to use dry Marsala instead of the more traditional sweet Marsala.

6 servings

1 cup all-purpose flour

1 teaspoon finely chopped fresh sage, or ½ teaspoon dried

Salt to taste

Freshly milled pepper to taste

3 pounds veal cutlets, well pounded

2 tablespoons unsalted butter

2 tablespoons extra-virgin olive oil

¼ cup dry Marsala wine

1 tablespoon chopped fresh Italian parsley

Combine the flour with the sage and some salt and pepper. Dredge the veal in this mixture and shake off the excess flour.

In a large skillet in which the veal can fit in one layer (or use two skillets), heat the butter and olive oil and sauté the veal on both sides over high heat for about 5 minutes. Add the wine, scrape the bottom of the skillet and let the wine evaporate. Sprinkle with parsley and serve.

NOTE   *For a more tangy flavor, substitute lemon juice for the Marsala.*

Veal Stew with Leeks | **SPEZZATINO DI VITELLO AI PORRI**

Leeks are more delicate than onions and have a fresher taste. They complement many delicate types of meat, such as veal and chicken. They are also an ideal base for a vegetable sauté. In this dish the leeks are combined with zucchini, but other vegetables—peas, mushrooms, potatoes—can be used. In my home in Naples, the rule for vegetables was "in season," therefore this stew was made with different vegetables year-round.

6 to 8 servings

2 leeks with some greens included, trimmed and sliced

2 teaspoons kosher salt

2 tablespoons extra-virgin olive oil

1 garlic clove, sliced

3 pounds lean boneless veal, cubed

¼ cup dry white wine

¼ cup homemade or canned chicken broth

2 or 3 medium zucchini, trimmed and diced

1 tablespoon chopped fresh dill or fennel greens

Place the sliced leeks in a bowl and cover with lukewarm water. Add 2 teaspoons kosher salt and stir. (The kosher salt will draw out the sand in the leeks.) Let stand for 15 minutes, then lift the leeks out of the water (you will see the sand at the bottom of the bowl) and rinse several times. Drain.

Heat the olive oil in a skillet, add the garlic, cook for 1 to 2 minutes. Add the leeks, cook until the leeks start to wilt, about 5 minutes. Add the veal, cook over high heat for 5 to 8 minutes stirring often. If the veal releases too much liquid, which is usually the case, let reduce. Add the wine, let the wine evaporate and then add the broth. Cover, reduce the heat and simmer 40 minutes, stirring every once in a while.

When the veal is almost tender, add the zucchini and dill. Simmer until the zucchini are cooked, about 10 minutes. Serve hot.

NOTE *If using mushrooms in this stew, sauté them in a little oil and add them at the last minute.*

Veal Stew with Broccoli and Cauliflower

VITELLO IN BIANCO E VERDE

This is a pretty dish, simple and tasty. It was another one of the recipes reinvented by my mother or one of our friends in Naples. While back then it was a convenience dish made to enhance the meat, I now proudly serve it to guests who admire the presentation and enjoy the flavor. I use a large round enameled cast-iron Le Creuset Dutch oven, which is just right to show off the pretty colors of the white and green vegetables.

6 servings

2 tablespoons extra-virgin olive oil

2 cloves garlic, crushed

2½ pounds veal, preferably shoulder, cut into 2-inch cubes

2 dry bay leaves

Salt to taste

Freshly milled pepper to taste

1½ teaspoons chopped fresh sage, or ½ teaspoon dried, crumbled

2 sprigs Italian parsley

½ cup dry white wine

1 (16-ounce) can crushed tomatoes

1 cup broccoli florets

1 cup cauliflower florets

In a large pot or Dutch oven, heat the olive oil and add the garlic. As soon as it starts to color add the veal and bay leaves. Cook over high heat, stirring until the veal is brown.

Add some salt, a good grinding of pepper, the sage, and parsley. Stir, cook for 2 to 3 minutes then add the wine. Let the wine evaporate and add the tomatoes with all their juice. Cover the pot, reduce the heat to a minimum and simmer the stew for 1 hour 15 minutes. Remove the bay leaves.

If the stems of the vegetable florets are long, cut and dice them and scatter them over the stew. Place the broccoli florets all around the pot, alternating with the cauliflower florets—do not stir. Cover and cook over low heat until the vegetables are tender, about 20 minutes. Serve in the pot.

NOTE   *I bring the pot to the table and uncover it in the presence of my guests.*

Herbed Veal Roast with Pearl Onions | **VITELLO AROMATICO**

The mixture of spices and herbs in this dish shows Saracen, Spanish, and French influence. It was during the Middle Ages that the use of spices, a sign of affluence, became popular. Another reason for the popularity of spices was very practical: due to lack of refrigeration, meat sometimes had an unpleasant odor that could be camouflaged by a lot of spices. The condiments give this dish an elegant, sophisticated flavor.

Keep in mind that veal often releases liquid, therefore add the broth a little at a time. The meat has to cook *in umido* (in humidity), with a little liquid all the time, but it should not have a soupy consistency.

6 servings

1/2 teaspoon freshly milled pepper

1/2 teaspoon ground cinnamon

1/2 teaspoon ground cloves

1/4 teaspoon ground nutmeg

Salt to taste

1 1/2 teaspoons each fresh thyme, marjoram, rosemary, and tarragon

3 pound veal roast, shoulder or loin, tied with kitchen twine

3 tablespoons extra-virgin olive oil

2 tablespoons butter

2 carrots, cut into pieces

1 stalk celery, cut in half

1 dry bay leaf

1/2 cup dry Marsala wine

2 cups or more homemade chicken or veal broth

24 pearl onions, peeled and with a crisscross cut at their root ends

1 teaspoon sugar

Sprigs of curly parsley for garnish

In a small bowl combine all the spices, some salt, and the herbs. Rub the veal all over with this mixture.

In a heavy pot into which the veal can fit snugly, heat 2 tablespoons of the olive oil and 1 tablespoon of the butter. Add the veal, carrots, celery, and bay leaf. Brown the veal. Add half of the Marsala and let evaporate. Add some of the broth, cover the pot and reduce to a simmer. Cook for about 1½ to 2 hours, adding more broth if necessary.

Remove the veal from the sauce, cover with aluminum foil and keep warm. Discard the bay leaf. Put the sauce and all the vegetables in a food processor and puree. Reserve the pot. Transfer the puree to a bowl.

Heat 1 tablespoon olive oil and 1 tablespoon butter in the pot and add the onions. Sauté until onions are soft and translucent, then sprinkle with sugar. Stir and add the remaining ¼ cup of Marsala. Cook over medium heat, stirring often, until the onions are tender, about 20 minutes. Transfer the onions to a plate. Keep warm.

Add a little broth to the pot and scrape the brown particles clinging to the bottom and sides. Gradually add more broth. You should have 1¼ cups of liquid. Bring to a boil and reduce to 1 cup. Add the pureed vegetables, stir and reheat.

Slice the meat and place it on a serving plate. Surround the meat with the onions. Pour some of the sauce on the meat, serve the remaining sauce on the side. Garnish the plate with the parsley.

Veal Braciole Stuffed with Artichokes

BRACIOLONA RIPIENA DI CARCIOFI

Braciole is perhaps the most well-known Neapolitan dish to cross the ocean and acquire instant popularity. This recipe is made with a large braciola, since it is a rustic recipe from the countryside of Campania. It is a seasonal dish that requires fresh baby artichokes. You also need a large slice of veal that your butcher should be able to prepare for you. If not, buy a loin of veal, and with a sharp knife, open it up like a book lengthwise (butterfly), then open the two sides of the loin the same way so you have a long piece of meat, and then pound the meat flat with a meat mallet.

4 to 6 servings

4 to 6 fresh baby artichokes

Juice of half a lemon

4 tablespoons extra-virgin olive oil

1 garlic clove, crushed

2 sprigs Italian parsley

3 eggs, well beaten

3 pound veal roast, preferably loin, butterflied as described above and pounded

Salt to taste

Freshly milled pepper to taste

¼ cup dry wine

1 large onion, peeled and with a crisscross cut at the root end

1 carrot, cut in half

¼ cup chicken broth plus more as needed

Trim the artichokes of the tough leaves and slice them into thin wedges. Place them in a bowl, add cold water and the lemon juice. (This will prevent the artichokes from discoloring before being cooked.)

In a skillet heat 2 tablespoons of the olive oil, add the garlic and 1 sprig of parsley. Drain the artichokes but reserve some of the lemon water. Add the artichokes to the skillet and sauté for about 5 minutes, then add ¼ cup of their reserved water. Cover, reduce the heat and cook the artichokes until tender, about 10 minutes. Remove the sprig of parsley and garlic and chop with the remaining sprig of parsley. Add back to the artichokes.

In a separate skillet heat 1 tablespoon olive oil and pour in the eggs. Cook on one side then turn and cook the *frittata* (omelet) on the other side until set.

Lay the veal flat on a working surface and sprinkle with salt and pepper. Cover with the *frittata* and place the artichokes lengthwise in the center. Roll the veal and tie with kitchen twine. Wrap both ends of the roll with aluminum foil to prevent the filling from falling out.

In a heavy pot heat 2 tablespoons olive oil, add the veal and brown on all sides. Remove the aluminum foil. Add the wine and let evaporate. Add the onion, carrot, and broth, reduce the heat and cook covered for about 1 hour, or until the veal is tender, turning it once in a while. Transfer the veal to a cutting board, cover with aluminum foil and let rest for 15 minutes before slicing it.

Remove the onion and carrot to a food processor and puree. Return the puree to the pan, bring to a boil, and if necessary, reduce the sauce. You should have 1 to 1½ cups. Slice the meat and serve with the sauce.

NOTE *The* braciolona *can be served cold. It is an ideal dish for a buffet that can be prepared one day in advance. It looks very appetizing when cut. You can also use other vegetables, such as zucchini, eggplants, or mushrooms.*

Veal Roast with Smoked Turkey Stuffing

ROTOLO DI VITELLO TURCHINATO

My father invented this elegant, tasteful roast. He used to sprinkle the stuffing with little pieces of pitted black olives and pretend they were truffles. Instead of the smoked turkey, my father used salami or mortadella. I changed it to smoked turkey once because that was what I had in the house when I was preparing this recipe. Since I liked the touch of smokiness, I continued making it this way. It is a good dish for family dinners. It can be prepared in advance and is also good cold.

6 to 8 servings

3 pound shoulder of veal, butterflied

Salt to taste

Freshly milled pepper to taste

8 slices smoked turkey

2 Italian sausages (about 8 ounces) (pork or turkey)

4 ounces ground veal

1 egg

2 teaspoons chopped fresh Italian parsley

¼ cup black olives, pitted and coarsely chopped (optional)

3 hard-boiled eggs

1 carrot

1 large onion

2 garlic cloves

2 celery stalks, cut into pieces

1½ teaspoons chopped fresh sage, or ½ teaspoon dried

1½ teaspoons chopped fresh rosemary, or ½ teaspoon dried

¼ cup extra-virgin olive oil

¼ cup dry Marsala wine

¾ cup chicken broth, plus more as needed

Place the veal flat on a working surface. Using a sharp knife, butterfly it a second time on both sides of the meat to open it up into a large slice. Pound the veal with a mallet or the flat of a heavy knife. Season with salt and pepper. Cover with 4 slices of the smoked turkey.

Remove the casings from the sausages and crumble the sausage in a mixing bowl. Add the ground veal, egg, and parsley. Mix well. Spread half of this mixture on the veal, leaving the edges of the meat clean. Sprinkle with the chopped olives. Line the hard-boiled eggs lengthwise in the center and cover with the remaining sausage mixture. Place the remaining slices of smoked turkey evenly on top. Fold the two sides of the veal to completely enclose the filling. Form into the shape of a roll, and secure with kitchen twine.

In a food processor place the carrot, onion, garlic, celery, and sage. If you are using fresh rosemary, reserve it, but if using the dry rosemary, add it to the food processor. Chop very fine.

Preheat the oven to 375 degrees F.

Heat the olive oil in an ovenproof casserole into which the veal can fit snugly. Add the meat roll and reserved fresh rosemary. Brown on all sides. Add the Marsala and let evaporate. Add the chopped vegetable mixture, cook briefly, stirring and turning the veal. Add ½ cup of the broth and place the veal in the oven. Cook basting often, adding a little more broth if necessary, for about 1 hour 15 minutes. Cool and slice.

Veal Meatballs with Bell Peppers

POLPETTINE APPETITOSE DI CARNE

Meatballs were such a common Italian dish that, being contrary children, my brother and I would say we didn't like them. Even so we ate the *polpette*, which were delicious, with great gusto. The addition of capers gives this sauce a savory taste.

6 servings

1½ pounds ground veal

¼ cup grated Pecorino Romano cheese

2 eggs, lightly beaten

5 slices toasted white bread, soaked in milk

1 tablespoon chopped fresh Italian parsley

Unflavored dry bread crumbs for dredging

⅓ cup extra-virgin olive oil

1 garlic clove

2 large red and yellow bell peppers, cored, seeded and cut into strips

1 tablespoon capers, drained

2 tablespoons balsamic vinegar

Freshly milled pepper to taste

2 teaspoons chopped fresh Italian parsley

4 or 5 basil leaves, chopped

In a mixing bowl combine the veal, cheese, and eggs. Squeeze the milk out of the bread and add the bread to the bowl together with the chopped parsley. Mix well. Shape the meat mixture into egg-size meatballs. Roll them in the bread crumbs. Set aside.

In a skillet large enough to contain all the meatballs in one layer, heat 3 tablespoons of the olive oil, add the meatballs, and cook over moderate heat, turning often until brown. Remove with a slotted spoon and drain on paper towels.

Add 2 more tablespoons of the olive oil to the skillet, heat and add the garlic and peppers. Sauté over medium heat for about 5 minutes. Cover the skillet, reduce the heat and cook for 5 minutes longer.

Return the meatballs to the skillet and add the capers and balsamic vinegar. Cook uncovered for 5 minutes longer while stirring. Add a generous amount of pepper. Sprinkle the meatballs with parsley and basil and serve hot.

NOTE *My mother used to add other ingredients to the meat mixture, for example prosciutto, salami, or small pieces of provolone, all chopped fine. I also make these meatballs with turkey or lamb in place of the veal, with excellent results.*

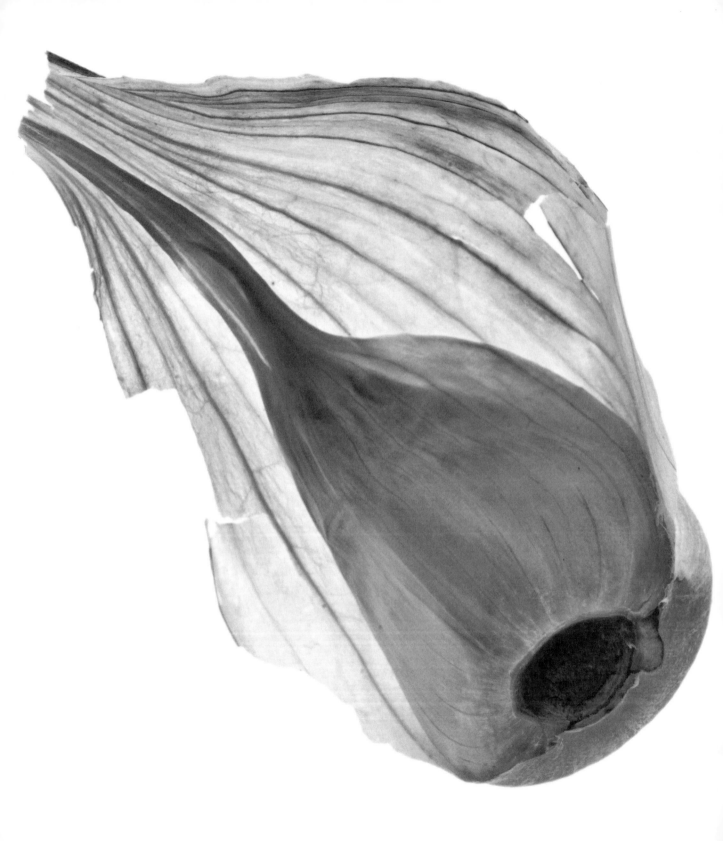

beef

I did not grow up with good beef. When I was a child, good tender steaks were only available in Florence and maybe Milan or Turin. Beef was always tough. This is the reason we Italians have such great recipes for pot roasts—called *arrosti morti* (meaning "cooked to death").

Despite the name, many of these dishes are earthy and comforting. Others, because of the choice of ingredients, are elegant, sophisticated, and at times quite expensive to make, for example the famous *carne al Barolo* from Piedmont, in which an entire bottle of expensive Barolo wine is used—but what a succulent dish!

Today you can eat good beef everywhere in Italy. In fact, the Italians are so proud of this new beef that my relatives and friends are always trying to entice me with a nice *bistecca*. But no matter how good this might be, I politely refuse. Nothing compares with a good American steak. And in Italy I can eat many other delicious things.

A story that I have told many times, that emphasizes the love of Europeans for American beef, happened at a conference. Jacques Pepin and I were part of a panel of food experts. People were asking questions, and someone wanted to know from Jacques what he liked to eat when traveling. Jacques hesitantly responded, "Oh, I don't know, maybe a soup…" He then turned to me, "What about you, Anna Teresa?" Without hesitating, I said, "A good American steak." And Jacques, with the unmistakable gesture of a Frenchman (or an Italian, for that matter), slapped his forehead, "Of course, why didn't I think of it!"

So do not laugh if I tell you that this chapter is dedicated to American beef.

Beef Roast | **L'ARROSTO**

In my family we simply called this "the roast." It was rarely made, only when we had a good piece of fillet of beef, which was hard to come by and expensive. But when we had one, it was treated with tender loving care by the cook, as well as those giving her instructions. This family recipe has a delicious herb flavor, and to obtain it you must use fresh herbs.

10 to 12 servings

2 garlic cloves

6 juniper berries

3 sprigs Italian parsley

5 blades chives

7 or 8 fresh basil leaves

2 to 4 fresh mint leaves

1 tablespoon fresh rosemary

¼ teaspoon ground allspice

½ stick unsalted butter

1 fillet of beef (about 6 pounds), trimmed of all fat

2 tablespoons extra-virgin olive oil

1 onion, thickly sliced

2 carrots, cut into small pieces

1½ cups homemade or canned beef or veal broth

4 or 5 strips prosciutto fat or same amount bacon

½ cup dry red wine

In a food processor place the garlic, juniper berries, parsley, chives, basil, mint, and rosemary. Chop very finely. Add the allspice and 3 tablespoons of the butter. Process until very fine. Reserve 2 tablespoons of this mixture and refrigerate it.

Tie the fillet to give it a round shape. Rub it evenly with the herb mixture. Cover loosely with aluminum foil and let it rest for 2 to 3 hours, or overnight in the refrigerator.

When ready to cook, let the fillet come to room temperature. Preheat the oven to 400 degrees F.

Put the olive oil, onion, carrots, and 1 cup broth in a roasting pan. Place the fillet in the middle and dot with 1 tablespoon butter. Arrange the prosciutto strips lengthwise on top of the meat. Roast for 30 minutes. Add the wine, and cook 1 hour or longer, according to your taste (my father always recommended that this meat should be cooked *al sangue*, bloody or rare). Baste every once in a while with the juices accumulating at the bottom of the pan. Transfer to a platter and keep warm.

Remove the vegetables from the pan and puree them in a food processor. Pour the mixture in a saucepan. Add a little broth to the roasting pan and scrape the brown particles clinging at the bottom and sides of the pan. Add to the vegetable puree. Add some or all of the remaining broth to the saucepan, depending on whether you like a thicker or thinner sauce. Bring to a boil and simmer for about 10 minutes. Add the reserved butter-herb mixture and stir. Remove the sauce from the heat, but keep warm.

Slice the meat and arrange on a serving platter. Pour some of the sauce on it and serve the remaining sauce on the side.

NOTE *My mother always served a creamy potato puree and a green vegetable with this dish.*

Filet Mignon with Mozzarella, Anchovies, and Peas

FILETTO DI MANZO DEI BORBONI

This is a succulent dish that requires very little time to cook. It is an old recipe, probably invented by one of the *Monzù*, chefs working for the local aristocracy during the reign of the French Bourbons.

6 servings

1 tablespoon extra-virgin olive oil

1 tablespoon unsalted butter

6 beef filet mignons
(about 4 ounces each)

Salt to taste

Freshly milled pepper to taste

¼ cup dry white wine

3 tablespoons Marsala wine

6 slices whole-milk mozzarella,
each about ½ inch thick

6 anchovies packed in oil

6 slices crusty Italian bread,
toasted

2 cups frozen peas, defrosted

Heat the olive oil and butter in a large skillet. Add the filets and cook for 2 minutes, then turn and cook for 2 more minutes. Season with salt and pepper. Add both wines and cook for 2 more minutes. Turn the filets and top each one with 1 slice of mozzarella and 1 anchovy.

Cover the skillet, leaving the lid a little askew. Cook for a few minutes until the mozzarella melts.

Place 1 slice of bread on each of six plates. With a slotted spoon, place a filet on top of each bread slice and keep warm.

Add the peas to the skillet, cook stirring for a few minutes until hot. Pour into a serving bowl and serve with the filets.

Filet Mignon with Prosciutto | **BISTECCHINE AL PROSCIUTTO**

This was one of the Sunday night specials in my home, perhaps because the dish could be prepared in advance and finished later. Sunday afternoon was the day the entire family went out together, so when we came home, we wanted a simple dinner like this one, which only needed to be placed in the oven.

6 servings

¼ cup extra-virgin olive oil

4 ounces prosciutto, coarsely chopped

1 pound mushrooms, trimmed and thinly sliced (about 6 cups)

2 teaspoons finely chopped fresh Italian parsley

Freshly milled pepper to taste

6 beef filet mignon, each about 1 inch thick, slightly pounded

Half a lemon

Preheat the oven to 375 degrees F.

Lightly oil a large baking dish from which you can serve.

In a mixing bowl combine 2 tablespoons of the olive oil with the prosciutto, mushrooms, parsley, and pepper. Toss well. Spread this mixture over the bottom of the baking dish in an even layer. Place the steaks on top of it in one layer. They may overlap a little. Drizzle the steaks with 2 tablespoons olive oil.

Bake for 15 minutes, then turn the steaks and drizzle with the lemon juice. Continue baking for 15 more minutes, until the steaks are medium done and the mushrooms have released their delicious liquid, which should have thickened into a light sauce.

NOTE *If you prefer a thicker sauce for this dish, drain the liquid into the bowl of a food processor, add ½ cup of the mushrooms and puree. Drizzle this sauce over the steaks and serve.*

Slow-Roasted Succulent Steak | **BISTECCONA SUCCULENTA**

You will see why this steak is called "succulent." Leave it to the Neapolitans to cook a rather inexpensive piece of meat and give it a superb flavor. The addition of a few vegetables, spices, and a good shot of Marsala wine do the job.

6 to 8 servings

1 large onion, quartered

2 carrots, cut into pieces

3 celery stalks, trimmed and cut into pieces

1 garlic clove

¼-inch piece ginger, peeled

2 cloves

¼ teaspoon ground allspice

¼ teaspoon freshly milled pepper

3 tablespoons extra-virgin olive oil

1 thick slice of beef chuck (3 pounds)

½ cup Marsala wine

1 teaspoon tomato paste

Place the onion, carrots, celery, garlic, and ginger in the bowl of a food processor and chop to a fine consistency. Remove to a bowl and add the cloves, allspice, and pepper. Mix well.

Preheat the oven to 375 degrees F. In a baking dish into which the meat can fit snugly, spread the vegetable mixture and 1 tablespoon olive oil. Place the meat on top and pour in the Marsala wine.

Combine the tomato paste with ¼ cup water and the remaining 2 tablespoons olive oil and pour this over the meat. Cover with aluminum foil and bake for 2 hours, or until the meat is tender, basting the meat with its own juices once or twice.

If at the end you have too much liquid at the bottom, transfer the meat to a platter and cover it with aluminum foil. Increase the oven temperature to 400 degrees F and reduce the liquid. Be careful though not to scorch the sauce. Slice the meat and serve with the sauce.

NOTE *A touch of soy sauce or Worcestershire sauce, combined with the Marsala, will give the dish an exotic taste.*

Pot Roast with Brandy | **BRASATO PRELIBATO**

My father called this dish *prelibato*, which means "special" or "delicious" in Italian. We usually made it with a simple local red wine. Ideally it should be made with Barolo wine, but not an entire bottle like in the Piedmontese version of the dish, considering that Barolo is a little pricey! I suspect that my father, if using Barolo, preferred to drink the rest of this wonderful wine and not use it all for cooking.

6 servings

1 carrot, cut into pieces

1 stalk celery, trimmed and cut into pieces

1 garlic clove

1 sprig Italian parsley

5 onions, peeled

2 tablespoons extra-virgin olive oil

1 rump roast (3 to 4 pounds)

4 cloves

Salt to taste

Freshly milled pepper

¾ cup dry red wine, or more

In a food processor place the carrot, celery, garlic, and parsley. Quarter one of the onions, add it and chop all the vegetables until very fine.

Thinly slice the remaining onions and set aside.

In a heavy skillet, heat the olive oil, add the chopped vegetables, and cook until soft. Add the roast and brown on all sides. Add the sliced onions and cloves and season with salt and pepper. Cook briefly, then add the wine. Cover the pan and simmer over low heat for about 3 hours, turning the meat once in a while. Add more wine if necessary. Cool for 15 to 20 minutes. Discard the cloves. Slice the meat and serve.

NOTE   *The sauce from the roast is also excellent on pasta.*

Slow-Cooked Beef with Cognac | **BRASATO AL COGNAC**

The flavor of this *brasato* is enhanced by the smokiness of the pancetta. Pancetta can be found in Italian food stores and many supermarkets. However, I have made this dish with good American smoked bacon with excellent results, very close to the Neapolitan taste that I remember so well.

6 to 8 servings

3 slices pancetta or smoked bacon

1 garlic clove

¾ teaspoon fresh sage, or ¼ teaspoon dried

1 bunch fresh rosemary

1 jigger cognac or brandy

1 bottom round roast (3 to 4 pounds)

1 tablespoon unsalted butter

1 tablespoon extra-virgin olive oil

2 onions, sliced

½ cup dry red wine

1 cup beef or veal broth

Salt to taste

Freshly milled pepper to taste

Chop very finely 1 slice of pancetta, the garlic, sage, and a few rosemary leaves. Reserve remaining rosemary. Add some of the cognac to moisten this mixture, then rub the roast with the herb mixture and tie with kitchen twine.

In a heavy pot heat the butter and olive oil. Add the roast and brown on all sides. Chop the remaining pancetta and add it to the pot together with the onions and bunch of rosemary. Cook stirring and turning the meat. Add the remaining cognac, let evaporate and then stir in the wine. Cover the pot and cook over low heat for 2 to 3 hours, stirring once in a while and adding the broth a little at a time, until the meat is very tender.

When done, transfer the roast to a platter and keep warm. Remove the rosemary bunch and discard. Pour a little broth into the pot, scrape the brown particles clinging at the bottom and sides of the pan. If you wish you can puree the onion mixture. Return the puree to the pot and reheat. Slice the roast and serve with the sauce.

Oxtail Stew | **CODA DI MANZO BRASATA**

This is such a delicious stew; the only problem is that everybody will want to chew on the bones—so don't forget the paper napkins. And as the Neapolitans do, drink a glass of red wine *alla salute*. It is better if made the day before, as it acquires more flavor and it will be easy to remove the fat on the surface that will congeal during the night.

6 servings

4 pounds oxtail

2 tablespoons extra-virgin olive oil

2 onions, coarsely chopped

2 carrots, cut into ½ inch slices

1 tablespoon all-purpose flour

½ cup dry wine (red or white)

2 celery stalks, trimmed and chopped

2 dry bay leaves

2 or 3 sprigs Italian parsley

8 peppercorns, crushed

3 cloves

4 cups hot water

1 beef bouillon cube

Trim as much fat off the meat as possible.

In a large pot, heat 1 tablespoon olive oil and brown the meat. Transfer the oxtail to a bowl and discard all the fat except 1 tablespoon.

Add 1 tablespoon olive oil to the pot and sauté the onions and carrots for 10 to 15 minutes, stirring often. Sprinkle the flour over the onions and carrots, stir well and return the meat to the pot.

Add the wine and let it evaporate, then add the celery, bay leaves, parsley, peppercorns, cloves, hot water, and bouillon cube. Cover the pot and cook at very low heat for 3 to 4 hours, stirring every once in a while. Remove the bay leaves and cloves before serving.

NOTE   *If you wish to eat the stew the same day, let it sit for a while and then skim the fat off the surface by placing some paper towels loosely on the top and peeling them off. You will see how much fat remains attached to the paper towels. Julia Child taught me this trick.*

Marinated Beef Shank Stew | **STINCO BRASATO**

I am aware that the Italian name of this dish sounds odd, but *stinco* is a perfectly polite Italian word meaning "shank." We Italians love shank meat, so much so that when we want to describe a very good person we call him or her *uno stinco di Santo* (a Saint's shank).

Stinco is often served in country *trattorie* where the people of Campania like to go in the summer to enjoy the fresh air and food. I remember a few years ago when my husband and I spent a vacation on the Amalfi coast as guests of my cousins, we wanted to go to a renowned local restaurant. But my cousins refused, saying that is was a tourist place and instead suggested a nearby *agriturismo*. I had vaguely heard of them, so we agreed. We were pleasantly surprised; the food was excellent and had the assertive flavor of home cooking. We started to call cousin Pasquale *uno stinco di Santo* since it was his idea to take us there.

In this recipe the meat is cooked on the bone, resulting in a succulent dish with a subtle hint of cinnamon and the harmonious taste of the clove. It can also be made with veal and pork shank. The meat must marinate 12 hours, so plan accordingly.

6 to 8 servings

1 or 2 beef shanks
(6 to 8 pounds total)

1 bottle of red wine, such as
Aglianico or Basilisco

3 carrots, cut into pieces

1 celery stalk, trimmed and cut
into pieces

3 red onions, quartered

10 cloves

5 juniper berries

5 dry bay leaves

1 cinnamon stick

10 peppercorns, crushed

¼ cup extra-virgin olive oil

Salt to taste

Freshly milled pepper to taste

The day before, place the meat in a large, noncorrosive bowl. Pour the wine over it and add all the rest of the ingredients except the last three. Cover and refrigerate for 12 hours, turning the meat a few times.

The next day, transfer the meat to a platter. Dry it with paper towels and set aside. Reserve the marinade.

In a heavy pot large enough to fit the shank, heat the olive oil and brown the meat on all sides, then transfer to a platter.

Remove the bay leaves and cinnamon stick from the marinade and reserve. Strain the marinade, reserving juices. Puree all the vegetables from the marinade in a food processor.

Return the pot to the heat, add the pureed vegetables and cook for 5 minutes.

Return the meat, bay leaves, and cinnamon stick to the pot. Add the marinade, season with salt and pepper. Bring to a boil, lower heat and simmer over very low heat for 4 hours or longer. The meat should be falling off the bone.

To serve, discard the bay leaves and cinnamon. Lift the shank on one end, and holding the bone with a paper towel, slice the meat or cut it into chunks. Serve with the sauce.

Beef Stew with Vegetables | **STUFATINO DI MANZO**

This is an old-fashioned stew that can be made with inexpensive cuts of meat. You can add all sorts of vegetables, including potatoes. This dish can be prepared in advance; in fact, the next day it is even better.

8 to 10 servings

3 to 4 pounds lean beef chuck, cut into 1-inch cubes

All-purpose flour for dredging

3 tablespoons extra-virgin olive oil

¼ cup dried porcini mushrooms, soaked in 1 cup lukewarm water

1 garlic clove, crushed

2 cups sliced mushrooms

2 large red onions, sliced

½ cup red wine

2 medium potatoes, peeled and cubed

2 carrots, cut into 1-inch pieces

2 celery stalks, trimmed and cut into 1-inch pieces

1 teaspoon tomato paste

1 (16-ounce) can tomato puree

1 cup string beans, cut into 1-inch pieces (optional)

1 cup broccoli florets (optional)

2 tablespoons chopped fresh Italian parsley

Dredge the beef cubes in the flour, shaking off the excess.

In a large pot, heat 2 tablespoons olive oil and brown the meat. Transfer the meat to a bowl, discard the fat and set the pot aside.

Gently remove the porcini mushrooms from the water as not to upset the sediments at the bottom. Filter the water through a paper towel and reserve it. Chop the porcini coarsely.

Return the pot to the heat and add the remaining olive oil and garlic. As soon as the garlic starts to fry, add the fresh mushrooms and porcini. Cook until all the water released by the mushrooms has been absorbed. Add the onions and cook, stirring, for 5 to 8 minutes.

Return the meat to the pot and cook for a few minutes. Add the wine and let evaporate. Add the reserved water from the porcini. Bring to a boil, cover, lower heat and simmer for 30 minutes. Add the potatoes and cook for 10 more minutes. Add the carrots and celery and cook for 20 more minutes.

Combine the tomato paste with ½ cup water and add to the pot together with the tomato puree. Rinse the can with half a can of water and add it to the pot. Cover and cook over low heat for an additional 1 to 1½ hours, or until the meat is tender.

Add the remaining vegetables if using and cook for 8 to 10 minutes. Add the parsley and serve.

pork

Today pork is often called the "other white meat," and rightly so, because pigs are now raised to produce meat that is not fatty. Unfortunately, pork often does not have the flavor it had in the past.

Pork dishes are popular all over Italy. In the north, there are pork chops cooked in grappa; Abruzzo and Lazio have their *porchette* (roasted piglets) as a specialty. Pork medallions done in the Neapolitan style with peppers and a touch of tomato have traveled far beyond Campania. Another easy and tasty staple of the region are sausages, usually served with broccoli. And of course, prosciutto is ever present on the antipasto plate and in the panini, the staple of picnics and afternoon snacks.

Some of the most succulent Neapolitan dishes are also made with organ meats, such as *soffritto di maiale* (a stew) or *la trippa* (tripe). Other succulent dishes are made with the head, the tongue, and the feet of the pig. In Naples, my dear reader, nothing of the pig is wasted, and the following recipes confirm that.

Pork Medallions with Bell Peppers and Mushrooms

LOMBATINE DI MAIALE ALLA NAPOLETANA

Even in Italy pork is not what it used to be. The meat is not always tender and flavorful; therefore it is a good idea to add some ingredients with pronounced flavors. A mixture of fresh mushrooms and some colorful peppers does the trick. In Naples, dried sweet peppers are used for this recipe instead of fresh ones. Dried peppers are not so easily available in America, but when I have some, I add one or two to the dish for extra flavor.

6 servings

¼ cup extra-virgin olive oil

2 garlic cloves, crushed

6 pork medallions from the loin, about 1 inch thick

3 sweet bell peppers, preferably of mixed colors, cored and sliced

1½ teaspoons chopped fresh rosemary, or ½ teaspoon dried

8 ounces mushrooms, sliced or quartered

1 tablespoon tomato paste

In a large pot heat 2 tablespoons of the olive oil and add 1 garlic clove. As soon as the garlic starts to sizzle, add the meat. Cook the medallions over medium heat, turning them over once or twice until nicely browned on both sides. Transfer to a platter and cover with aluminum foil.

Add 2 tablespoons of the olive oil to the skillet and the remaining garlic, heat and add the peppers and rosemary. Cook over medium heat, stirring often, for about 10 minutes. Add the mushrooms and cook for 5 more minutes.

Dilute the tomato paste in ¼ cup water and add to the pot. Mix well and continue cooking the vegetables for 5 to 8 more minutes. Return the pork medallions to the pot. Cover and simmer over low heat for 30 more minutes. Serve hot.

Pork Chops with Orange | COSTOLETTA DI MAIALE ALL'ARANCIA

We Italians do not particularly like fruit with meat. But pork, and sometimes duck, are exceptions. This recipe comes from my cousin Franca who lives in Naples and is a good, imaginative cook.

6 servings

6 center-cut pork chops (about 12 ounces each), trimmed of excess fat

Freshly milled pepper to taste

2 tablespoons extra-virgin olive oil

3 garlic cloves, crushed

¾ cup chicken broth

1½ teaspoons chopped fresh sage, or ½ teaspoon dried

2 large strips orange zest

Salt to taste

1 orange

Sprinkle the pork chops with some pepper. Let stand for 15 minutes.

In a large skillet, heat the olive oil and add the garlic. As soon as the garlic starts to sizzle, add the chops and brown on both sides. Transfer the chops to a platter.

Discard the fat in the skillet and add a little of the broth. Stir with a wooden spoon to dislodge the brown particles clinging at the bottom and sides of the skillet. Add the remaining broth, sage, and orange zest. Cook for 2 to 3 minutes and then return the chops to the skillet. Cover the skillet, reduce the heat and simmer for 10 more minutes, turning the chops once or twice. Remove the lid and continue cooking until the chops are tender, about 5 minutes longer. If necessary, add a little more broth or water. Season with some salt.

Peel the orange, cut into slices, section the slices and add to the skillet. Stir and leave it on the heat just long enough to reheat the dish. Remove the orange zest and discard. Serve the chops with the sauce spooned over it.

NOTE   *I like to garnish these chops with a few curls of orange zest. To make sure that the meat is not overcooked, I cut a little piece and taste it.*

Roasted Pork Ribs | **ARROSTICINI COL MANICO**

This is another extremely tasty pork dish that my brother Mimmo called *col manico*, "with the handle." Indeed these ribs have a handle, and it is wonderful to eat one of them with your hands. But make sure you have plenty of napkins available on the table.

6 servings

6 pounds pork spareribs

1 teaspoon kosher salt

Freshly milled pepper to taste

1 cup red wine vinegar

¾ cup water

1 teaspoon tomato paste

1 cup beef or chicken broth

Sprinkle the salt and some pepper over the spareribs. Cover and refrigerate for 6 hours or longer.

Preheat the oven to 400 degrees F.

Place the ribs in a roasting pan and pour the vinegar and water over them. Roast for about 1 hour, rotating the ribs once in a while and basting with the juices at the bottom.

Combine the tomato paste with ½ cup of the broth. Brush the ribs with this mixture and bake 1 hour longer, or until the ribs are tender. Remove them from the oven and keep warm.

Pour the remaining broth into the pan. With a wooden spoon, scrape to remove the brown particles clinging at the bottom of the pan. Cut the ribs into serving sizes and serve them with the sauce.

Drunken Pork Cutlets with Fennel and Red Wine

BRACIOLE DI MAIALE UBRIACHE

Simple and delicately perfumed with fennel, these *braciole* are a cinch to make. My mother used to prepare them in the afternoon, before our ritual *passeggiata* on the elegant Via Sparano in the Vomero area of Naples where we lived. On our return, and after relaxing a little, she would move to the kitchen to cook them, followed by my father who liked to supervise the proceedings while we kids set the table.

6 servings

3 tablespoons chopped fresh Italian parsley

1 tablespoon chopped fennel greens

2 garlic cloves, chopped

3 pounds pork cutlets, pounded

3 tablespoons extra-virgin olive oil

1 cup dry red wine

Freshly milled pepper to taste

Salt to taste

Combine the parsley, fennel, and garlic. Spread an even amount of this mixture on the pork cutlets, roll them and tie with kitchen twine.

In a large skillet in which the cutlets can be placed in one layer, heat the olive oil and brown the cutlets on all sides.

Add the wine, cover the skillet, reduce the heat, and simmer until the wine is reduced, about 45 minutes. If it gets too dry, add more wine or water. Add a good amount of pepper and some salt.

Pork Cutlets with Capers | **PICCATA DI MAIALE AI CAPPERI**

As a variation of veal *piccata* this is a Neapolitan version that is as easy to prepare and quite delicious. In my home it was usually served with a delicate potato puree, which provided a perfect counterpoint to the tanginess of the capers.

6 servings

12 pork cutlets from the loin (about 1½ pounds), pounded

All-purpose flour for dredging

3 tablespoons extra-virgin olive oil

1 tablespoon unsalted butter

Salt to taste

Freshly milled pepper to taste

Juice of half a lemon

½ cup red wine

2 tablespoons capers, drained

Dredge the cutlets in flour, shaking off the excess.

Using a large skillet in which the cutlets can fit in one layer (or cook them in batches), heat the olive oil and butter and quickly sauté the cutlets on both sides until brown. Sprinkle with salt and pepper. Add the lemon juice, cook for a few minutes and transfer the cutlets to a plate.

Add the wine to the skillet and deglaze the pan. Return the cutlets to the skillet. Let the sauce reduce a little and add the capers. Serve immediately.

Poached Pork Loin with Water and Spices

MAIALE ALL'ACQUA E SPEZIE

This is another delicious and tasty *brasato*. The addition of raisins and almonds suggests an Arab influence that is not surprising since the region was once under Arab domination. In Campania, pigs are grass-fed, therefore pork is tender and flavorful. We were lucky when we lived in Naples that an employee of my father had a farm in a small town not too far from the city. Once in a while he would bring us a nice piece of pork. The meat was usually braised and, like in this recipe, coarsely shredded. This way it could be stretched, served over toasted bread. If there were any leftovers, we would use them to dress pasta.

6 servings

1 bone-in pork loin
(about 5 pounds)

1 garlic bulb, unpeeled,
cut in half horizontally

1 teaspoon peppercorns, crushed

3 dry bay leaves

3 or 4 cloves

2 tablespoons extra-virgin
olive oil

1 large onion, coarsely chopped

3 ripe tomatoes, coarsely
chopped

5 or 6 fresh basil leaves, chopped,
or ½ teaspoon dried,
or 1 sprig oregano, chopped,
or ½ teaspoon dried

2 tablespoons raisins

¾ cup almonds, blanched

2 tablespoons toasted
sesame seeds

Place the pork in a heavy pot. Add the garlic, peppercorns, bay leaves, and cloves. Cover with water up to 2 inches above the solids. Bring to a boil, reduce the heat to a minimum, cover the pot and simmer for about 2 to 2½ hours.

Remove the pork from the pot. Set aside to cool. Reserve the broth and discard the garlic and bay leaves. (At this point the meat and broth can be kept overnight in the refrigerator.)

While the meat cools, heat the olive oil in a large skillet, add the onion and cook covered over low heat, stirring often, until the onion is soft and translucent, about 10 minutes. Add the tomatoes and herbs, and cook stirring for 10 minutes longer.

Remove all visible fat from the meat and cut it into small pieces or shred it. Add the meat to the skillet and stir. Add the raisins and 1 cup of the reserved broth, or more if you prefer the dish more liquid. Cook until the meat is heated through. Sprinkle with the almonds and sesame seeds and serve.

NOTE   *This dish is usually accompanied by croutons or toasted slices of crusty Italian bread.*

Fresh Ham with Fennel | **PROSCIUTTO FRESCO AL FINOCCHIO**

During wartime in Naples, we would never "waste" the fresh meat of the prosciutto and cook it—it was too precious. The cured meat would be a glorious prosciutto to be cut in thin, satiny slices for *antipasti* or *panini*. For us children, *panini* with prosciutto was our favorite snack after school.

Even here in America, it isn't easy to find a fresh backside leg of pork, with which the prosciutto is made. However, a good butcher will get it for you. If all fails, you can use a rib side roast. Ask the butcher to remove the meat from the bones so you can use the bones as a rack. You can also cook this meat on the bone, but it will be a little difficult to slice.

8 to 10 servings

4 to 5 pounds backside leg of pork (see above)

2 sprigs wild fennel or fresh fennel greens, plus more for garnish

1 tablespoon fresh rosemary, or 1 teaspoon dried

1 garlic clove

Extra-virgin olive oil for rubbing

1½ cups dry red wine

Freshly milled pepper to taste

Salt to taste

1 celery stalk, cut into 2 inch pieces

1 carrot, cut into 2 inch pieces

1 onion, sliced

Trim the leg of pork of excess fat and reserve 1 tablespoon of the fat.

Chop the fennel, rosemary, garlic, and reserved fat together. Rub the pork with this mixture and tie to keep in shape. Pour a little oil in your hands and "massage" the meat with it.

Preheat the oven to 400 degrees F.

Lightly oil a roasting pan. Combine ¼ cup wine and ¼ cup water, pour into the pan and add the meat. Roast for 45 minutes, turning the roast once, and basting often with its own juices.

Reduce the heat to 375 degrees F. Sprinkle the meat with pepper and salt. Cook 2 more hours, basting often and adding more of the remaining wine.

Scatter the vegetables all around and continue roasting until the meat is cooked, about 45 minutes. The meat is done if the juices run clear when pierced with a skewer.

Remove the roast from the pan and keep warm. Remove the vegetables with a slotted spoon, pass them through a food mill or puree in a food processor. Spoon off excess fat from the pan, combine the remaining sauce with the vegetable puree. Warm up the sauce.

Slice the roast, pour some sauce over and serve the rest in a gravy boat. I like to garnish the dish with sprigs of fennel.

Fennel-Flavored Pork Roast "My Home"

ARROSTO DI MAIALE CASA MIA

This is a succulent roast whose special flavor comes from the fennel. We loved this roast. I still remember how the scent wafted through the entire house. My brother Mimmo and I would anticipate with glee the moment we were given some of the bones to chew on. We had to bring our dishes to the kitchen, though, since mother was a bit finicky about manners. But we didn't mind it at all. Although this is a definite Campanian dish, we called it *casa mia* (my home) because my mother or father surely had a hand in it.

6 to 8 servings

1 fresh rosemary sprig

1 sprig fresh fennel greens or dill

2 garlic cloves

Freshly milled pepper to taste

1 bone-in pork loin (6 pounds)

2 tablespoons extra-virgin olive oil

3 carrots

½ cup dry wine, preferably red

1 stalk celery, trimmed and cut into 1-inch pieces

1 large onion, cut into thick slices

Salt to taste

In a food processor chop the rosemary, fennel greens, and garlic. Add a good amount of pepper.

With a sharp knife detach, but not completely, the loin from the bone. Spread the herb and garlic mixture all along the meat on the side of the bone. Tie the meat and bone securely together with twine.

Preheat the oven to 400 degrees F.

Pour the olive oil in a roasting pan and roll the meat in it. Sprinkle with a little pepper.

Cut the carrots lengthwise into 2 sticks, or 4 sticks if large. Insert the sticks under the meat to make a rack. Roast for 15 minutes. Reduce the heat to 350 degrees F, and continue roasting for 30 minutes, then add some of the wine, the celery and onion. Sprinkle with salt. Roast for 30 more minutes, or until the meat is done, basting often, and adding the remaining wine.

When the meat is cooked, transfer it to a plate and keep warm. Puree all the vegetables in a food processor. Degrease the pan juices and add them to the vegetables. Reheat this sauce and serve it with the sliced meat.

Poached Sausages | **SALSICCE IN PADELLA**

In the provinces of Benevento, Aversa, and Caserta, pigs are raised on every farm. The meat is so flavorful, especially the sausages. We used to cook them in the simplest way—just in water. I do the same today with quite good results. Try to buy fresh sausages from a good butcher, and you will see how good they can be.

The students in my cooking school always ask me how to cook sausages. I teach them this simple method, and when they return, they always tell me how juicy and well cooked-through the sausages came out.

6 servings

1½ pounds sweet or hot Italian sausages

Place the sausages in a skillet. Pierce them with a pointed knife in several places and cover with water. Cook over medium-high heat until the water evaporates, about 30 minutes.

Continue cooking the sausages in their own fat until brown, about 5 to 8 minutes, turning them often.

NOTE *The best accompaniment for these sausages is a nice bowl of broccoli rabe, sautéed in olive oil with garlic. I often serve these sausages as* spiedini *with drinks. After cooking, cut them into 1-inch slices and serve with toothpicks.*

*variety
meats*

LE FRATTAGLIE

A book on Italian food, especially one on the cooking of Campania, would not be complete without a chapter on innards. Still I had to convince myself to include one. Americans often turn up their noses when I mention a savory dish of tripe or a succulent *coratella Napoletana*, which is a delicious mixture of organ meats. Most of the recipes are easy to make so do not hesitate to try them. Perhaps you can invite an Italian friend for dinner. I am sure that he or she will be quite happy to share this meal with you.

Sautéed Pig Innards | **IL SOFFRITTO**

This is a typical Neapolitan dish. The *soffritto* consists of stewed offal: lung, heart, kidney, spleen, and liver. In Campania and other regions of Italy, this dish is made with pig offal. In Abruzzo it is made with the organs of the lamb. At some points in history *soffritto* did not contain liver, which was too precious and reserved for other dishes, but today liver is sometimes included.

Vittorio Gleijeses, the author of many interesting books on Campania, praises *soffritto*, calling it a "food for a Hercules whose fine, courageous palate is capable to stand the powerful effect (of the ingredients) without cringing, and, once in a while, subdues the hottest flashes on his forehead with a good sip of dry red (wine)." I hope that my readers will not shy away from trying this delicious dish. But first of all, find a good butcher who knows what you are talking about. Spleen is not easy to find, but if possible, give it a try.

6 servings

3 pounds pig offal (lung, spleen, kidney, heart)

1 tablespoon kosher salt

3 tablespoons extra-virgin olive oil

1 bay leaf

1 tablespoon chopped fresh rosemary, or 1 teaspoon dried

1½ teaspoons chopped fresh sage, or ½ teaspoon dried

1 small hot pepper (optional)

2 tablespoons pepper paste (available in Italian food stores) or tomato paste

Salt to taste

Freshly milled pepper to taste

1 tablespoon chopped fresh Italian parsley

Place the pig offal in a bowl, cover with cold water, add the kosher salt and stir. Let stand for 20 minutes, then wash under running water and cut each piece into 1-inch cubes.

In a pot large enough to contain all the meats, heat the olive oil. Add the bay leaf, rosemary, sage, and hot pepper if using. Add the offal and sauté, stirring until nicely browned. Add the pepper or tomato paste and cook stirring for a few minutes. Add 2 cups water, cover the pot, bring to a boil and then reduce the heat. Continue simmering gently for about 30 minutes. Taste a piece of kidney—if it is soft, all the other offal are done as well. Season with salt and pepper.

Discard the hot pepper. Transfer the mixture to a bowl. Sprinkle with parsley and serve.

NOTE *Instead of olive oil, the Neapolitans use lard. For flavor, I add a little prosciutto fat, about 1 tablespoon.*

Calf's Liver with Onions and Capers

FEGATO DI VITELLO CON LE CIPOLLE E CAPPERI

In my home, liver was a must because my father believed it was a nutritious food for children that helped them grow. When available, lungs, hearts, and sweetbreads were also included in this dish, but then it's called *soffritto* in Naples (see recipe on page 233).

6 servings

3 tablespoons flour

¼ teaspoon dried sage

¼ teaspoon dried thyme

6 slices calf's liver
(about 4 ounces each)

1 to 2 tablespoons unsalted butter

1 to 2 tablespoons extra-virgin
olive oil

1 large red onion, sliced

1 tablespoon capers, drained

1 small bunch rosemary

2 tablespoons Marsala wine

1 tablespoon chopped fresh
Italian parsley

Combine the flour with the sage and thyme. Dredge the liver in it and shake off the excess flour. Set aside.

In a skillet heat 1 tablespoon butter and 1 tablespoon olive oil. Add the onion, sauté over low heat until the onion is quite soft. Add the capers and cook briefly. With a slotted spoon transfer the onion mixture to a bowl and keep warm.

If you have enough fat left in the skillet, add only the remaining butter or the remaining olive oil—not both. Add the rosemary and liver and quickly sauté, about 2 minutes on each side. Transfer the liver to a serving plate.

Add the Marsala to the skillet and let evaporate. Return the onion and capers to the skillet and reheat. Remove the rosemary and then spoon the onion mixture over the liver. Sprinkle with the chopped parsley and serve.

Tripe with Prosciutto in Tomato Sauce | **LA TRIPPA**

It wasn't an everyday meal, but when our butcher would tell my father that he had some nice tripe, Papa would buy it immediately. My mother was a master at cooking it, although my father wouldn't leave her alone, showing up several times in the kitchen to tell her to add this or that. I was always around, too, because this dish was, and still is, one of my favorites.

There are only two types of tripe, because only certain parts of the intestine are allowed to be sold—the honeycomb and the flat tripe. When you buy it, make sure it is well cleaned and partially boiled. In any case, I always boil my tripe for a couple of hours before using it.

6 servings

4½ pounds tripe, cleaned and partly boiled

2 leeks, just white parts

2 celery stalks, trimmed and cut in half

2 carrots

2 tablespoons extra-virgin olive oil

3 slices prosciutto with fat included, chopped

1 small *diavoletto* (hot red pepper) (optional)

Salt to taste

Freshly milled pepper to taste

½ cup dry white wine

1 (28-ounce) can tomato puree

Freshly grated Parmesan or Grana Padano cheese

Wash the tripe, changing the water several times. Put it in a large pot.

Wash the leeks well and add 1 to the tripe. Add 1 celery stalk and 1 carrot. Bring to a boil, reduce heat, and simmer for 2 hours. Cool the tripe in its own broth until it can be handled.

Transfer the tripe to a cutting board. Discard the broth and vegetables. Cut the tripe in thin strips.

Chop the remaining uncooked leek, celery, and carrot finely. This can be done in a food processor.

In a large skillet heat the olive oil and add the prosciutto. Cook for a few seconds and add the tripe, the *diavoletto* if using, and the chopped vegetables. Season with salt and pepper. Cook stirring for 10 minutes and then add the wine. Let the wine evaporate and add the tomato puree. Rinse the can with some water and add it to the pot. Cover, reduce the heat and simmer over very low heat until the tripe is tender, about 2 hours. Serve sprinkled with the grated cheese.

NOTE *This tripe is better the day after. Reheat and simmer 15 minutes.*

Sweetbreads with Porcini Mushrooms

ANIMELLE DI VITELLO CON PORCINI

Organ meats, all of them, are an absolute passion of mine. Sweetbreads and brains are my favorites. In Naples, these are considered a delicacy. Both can be cooked the same way, and they are so easy to prepare. I like to serve them as an *antipasto*.

6 servings

2 pounds sweetbreads

1 teaspoon kosher salt

¼ cup dried porcini mushrooms

2 tablespoons unsalted butter

1 teaspoon extra-virgin olive oil

2 tablespoons Marsala wine

½ a leek, or 3 scallions, washed, trimmed, and chopped

2 cups sliced fresh porcini mushrooms (see note)

Salt to taste

Freshly milled pepper to taste

1 tablespoon chopped fresh Italian parsley

Place the sweetbreads in a bowl and cover with water. Add the salt, stir and let stand for 1 hour. Blanch the sweetbreads in boiling water, drain, rinse under cold water and cut into slices or cubes.

Soak the dried porcini mushrooms in lukewarm water for 20 minutes. Carefully remove them from the water without disturbing the sediment. Chop the porcini coarsely. Discard the water or reserve for another use after filtering it.

In a skillet heat the butter and olive oil. Add the sweetbreads and sauté them for about 5 minutes. Add the Marsala and let evaporate. Transfer the sweetbreads to a bowl.

Add the leek to the skillet and sauté for a few minutes. Add the dried porcini and fresh mushrooms and cook until the liquid released by the mushrooms has evaporated.

Return the sweetbreads to the skillet and season with salt and pepper. Cook for 5 minutes to reheat thoroughly. Sprinkle with parsley and serve.

NOTE *My mother made this dish with small, fresh porcini mushrooms. In the United States, fresh porcini are not easy to find, and they are expensive. However, you can use fresh shiitake or other wild mushrooms. If using shiitake, I would omit the dried porcini, as their tastes obliterate each other.*

Ox Tongue Stew | **LINGUA DI BUE ALLA CASALINGA**

We were so happy when my father, the shopper of the house, would announce that he had gotten a tongue. Mother used to cook it so well with the *aromi di cucina* (the perfumes of the kitchen), which include onions, carrots, and celery. She also served the tongue with one of her marvelous sauces. Our favorite was the *salsa verde* (recipe on page 87), which is quite appropriate for this recipe. When you buy the tongue make sure that it is ready to cook (skinned); otherwise ask the butcher to do the job for you. This is delicious as an antipasto or a light lunch.

6 to 8 servings

1 ox or veal tongue
(2 to 3 pounds), skinned

¼ cup red wine vinegar

¼ tablespoon kosher salt

1 large onion

4 cloves

2 carrots, cut in half

1 celery stalk including leaves
(see note)

2 sprigs Italian parsley

2 dry bay leaves

Green Sauce (recipe on page 87)

1½ cups cherry tomatoes,
washed

1 tablespoon extra-virgin olive oil

1 tablespoon balsamic vinegar

1 tablespoon chopped fresh
Italian parsley

Place the tongue in a large pot and cover with water. Add the vinegar and salt. Bring to a boil and cook for 10 minutes at a steady simmer. Let the tongue cool in its water. (This step can be done in advance.)

When ready to continue, remove the tongue from the water. Discard the water and return the tongue to the pot.

Stud the onion with the cloves and add to the pot together with the carrots, celery, parsley, and bay leaves. Add water to come up 2 to 3 inches above the solids. Bring to a boil, reduce the heat and simmer for about 2 hours. Let the whole cool in the broth completely.

When ready to serve, remove the tongue from the broth, reserving the broth and vegetables for another use (see note). Cut the tongue into thin slices. Place the slices around the border of a serving plate letting each slice overlap a little. Leave the space in the middle of the plate empty. Spoon the Green Sauce over the slices. Put the cherry tomatoes in a mixing bowl. Add the olive oil, vinegar, and chopped parsley and pour the tomato mixture in the middle of the serving plate.

NOTE   *If you have a bunch of celery with leaves, wash and add the leaves to the broth, otherwise add 1 other stalk of celery.*

When making the broth, my mother used to add a piece of beef or veal, which made the broth more flavorful. All the vegetables in the broth can be pureed to make a delicious soup. You can serve it with a sprinkling of grated Parmesan cheese. And if you have a good amount of broth left over, you can use it for a risotto.

vegetables

The fertile, well-irrigated heart of Campania produces an abundance of vegetables and fruits. Since antiquity Campania has been renowned for its lush vegetation and the high quality of its produce. When you travel in the region, it is a pleasure to see the neat fields, the golden sea of wheat, the olive trees with their silvery leaves, and row after row of zucchini, string beans, artichokes, potatoes, and so much more. It is for good reason that the ancient Romans called this region *Campania Felix*—happy Campania!

For the Neapolitans vegetables are never secondary but an important part of the meal and cooked with great care. In fact, during the Renaissance, Neapolitan cooking was mostly vegetarian. The 15th-century Florentine ruler Lorenzo de Medici, aka Lorenzo the Magnificent, was the first who wittily called the Neapolitans *mangiafoglia* (leaf eaters). The Neapolitans retaliated by calling the people of the north *polentoni* (polenta eaters) (sic). This verbal skirmish between northerners and southerners continues to this day.

Some of the best and most original Italian vegetable dishes are from Campania. Vegetables are not only an accompaniment for meat or fish, they are also turned into delectable casseroles in their own right. Remember that the cooking of this region is that of the *cucina povera*, the cooking of the poor. For this reason vegetables take a central place in the casserole when there is no meat. Zucchini, peppers, potatoes, eggplants, spinach, or broccoli are stuffed or layered with cheese, sausage, prosciutto, sauce, bread crumbs, rice, and more. Together with a soup and a salad, these dishes can make satisfying main courses for a family dinner.

Sautéed Broccoli Rabe

BROCCOLI STRASCINATI OR "FRIARIELLI"

Broccoli rabe is a quintessential Italian green, with a pleasant, slightly bitter flavor that blends splendidly with fruity olive oil and garlic. I also like it just boiled, dressed with a little oil and lemon or a touch of balsamic vinegar. This simple classic recipe is a perfect accompaniment for meat or fish.

6 servings

2 bunches broccoli rabe
(about 2 pounds)

¼ cup extra-virgin olive oil

2 garlic cloves, crushed

1 small dried hot red pepper
(optional)

Salt to taste

Trim the broccoli rabe. Do not remove the stems, which are good to eat, just peel them. Cut each stalk into 3 or 4 pieces. Wash the greens well and keep them in water until ready to use, not more than an hour.

In a skillet place the olive oil, garlic, and hot pepper. Place over medium heat.

Lift the broccoli rabe with your hands, without shaking off the excess water and place in the skillet. Stir, cover, reduce the heat and let the broccoli cook in its own liquid for 5 minutes. Remove the lid. If you still have too much liquid, cook some more to reduce. Otherwise, raise the heat and sauté for 5 to 6 minutes, or until they are done. The total amount of cooking should not exceed 15 minutes. Remove the hot pepper if used. Add salt and serve.

NOTE   *In Campania this dish is also used to dress pasta, preferably short ones like penne. Other vegetables that the Neapolitans cook with garlic and oil are escarole and chicory.*

Asparagus with Hard-Boiled Eggs | **ASPARAGI MIMOSA**

During Spring, the first asparagus of the year is available and the mimosa trees are all in bloom—this is what inspired the Neapolitans to call this dish *mimosa*.

6 servings

36 asparagus stalks

¼ cup extra-virgin olive oil

¼ cup lemon juice

½ teaspoon grainy mustard

3 hard-boiled eggs

Trim the tough ends of the asparagus and discard; peel the stems if you wish. Put the asparagus in a skillet, cover with water, bring to a boil and cook until tender, about 5 minutes. The asparagus are done if their heads bend slightly when lifted with tongs.

Drain the asparagus, place in a bowl, and rinse under cold running water. Wrap in paper towels.

Whisk together the olive oil, lemon juice, and mustard.

Peel the eggs. Chop the yolks and whites separately.

Place the asparagus on a serving platter. Pour the olive oil mixture on the tip ends. Sprinkle with the egg yolks. Distribute the whites all around. If you wish, you can divide the asparagus among individual plates and dress them accordingly.

Pea Stew | **PISELLI STUFATI**

This is the most common way of cooking peas in Italy. I seldom use fresh peas, unless I find them at the very beginning of the season in the green market. Later in the season peas become starchy and hard, and they loose natural flavor and sweetness. Since in Italy fresh peas are very tender and cook in a minute, to call them "stewed," as in this recipe, is a little misleading—but this is what they are called in Campania!

6 servings

1 tablespoon extra-virgin olive oil

3 ounces pork cheeks, pancetta, or prosciutto, diced (see note)

1 onion, chopped

2 cups frozen peas, defrosted

1 tablespoon chopped fresh Italian parsley

In a skillet heat the oil and pork cheek. Add the onion, reduce the heat, cover and let the mixture cook for about 10 to 15 minutes, stirring often. If you feel you have too much fat in the skillet, remove some and discard.

Add the peas and cook for 5 minutes. Add the parsley and serve.

NOTE *If using prosciutto, buy it in one slice, so you will be able to dice it.*

Fava beans are also excellent cooked this way, but they need to cook longer.

String Beans with Cinnamon | **FAGIOLINI ALLA CANNELLA**

During the Kingdom of the Two Sicilies, Campania had a glorious period. The Arab domination of these regions in the 9th century A. D. lasted only one century, but traces of their civilization are still visible today in the architecture, art, science, and, of course, the cuisine. The Arabs loved spices, so they imported many spices that had been unknown in this region before. One of these spices was cinnamon.

6 servings

2 tablespoons extra-virgin olive oil

2 garlic cloves, chopped

2 pounds string beans, trimmed

Salt to taste

Freshly milled pepper to taste

1 teaspoon cinnamon

In a saucepan heat the olive oil and add the garlic. As soon as the garlic starts to sizzle, add the string beans and toss. Season with salt and pepper and add the cinnamon. Toss again and add 1 cup water. Cover and simmer over medium heat for 10 minutes, or until the beans are tender. Do not overcook.

If you have too much water at the end, remove the lid, increase the heat and let the water evaporate. Serve hot.

Sautéed String Beans and Bell Peppers

FAGIOLINI E PEPERONI IN PADELLA

In Campania, at least at one time, it was almost sacrilegious to eat vegetables that were not in season anymore. I remember how sorry my mother felt when the *fagiolini* were no longer available. So she made good use of them during the summer. The touch of butter and the nuts denote that this dish must have been the invention of a *Monzù*, the French chefs of the nobility.

6 servings

1½ pounds fresh string beans, trimmed

2 tablespoons extra-virgin olive oil

1 tablespoon unsalted butter

1 large onion, finely sliced

1 yellow or red bell pepper, cored and cut into thin strips

Salt to taste

Freshly milled pepper to taste

¼ cup toasted almonds or pine nuts, finely chopped

Blanch the string beans in boiling water for 5 minutes. Drain.

In a skillet heat the olive oil and butter. Add the onion and pepper strips. Cook until the onion is soft and translucent, stirring often, about 10 minutes. Season with salt and pepper.

Add the string beans and ¼ cup water. Cover loosely with a lid and cook for 10 to 15 minutes, or until the vegetables are tender. Add the almonds during the last minutes.

At the end the vegetables should be almost dry. If not, remove the lid and let the liquid evaporate. Serve hot.

Cauliflower with Tomatoes

CAVOLFIORE CU' A' PUMMAROLE

The Italian name for this recipe is Neapolitan dialect which means "cauliflowers with the always loved tomato."

6 servings

1 large head cauliflower, trimmed and cut into florets

1 tablespoon kosher salt

2 tablespoons extra-virgin olive oil

2 garlic cloves, crushed

1 cup peeled, coarsely chopped tomatoes

2 basil leaves, chopped

Salt to taste

Freshly milled pepper to taste

Place the cauliflower in a bowl, cover with water and add the salt. Stir and let stand for 10 to 15 minutes. Rinse and drain well.

In a skillet heat the olive oil and add the garlic. As soon as the garlic starts to sizzle, add the florets. Cook tossing the vegetables for about 5 minutes, then add the tomatoes. Cover the skillet, reduce the heat and cook for about 20 minutes. Add the basil, salt, and pepper and continue cooking until the cauliflower is tender. Serve hot.

Cauliflower with Raisins and Pine Nuts | **CAVOLFIORI AFFOGATI**

In Campania, a touch of fruit, fresh or dried, is often added to vegetables. In this easy recipe, the cauliflower is combined with raisins and pine nuts, and the whole is *affogati* (drowned in wine).

6 servings

1 large head cauliflower, trimmed and cut into florets

1 tablespoon kosher salt

3 tablespoons extra-virgin olive oil

¼ cup white wine

¼ cup raisins

¼ cup pine nuts

Place the cauliflower in a bowl, cover with water, add the kosher salt, mix and let stand for 15 to 20 minutes. When ready to cook, drain and rinse.

In a skillet, heat the olive oil and add the cauliflower. Cook, tossing for 5 to 10 minutes. Add the wine, cover the pot, reduce the heat to a minimum and cook the cauliflower for 10 minutes until tender. If there is not enough liquid, add a little water.

Stir in the raisins and pine nuts and remove from the heat. Serve hot.

Cauliflower Casserole | **SFORMATO DI CAVOLFIORI**

Campania has an abundance of vegetables, and many elegant dishes have been created by chefs and home cooks to show them off. They are called *sformati*, which can be translated into English as "casserole" or "mold."

6 servings

2 tablespoons unsalted butter

2 tablespoons fine unflavored dry bread crumbs

1 head cauliflower, trimmed

1 egg, beaten

1 cup Béchamel Sauce (recipe on page 79)

4 slices prosciutto or ham, finely chopped

4 ounces Gruyere cheese, diced

4 ounces smoked whole-milk mozzarella, coarsely chopped

3 tablespoons freshly grated Parmesan cheese

Preheat the oven to 350 degrees F. Butter a pie pan from which you can serve with 1 tablespoon of the butter. Sprinkle with bread crumbs.

Cut the cauliflower into small florets and peel the stems. Blanch the cauliflower in boiling salted water for 3 to 5 minutes. Drain.

Place the cauliflower in a mixing bowl and add the egg. Toss well. Add 2 to 3 tablespoons of the béchamel, all of the prosciutto, Gruyere, smoked mozzarella, and 2 tablespoons of the Parmesan. Toss well. Pour the mixture into the prepared pan. Drizzle the remaining béchamel all over, sprinkle with the remaining Parmesan and dot with the remaining butter.

Bake for 30 to 40 minutes, or until the top is nice and golden. Serve hot.

Cabbage in Sweet-Sour Sauce

CAVOLO IN AGRO-DOLCE

For this recipe you can also use a mixture of greens, such as curly endive, spinach, or escarole. The Neapolitans say the more the better, but I prefer to make it just with cabbage because I feel that the combination of sweet and sour goes perfectly with it.

6 servings

1 tablespoon extra-virgin olive oil

1 tablespoon prosciutto or bacon, chopped

2 garlic cloves, chopped

1 green or red cabbage, or a mixture of the two, shredded

¼ cup wine vinegar

1½ teaspoons sugar

Freshly milled pepper to taste

Salt to taste

Heat the olive oil in a heavy skillet. Add the prosciutto and garlic and cook stirring for 5 minutes. Add the cabbage, vinegar, sugar, pepper, and salt. Cover, reduce the heat to a minimum and simmer the cabbage for 30 to 35 minutes. Check the liquid in the skillet and, if necessary, add a little water.

NOTE   *This dish can be made in advance. Add a little water before reheating it.*

Fresh Fava Beans | **FAVE FRESCHE**

Not only did we eat fava beans raw in Naples, but we also made wonderful soups and side dishes with them. This recipe is made with fresh fava beans. It is a delicious accompaniment to fish or chicken, and if you add more water or broth, it makes a soup.

6 servings

4 pounds fresh fava beans

3 tablespoons extra-virgin olive oil

2 onions, thinly sliced

3 or 4 thin slices pancetta or bacon, chopped

1 tablespoon chopped fresh Italian parsley

Pod the fava beans but do not peel them. Place the beans in a bowl of cold water for a few minutes and drain.

In a skillet, heat the olive oil and add the onions and pancetta. Cook until the onions are soft and translucent.

Add the fava beans. Cook for about 5 minutes stirring, then add ½ cup water. Cover, reduce the heat, and simmer for about 15 to 20 minutes, or until the fava beans are tender. If necessary, add a little more water. Add the parsley and serve.

Fava Beans and Potatoes | **FAVE E PATATE**

In spring, the first, most tender fava beans are eaten like a fruit. As children it was such fun to remove them from their green velvety pods, peel the skin and eat the succulent beans. But the season doesn't last long, so the Neapolitans turn to dried fava beans, which can be eaten in every season. This recipe is very filling, a winter dish to satisfy healthy appetites.

6 servings

1 pound dried fava beans, soaked in water overnight

1 sprig thyme, or 2 dry bay leaves

2 or 3 medium potatoes, peeled and cubed

3 tablespoons extra-virgin olive oil

1 onion, thinly sliced

3 ripe tomatoes, cubed

Salt to taste

Freshly milled pepper to taste

1 tablespoon chopped fresh Italian parsley

Drain the fava beans and rinse. Put them in a pot, cover with water to come up 2 inches above the beans. Add the thyme, bring to a boil and cook over medium heat until the beans are almost tender, about 30 to 45 minutes, stirring once in a while.

Add the potatoes and continue to simmer for an additional 15 to 20 minutes.

In a large skillet heat the olive oil and sauté the onion until soft and translucent. Add the tomatoes and cook for 5 minutes.

Drain the fava beans and potatoes. Add them to the skillet and cook, stirring, for 10 minutes over medium heat. If necessary add a little hot water or broth. Season with salt and pepper. Serve sprinkled with parsley.

ABOUT ARTICHOKES

When you buy artichokes, baby or medium-size, make sure their leaves are closed into a solid ball. To see if they are fresh, squeeze the artichokes with your hands, they should squeak. Avoid those monstrous American types with spiked leaves—they might look impressive but they are tough, and there will be a lot of waste. They will also contain a large choke, which must be removed.

If you want to make stuffed artichokes, go to a green market and pick the largest baby artichokes you can find. They will be tender and without chokes. Do not throw away the stems if there are any attached, they are edible. Just peel and add to the dish or chop them and use them for a stuffing.

Artichokes and Fava Beans
SPEZZATINO DI CARCIOFI E FAVE

This is truly a spring dish. In fact, when my mother found a choke (the inedible prickly part) in an artichoke that she was preparing for stuffing, she would sigh and say, "Ah! The artichoke season is finished!"

Snap back the tops of the leaves of the artichokes and discard. Do this all around the artichokes until you reach the pale green leaves. Cut off about ½ inch of the tops of the trimmed artichokes. Peel the stems, if any, leaving them attached. Cut the artichokes into wedges and place them in a bowl of water. Add the lemon juice to prevent discoloration.

Shell the fava beans and blanch them for a few minutes in boiling water. Cool and squeeze the beans out of their skins. Set aside.

In a nonreactive skillet, heat the olive oil over medium heat. Add the sprig of parsley and garlic. Cook for a few minutes, then add the fresh artichokes and ½ cup of their lemon water. Cover and cook the artichokes for 10 minutes over low heat, stirring once or twice.

Add the fava beans and continue cooking until the vegetables are tender. Season with salt and pepper, sprinkle with the chopped parsley and serve.

6 servings

8 fresh baby artichokes, with stems if possible

Juice of half a lemon

2 pounds fresh fava beans, shelled

3 tablespoons extra-virgin olive oil

1 sprig Italian parsley

2 garlic cloves, crushed

Salt to taste

Freshly milled pepper to taste

1 heaping tablespoon chopped fresh Italian parsley

Artichokes and Peas | **SPEZZATINO DI CARCIOFI E PISELLI**

This has been one of my favorite vegetable dishes since childhood. Sometimes I make it just for myself for lunch. And if I have leftovers, I scramble a couple of eggs into the *spezzatino*—what a feast!

6 servings

8 fresh or frozen baby artichokes

Juice of half a lemon

¼ cup extra-virgin olive oil

1 sprig Italian parsley

2 garlic cloves, peeled and crushed

10 ounces frozen peas, defrosted

Salt to taste

Freshly milled pepper to taste

1½ to 2 tablespoons chopped fresh Italian parsley

If using fresh artichokes, snap back the tops of the leaves of the artichokes and discard. Do this all around the artichokes until you reach the pale green leaves. Cut off about 1 inch of the top of the trimmed artichokes. If there are stems, peel them. Quarter the artichokes and place in a bowl of water. Add the lemon juice to prevent discoloration.

In a nonreactive skillet, heat the olive oil over medium heat. Add the sprig of parsley and garlic. Cook for a few minutes and add the fresh artichokes and ½ cup water. Cook until almost tender, about 15 minutes. If using frozen artichokes, do not add water and cook them for only 5 to 6 minutes.

Add the peas and season with salt and pepper. Cook until the peas are heated through. Sprinkle with the chopped parsley and serve.

NOTE *You can cook just the artichokes this way, and you will have* carciofi trifolati. Trifolati *is a term for any cut-up vegetable, such as mushrooms, eggplants, zucchini, cooked in oil and garlic.*

Spinach and Artichoke Casserole

SFORMATO DI SPINACI E CARCIOFI

The vegetables give this dish its unique texture, and the beautifully intense flavor of the cheeses combines well with them. This is one of the dishes of the *cucina povera* or "cooking of the poor." Sometimes more eggs are added and the whole is cooked like a *frittata* (omelet), but since it is too big to turn, it is finished in the oven or under the broiler.

6 to 8 servings

3 tablespoons unsalted butter plus more for the pan

1 tablespoon extra-virgin olive oil

1 onion, chopped

1 (9-ounce) package frozen artichoke hearts, thawed, or 10 to 12 baby artichokes, trimmed and quartered

2 pounds fresh spinach, washed and coarsely chopped

1/2 teaspoon dried tarragon

1 tablespoon chopped fresh Italian parsley

1/2 cup unflavored dry bread crumbs

3/4 cup shredded Caciocavallo or Fontina cheese

2 tablespoons freshly grated Pecorino Romano cheese

3 eggs, lightly beaten

Preheat the oven to 350 degrees F. Butter a pie pan from which you can serve.

In a large skillet, heat the butter and olive oil. Add the onion and cook stirring for 5 minutes, then stir in the artichokes and cover. If using frozen artichokes cook for 5 to 10 minutes. For the fresh artichokes add 1/2 cup water and cook for 10 to 15 minutes, or until tender. Add the spinach and toss until wilted.

Transfer the vegetables to a mixing bowl and add the tarragon, parsley, bread crumbs, cheeses, and eggs. Mix well and transfer to the prepared pan. Smooth the top and bake for 25 to 30 minutes, or until set. Cool slightly before serving.

Breaded and Baked Artichokes | **CARCIOFI INDORATI E FRITTI**

To call these artichokes simply "fried" is not enough for the Neapolitans. They like to magnify things, therefore the artichokes are *indorati*, which means "gilded." Fried artichokes are often part of a *fritto misto*, which is a mixture of vegetables and sometimes fish, usually served at important occasions.

6 to 8 servings

8 baby artichokes

Juice of 1 lemon

Canola oil for frying

All-purpose flour for dredging

4 eggs, well beaten

½ teaspoon salt

1 or 2 lemons, cut into wedges

Remove the tough leaves of each artichoke and cut 1 inch off the tops. Add the lemon juice to a bowl of cold water. Cut each artichoke into quarters and add to the bowl. When ready to cook, drain and rinse the artichokes. Dry them with paper towels.

Pour some canola oil into a skillet and set over medium heat. The oil is ready when it starts to shiver. Preheat the oven to 350 degrees F.

Put some flour on a plate, add a handful of artichoke pieces, toss them in the flour and shake off excess flour. Do this with a few artichoke pieces at a time until all are coated.

Beat the eggs and add in the salt. Dip the artichoke pieces, a few at a time, into the beaten eggs. Slide them into the hot oil.

When the artichoke pieces are nice and golden, remove them with a slotted spoon. Place them on paper towels to absorb oil and then transfer them to a serving platter. Switch off the oven and keep the artichokes warm in the oven until you finish frying all the pieces. Serve hot, with wedges of lemon, if you like.

NOTE *I add a shot of olive oil to the canola oil for flavor. If you have some of these artichokes left, which I doubt, make a Parmigiana with them. Layer the artichokes with a little mozzarella and grated Parmesan and bake for 10 to 15 minutes, or until the mozzarella starts to melt.*

Stuffed Artichokes | **CARCIOFI RIPIENI**

This is one of the most common ways of eating artichokes in Italy. The stuffing might vary, but the idea remains the same. Bread is the main ingredient of the stuffing; after that, just use your imagination as the Neapolitans do—they usually include olives, capers, and anchovies.

6 servings

6 large artichokes

Juice of 1 lemon

6 anchovies packed in oil, chopped

½ cup black olives, pitted and chopped

1½ tablespoons capers, drained

3 garlic cloves, chopped

¼ cup chopped fresh Italian parsley

2 slices stale bread, soaked in a little water

¼ cup extra-virgin olive oil plus more for drizzling

Salt to taste

Freshly milled pepper to taste

Unflavored dry bread crumbs

Sprigs of Italian parsley for garnish

Cut 1 inch off the tops of each artichoke. Cut the stems if any, peel and chop them and set aside. Discard the toughest leaves. Insert your fingers into the middle of each artichoke and remove the choke if any. Place the artichokes in a bowl, cover with cold water and add the lemon juice.

In a bowl combine the anchovies, olives, capers, garlic, and parsley. Squeeze the water out of the bread and add to the mixture. Add the olive oil and mix well. Add salt and pepper to taste.

Oil a pot into which the artichokes can be placed standing up and close to each other.

Fill the centers of the artichokes with the bread mixture and place them in the prepared pot. Sprinkle them with bread crumbs and drizzle with olive oil. Add 2 cups of water, cover, and bring to a boil. Reduce the heat and simmer for about 30 to 40 minutes, basting once in a while. If the water evaporates, add a little more. The artichokes are done when a leaf can be pulled out easily. Garnish each artichoke with a sprig of parsley and serve.

Fresh Cranberry Beans | **FAGIOLI FRESCHI**

I am so glad to see more and more fresh cranberry beans in their bright red pods sold in green markets and some supermarkets. They cook quickly and can be just boiled and dressed with oil and lemon juice, or in a more modern way, with oil and balsamic vinegar. The Neapolitans call them *spolichini,* and one of their best *pasta e fagioli* (recipe on page 52) is made with them.

6 to 8 servings

1½ pounds fresh cranberry beans, shelled

⅓ cup extra-virgin olive oil

2 garlic cloves, peeled

1½ teaspoons chopped fresh sage, or ½ teaspoon dried

1 ripe firm tomato

Salt to taste

Freshly milled pepper to taste

In a pot place the beans, 2 tablespoons of the olive oil, the garlic cloves, sage, and whole tomato. Add water to come up 1 inch above the beans. Cover the pot, bring to a boil, then reduce the heat and simmer until the beans are tender, about 20 to 30 minutes.

Drain the beans. Remove the garlic and tomato and set aside. Return the beans to the pot.

Puree the garlic, peel and chop the tomato, and then stir both back into the beans. Add salt, a good grinding of pepper and 3 tablespoons olive oil. Mix well and serve.

Sweet-and-Sour Pearl Onions and Carrots

CIPOLLINE E CAROTE AGRO-DOLCI

Sweet and sour food, both for simple daily meals or festive occasions, is much loved in Campania, especially when served as an accompaniment for plain meat dishes or fish. Pearl onions have an assertive flavor, so you do not want to pair them with a strong-flavored sauce.

6 servings

¼ cup honey

⅓ cup white wine vinegar

1 pound pearl onions, peeled and with a crisscross cut at the root ends

3 carrots, cubed

2 tablespoons unsalted butter, at room temperature

1 teaspoon extra-virgin olive oil

Freshly grated pepper to taste

1 tablespoon chopped fresh Italian parsley

Preheat the oven to 375 degrees F.

In a saucepan combine the honey and vinegar. Heat and reduce to ⅓ cup liquid.

In a mixing bowl, combine the onions and carrots. Pour the honey mixture over them. Add 1 tablespoon of the butter, the olive oil, and pepper, and toss well.

Grease a sheet of heavy-duty aluminum foil with the remaining butter. Place the vegetables in the center, bring up the side, and seal well. Bake for 50 minutes. Unwrap, place in a serving bowl and serve sprinkled with the parsley.

Mixed Grilled Vegetables | **GRIGLIATA DI VERDURE**

In Campania with its abundance of vegetables, this *grigliata* is prepared almost on a daily basis. It is a cheap dish and needs only a little oil to make the vegetables taste delicious. The balsamic vinegar is my modern addition.

6 to 8 servings

1 garlic clove, chopped

3 tablespoons extra-virgin olive oil

Juice of half a lemon

2 tablespoons balsamic vinegar

½ teaspoon mixed fresh herbs (basil, oregano, rosemary, etc.)

2 bell peppers, sliced into ½-inch strips

1 or 2 zucchini, sliced ¼ inch thick

8 white mushrooms, sliced in half

1 or 2 large red onions, sliced thick

3 firm tomatoes, sliced into ¼-inch slices

6 lemon wedges

In a large bowl, combine the garlic, olive oil, lemon juice, balsamic vinegar, and herbs. Add all the vegetables except the tomatoes. Toss gently.

Lift the vegetables from the bowl and line them on a grill. Add the tomato slices to the dressing, toss gently and place them on the grill. You may have to do this in batches. Grill the vegetables for 15 to 20 minutes, turning the vegetables once. Serve with lemon wedges if desired.

Grilled Portobello Mushrooms

FUNGHI PORTOBELLO ALLA GRIGLIA

In Campania and some other regions of Italy grows a very meaty, ball-shaped mushroom with the unappealing name *testa di morto* (skull). The flavor, however, is exceptional and quite similar to steak. Since it is not possible to find these mushrooms in the United States, I use portobello mushrooms.

6 servings

12 large portobello mushrooms

1 tablespoon kosher salt

¼ cup extra-virgin olive oil

1 bunch fresh rosemary, chopped

1 garlic clove, chopped (optional)

Juice of 1 lemon

Sprigs of Italian parsley for garnish

Place the mushrooms in a large bowl and add the salt. Pour lukewarm water into the bowl to cover the mushrooms. Quickly swirl the mushrooms around to clean them well. Place in a colander, rinse with cold water, drain and gently dry with paper towels.

In a bowl, combine the olive oil, rosemary, and garlic.

Place the mushrooms on a platter in one layer and pour the oil mixture over them. Add the lemon juice and toss. Marinate for 20 minutes.

Preheat the grill. Cook the mushrooms for 5 to 6 minutes on both sides. Serve hot, garnished with the parsley sprigs.

Fried Bell Peppers

PEPERONI FRITTI

These fried peppers go with everything—fish, meat, poultry—and choosing peppers of different colors makes an attractive presentation.

Heat the olive oil in a large skillet. Add the garlic and rosemary, if using fresh. As soon as the garlic starts to sizzle, add the peppers and, if using, the dried rosemary. Cook stirring often until the peppers are soft and slightly brown, about 15 minutes. Transfer the peppers to a serving plate and serve hot.

6 servings

¼ cup extra-virgin olive oil

2 garlic cloves, crushed

1 tablespoon chopped fresh rosemary, or 1 teaspoon dried

5 or 6 large bell peppers of mixed colors, washed, cored and cut into strips

ABOUT PEPPERS

When it comes to peppers, the Neapolitans become poetic. The native writer Mario Stefanile, in his book *Partenope in Cucina*, describes how the locals "cultivate their peppers with love to devour them raw in a salad, fried in a skillet, roasted, peeled, cooked in oil with a veil of bread crumbs and a fistful of black olives."

A bit of advice: Buy your peppers in advance and keep them in a basket for a few days. They are a lovely still life in your kitchen or living room. When they start to get wrinkly, it means that they are getting more mature and therefore more flavorful.

If you buy them at a green market, choose the peppers that have spots of colors and let them turn fully red or yellow. Green peppers are actually unripe peppers which are good for eating at any time.

Roasted Bell Peppers | **PEPERONI ARROSTITI**

When summer came, the ritual of roasting peppers every day for our daily meal would begin. The smoky scent permeated the house and wafted out of the window. The peppers were served as a *contorno*, an accompaniment to the main course. The leftovers went into a delicious *frittata* or were pureed to dress spaghetti.

6 servings

6 bell peppers, a mixture of green, yellow, and red

1 garlic clove, chopped

2 to 3 tablespoons extra-virgin olive oil

1 tablespoon chopped fresh Italian parsley

Roast the peppers by placing them directly on the flame of the gas stove until their skin is charred, turning the peppers often. Drop the blackened peppers in a paper bag and seal the top. (This will facilitate peeling.) Let the pepper cool then peel, core and seed them (see note). Cut into strips.

In a serving bowl combine the garlic, olive oil, and fresh parsley. Toss with the peppers and serve.

NOTE *Do not succumb to the temptation of peeling the peppers under running water. You will also wash the flavor away. If you do not have a gas stove, use a grill pan, or even better, a barbecue!*

Stuffed Bell Peppers | **PEPERONI RIPIENI ALLA RAFFAELLA**

Mario Stefanile, the Neapolitan writer who uses poetic language to describe his love for *peperoni*, thinks that stuffed peppers are the best. And this is what he says about a platter of stuffed peppers, "... a still life for amateur painters, a strong dish for any dinner with a Neapolitan brand."

My mother, Raffaella, was famous for her stuffed vegetables. Her beautiful tray of peppers also contained stuffed tomatoes, stuffed onions, stuffed zucchini, and stuffed eggplants. This is her recipe. It suits peppers quite well, but you can also use other kinds of vegetables, just as she did.

6 servings

6 bell peppers, any color

6 sprigs Italian parsley, chopped

2 garlic cloves, chopped

1 heaping tablespoon capers, drained

2 anchovies packed in oil, chopped, or 1 teaspoon anchovy paste (optional)

2 cups unflavored dry bread crumbs

3 tablespoons grated Pecorino Romano cheese

8 ounces whole-milk mozzarella, coarsely chopped

⅓ cup extra-virgin olive oil

1 tablespoon chopped fresh rosemary, or 1 teaspoon dried

¼ cup homemade chicken broth or water

Freshly milled pepper to taste

Preheat the oven to 375 degrees F. Evenly cut the tops off each pepper and set them aside. Remove the core and seeds from the peppers.

Combine the parsley, garlic, capers, anchovies, bread crumbs, grated cheese, and mozzarella. Add 5 tablespoons of olive oil, mix well and stuff the peppers with this mixture. Top each pepper with the reserved tops.

Oil a roasting pan in which the peppers can be placed upright in one layer. Add the peppers. Mix the rosemary and broth and pour around the bottom of the pan. Drizzle a little olive oil over the peppers and sprinkle with a good amount of pepper. Bake for 1 hour or more, or until the peppers are tender, basting them with their own juices once in a while. If necessary, add a little more broth.

ABOUT EGGPLANTS

Some people believe in salting eggplants before cooking them. The Neapolitans do this for their *Parmigiana*. This removes the natural bitterness of the vegetables. I sometimes do it too, especially if I cannot find small eggplants and have to use large ones. But personally I do not mind a little bitterness in my eggplants.

Eggplants are guzzlers of oil. I remember my mother using quite a bit of it and always adding a little more while cooking them. But I have a trick—I add a little broth so I do not need more oil.

Eggplant Sauté | **MELANZANE A FUNGHETTO**

Melanzane a funghetto means that the eggplants are cooked in the style of mushrooms. This is a common method of cooking vegetables in Italy. It is a sauté with oil and garlic.

Heat the olive oil in a large skillet. Add the garlic, and sprigs of parsley and cook briefly. Add the eggplants. Cover the skillet and reduce the heat. Cook for 10 minutes, stirring once or twice.

Remove the lid and continue cooking until the eggplants are slightly browned. If they start to stick to the skillet, add some broth.

Season with salt. Remove the garlic and sprigs of parsley. Serve sprinkled with the chopped parsley.

6 servings

3 tablespoons extra-virgin olive oil

2 garlic cloves, peeled

2 sprigs Italian parsley

3 medium eggplants, stemmed and cut into small cubes

1 or 2 tablespoons homemade or canned chicken or beef broth, if necessary

Salt to taste

1 tablespoon chopped fresh Italian parsley

NOTE *For a stronger garlic flavor, chop the garlic, but be careful not to let it color, otherwise the dish will taste bitter.*

Eggplant with Capers

MELANZANE ALLA MEDITERRANEA

This simple recipe from Campania combines classic Mediterranean staples—olive oil, garlic, lemon, and capers—that perfectly complement the earthy flavor of eggplant.

6 servings

6 medium eggplants

¼ cup extra-virgin olive oil

2 garlic cloves, finely chopped

1 teaspoon tomato paste

Juice of 1 lemon

1½ teaspoons capers, drained

1 tablespoon chopped fresh Italian parsley

With a fork, pierce the eggplants in 2 or 3 places. Roast them over a gas flame or grill, turning them often until their skin is charred; or, without piercing the skin, bake in a 375 degree F oven until they "collapse." Peel and cube the eggplants, removing some of the seeds if there are any.

Combine the olive oil, garlic, tomato paste, lemon juice, and capers. Pour over the eggplants and toss well. Serve with a sprinkling of chopped parsley.

Baked Eggplants and Tomatoes | **MELANZANE ALLA PIZZAIOLA**

Pizzaiola evokes an association with pizza. However, in this dish the main ingredients are eggplants and the ubiquitous tomatoes.

6 servings

3 medium eggplants

1 pound ripe tomatoes

2 garlic cloves, chopped

Fresh oregano to taste

Extra-virgin olive oil for drizzling

Preheat the oven to 375 degrees F.

Peel the eggplants and slice them lengthwise. Set aside.

Oil a large baking dish from which you can serve. Place the slices of eggplant in the dish. You can let them overlap a little.

Slice the tomatoes, preferably lengthwise and place them in a layer over the eggplants. Sprinkle the oregano over all and drizzle the dish with olive oil.

Bake for 30 to 35 minutes, or until the eggplants are soft. Serve hot as an accompaniment to meat or fish.

Belgian Endive with Pine Nuts | **INDIVIA ALLA NAPOLETANA**

This recipe, whose origins are Sicilian, is a complex dish full of different flavors. It goes well with roasted pork and other roasted meats.

6 servings

2 bunches curly endive, trimmed and washed

3 tablespoons extra-virgin olive oil

1 small onion, thinly sliced

2 or 3 sun-dried tomatoes, chopped

¼ cup black olives, pitted and coarsely chopped

1 tablespoon capers, drained

1 tablespoon pine nuts

1 tablespoon raisins

1 teaspoon anchovy paste (optional)

Cut the leaves of the endive into 3 to 4 pieces, blanch in boiling water for 5 minutes and drain.

In a skillet heat the olive oil. Add the onion and sun-dried tomatoes, and cook for a few minutes while stirring. Add the endive and cook for 5 to 10 minutes, stirring once in a while. Add the chopped olives, capers, pine nuts, raisins, and anchovy paste. Cook for a few more minutes and serve.

Sautéed Swiss Chard | **BIETOLE AL BURRO**

As it is well known, the Neapolitans are called *mangiafoglia* (leaf eaters). This recipe contributes to that image. The delicate leaves of the chards are simply cooked in butter and a little oil. I reserve the white core of this vegetable to use in a salad.

6 servings

2 tablespoons unsalted butter

1 tablespoon extra-virgin olive oil

1 bunch Swiss chard, washed, trimmed and chopped

Salt to taste

Freshly milled pepper to taste

1 cup homemade beef or chicken broth

Freshly grated Parmesan or Grana Padano cheese

Heat the butter and oil in a skillet. Add the chard and cook, stirring, for a few minutes. Add salt and pepper and the broth. Cover and simmer for about 8 minutes. Serve sprinkled with the grated cheese.

NOTE   *Brussels sprouts can also be cooked this way.*

Tomato Gratin

POMODORI GRATINATI

This is an elegant accompaniment to meat or fish, especially fish, either grilled or roasted. The word *gratin* is of course of French origin; and the dish was probably concocted by a *Monzù*, the French chefs of the Neapolitan nobility.

6 servings

2 pounds ripe tomatoes, washed and cut in half

¾ cup dry unflavored bread crumbs

½ cup black olives, pitted and coarsely chopped

2 tablespoons capers, drained

2 or 3 anchovies packed in oil, coarsely chopped, or 1 teaspoon anchovy paste

1½ teaspoons chopped fresh oregano, or ½ teaspoon dried

Salt to taste

Freshly milled pepper to taste

2 to 3 tablespoons extra-virgin olive oil

Preheat the oven to 350 degrees F. Oil a large baking dish from which you can serve.

Place the tomatoes, cut side down, in a colander to drain.

Combine the bread crumbs, olives, capers, anchovies, oregano, salt, and pepper. Add 2 to 3 tablespoons olive oil and mix well.

Place the drained tomatoes, cut-side up, in the prepared pan. Spoon the breadcrumb mixture evenly over all the tomatoes. Drizzle with a little olive oil.

Bake for 25 to 30 minutes and serve hot.

Ratatouille with Basil | **LA CIANFOTTA**

The name of this recipe, which is a real example of the *cucina povera*, means "an assortment." It is made with a mixture of vegetables including the "sacred" tomato.

6 to 8 servings

3 medium potatoes,
peeled and cut into small cubes

⅓ cup extra-virgin olive oil plus
more as needed

2 garlic cloves

3 bell peppers of mixed colors,
seeded and cut into small pieces

2 or 3 medium eggplants, peeled
and cubed

1 (28-ounce) can peeled tomatoes

8 to 10 fresh whole basil leaves

Salt to taste

Freshly milled pepper to taste

Put the potatoes in a bowl of cold water to prevent discoloration.

In a large skillet heat the olive oil and add the garlic. As soon as it starts to brown, remove the garlic and discard.

Add the potatoes and sauté until they are almost soft. Remove with a slotted spoon and set aside. Sauté the peppers the same way. Remove and set aside.

Heat more oil if necessary and sauté the eggplants for about 15 minutes. Remove with a slotted spoon and set aside.

Add the tomatoes with their juices to the skillet and crush them with a wooden spoon. Bring to a boil, reduce the heat and simmer for 10 minutes. Add the basil and return all the vegetables to the skillet. Stir well. Cover the skillet and continue simmering over low heat for about 10 minutes, or until the vegetables are cooked. Season with salt and pepper and serve hot.

Roasted Potatoes | **PATATE AL FORNO**

When you make a roast, add some potatoes to the pan. The flavor of the meat gives the potatoes a delicious taste. However, if you are not making a roast and you would still like delicious potatoes, this is a good recipe. You can use any kind of potatoes, but small red ones are my favorite for this dish. I do not peel them.

6 servings

2 pounds small red potatoes

2 tablespoons extra-virgin olive oil

1 tablespoon unsalted butter

1 bunch fresh rosemary

1 large onion, coarsely chopped

Salt to taste

Freshly milled pepper to taste

1 tablespoon chopped fresh Italian parsley

Boil the potatoes in their jackets. Drain. Do not peel them, but cut potatoes into slices.

Preheat the oven to 375 degrees F. Oil a baking dish from which you can serve.

In a large skillet, heat the olive oil and butter. Add the rosemary and onion. Cook for 5 minutes, stirring, then add the potatoes. Cook for five minutes tossing them around.

Transfer the potatoes to the prepared dish. Discard the rosemary, season with salt and pepper. Bake for 15 minutes, or until the potatoes are slightly brown. Serve sprinkled with parsley.

Potatoes with Bay Leaves | **PATATE ALL'ALLORO**

A great, aromatic, simple side dish to accompany roasted meats, it is the combination of bay leaves and garlic that gives this dish its special taste.

6 servings

3 baking potatoes (about 1½ pounds)

2 tablespoons extra-virgin olive oil plus more for drizzling

Salt to taste

2 garlic cloves, sliced

4 or 5 dry bay leaves

Peel the potatoes, slice them into thin slices and place in a mixing bowl. Add the olive oil and salt and toss.

Preheat the oven to 375 degrees F.

Layer the potatoes in a baking dish with the garlic and bay leaves. Drizzle with a little more olive oil and bake for 45 minutes to 1 hour. Remove bay leaves before serving.

Potato Puree with Parmesan | **PURÉ DI PATATE**

Creamy and delicious, this classic puree makes an elegant accompaniment for many dishes. It is a favorite *contorno* (side dish) all over Italy.

6 servings

5 medium potatoes (about 2 pounds)

5 tablespoons unsalted butter, at room temperature

¼ cup milk, plus more as needed

Pinch of salt

3 to 4 tablespoons freshly grated Parmesan cheese

Boil the potatoes until soft; peel and strain them through a food mill or a potato ricer into a mixing bowl. Add the butter and mix well. Add milk and continue mixing until smooth.

Transfer the mixture to a heavy pot and cook over low heat, stirring constantly until the puree is light and soft, about 10 minutes. If necessary add a little more milk. Remove from the heat and stir in some salt and the Parmesan. Serve hot.

NOTE *Leftover puree makes delicious pancakes, or it can be layered with mozzarella and baked.*

Potato Casserole with Smoked Mozzarella

GATTÒ DI PATATE GIANNA AMORE

The Italian word *gattò* comes from the French word *gateau*. This is a classic Neapolitan dish whose origins go back to the French domination of Campania. My mother learned to make it when we lived in Naples. She loved the dish and served it often at our Sunday dinners. My cousin Gianna Amore, who lives in Campania, has made it even more special. Adding smoked mozzarella was a stroke of genius; it lends a subtle, unexpected flavor to the dish. And my mother, after tasting Gianna's version, started to make her *gattò alla Gianna*.

6 to 8 servings

4 or 5 baking potatoes

6 tablespoons unsalted butter

⅓ cup freshly grated Parmesan cheese

1 cup milk

2 eggs, lightly beaten

8 ounces smoked whole-milk mozzarella, diced

4 ounces prosciutto, chopped

1 tablespoon chopped fresh Italian parsley

Salt to taste

Freshly milled pepper

Unflavored dry bread crumbs for the dish

4 ounces whole-milk mozzarella, thinly sliced

Boil the potatoes, peel, mash, and transfer to a mixing bowl. Add 5 tablespoons of the butter and the Parmesan and mix well. Add the milk, eggs, smoked mozzarella, prosciutto, parsley, salt and pepper. Mix well.

Preheat the oven to 375 degrees F. Butter a pie pan from which you can serve. Sprinkle it with bread crumbs.

Spoon half of the potato mixture into the pan, smooth the top and cover with the mozzarella slices in one layer. Spoon the remaining potato mixture into the pan, smooth the top, sprinkle with bread crumbs and dot with the remaining tablespoon butter. Bake for 40 to 45 minutes, or until the top is golden.

NOTE *My mother made several variations of this dish. She would make it meatless, leaving out the prosciutto and adding a layer of sautéed fresh vegetables, such as broccoli, zucchini, or baby artichokes. When she used peas, she would stir them into the potato mixture and cook the* gattò *in a deeper dish so that when it was cut, the slices were dotted with peas.*

Zucchini in Tomato and Basil Sauce | **ZUCCHINE IN UMIDO**

Many recipes in Italy are cooked *in umido*, which means "in liquid." This savory dish is particularly suitable as a side dish for roasts.

6 servings

1 teaspoon extra-virgin olive oil

1 slice pancetta (about 2 ounces), coarsely chopped

1 onion, chopped

5 or 6 medium zucchini

4 or 5 ripe tomatoes, peeled, seeded and cubed

5 or 6 basil leaves, chopped

1 sprig Italian parsley, chopped

In a skillet, heat the olive oil and pancetta, cook for 5 minutes, and then add the onion and cook stirring for 5 more minutes. Add the zucchini, stir again, and cook for a few more minutes.

Add the tomatoes, reduce the heat and cook, stirring often until the liquid has almost evaporated. Stir in the basil and parsley at the end. Serve hot.

NOTE *This sauce can also be used to dress any short type of pasta.*

Zucchini in Wine Sauce | **ZUCCHINE AL VINO ARMANDINO**

We always called this dish Armandino because it rhymes with *vino* (wine), and because it was given to my father by a fine waiter named Armandino in a restaurant in Naples where we used to go for special occasions. I remember him very well because, when the *padrone* was not looking, he would slip a little more food onto the plates of us children. The unusual addition of wine and herbs makes this dish quite special.

6 to 8 servings

2 tablespoons extra-virgin olive oil

3 medium to small zucchini, cut into slices

½ cup white wine

2 dry bay leaves

¼ teaspoon dried thyme, crumbled

Salt to taste

Freshly milled pepper to taste

In a skillet, heat the olive oil, add the zucchini and sauté until they start to color. Add the wine, bay leaves, thyme, salt, and pepper. Cover and cook over medium heat until tender, about 12 minutes, stirring often. If you have too much liquid, uncover the skillet to reduce it. Remove bay leaves before serving.

Zucchini Gratin with Mozzarella and Tomatoes

ZUCCHINE GRATINATE CON MOZZARELLA E POMODORO

We used to have this dish on Fridays, when we were not supposed to eat meat. My vegetarian friends love it, so I make it often for them. But when they are not around, I love to add a little prosciutto or mortadella to the vegetables—you can do the same.

6 servings

4 zucchini (about 1½ pounds)

1 pound ripe plum tomatoes

2 tablespoons extra-virgin olive oil, plus more for drizzling

Salt to taste

Freshly milled pepper to taste

1½ teaspoons chopped fresh oregano, or ½ teaspoon dried, crumbled

8 ounces whole-milk mozzarella, diced

1 tablespoon unsalted butter (optional)

Preheat the oven to 400 degrees F.

Cut the zucchini into thin slices. Slice the tomatoes thinly with a serrated knife.

Put the zucchini slices in an oiled baking dish. Add the olive oil, season with salt and pepper, sprinkle with half of the oregano and toss.

Insert half of the tomato slices in between the zucchini slices and drizzle with a little oil.

Scatter half the mozzarella cubes evenly over the vegetables and top with the remaining tomato slices. Sprinkle the remaining oregano on top and scatter the remaining mozzarella. Drizzle evenly with oil.

Bake for about 35 minutes, or until the zucchini are tender when pierced with a fork.

Zucchini Casserole | **TORTINO DI ZUCCHINE**

A *tortino* is a baked *frittata* (omelet). Like *frittata*, this dish lends itself to many variations. You can use any kind of vegetables, or a mixture, such as spinach, artichokes, cauliflower, or broccoli. This is another dish that is great for using leftovers, as the parsimony of the Neapolitans dictates. It was an absolute favorite in my house and still is today. It is a good dish for lunch or a light dinner. Leftover *tortino* can be cut into small squares and served cold with drinks.

6 or more servings

3 tablespoons extra-virgin olive oil

2 cups thinly sliced zucchini

1 garlic clove, chopped

2 teaspoons chopped fresh Italian parsley

1 cup tomato sauce (optional)

5 eggs

1 tablespoon all-purpose flour

Salt to taste

Freshly milled pepper to taste

8 ounces whole-milk mozzarella, shredded

1 tablespoon freshly grated Parmesan or Grana Padano cheese

Preheat the oven to 375 degrees F.

In an ovenproof skillet, preferably iron, heat the olive oil and add the zucchini and garlic. Cook stirring until the zucchini starts to color, about 5 to 10 minutes. Stir in the parsley, and tomato sauce if using, and set aside.

In a mixing bowl, beat the eggs until foamy. Add the flour, salt, and pepper and mix well. Add the mozzarella and grated cheese and mix. Pour the mixture over the zucchini. Cook a few minutes to let the bottom set, then put the skillet in the oven.

Bake for 30 to 35 minutes, or until the eggs are set and the top starts to brown. Cut into wedges and serve.

NOTE   *A variation of this dish was invented one Sunday when we came back from a friend's farm with a basket full of zucchini. Our friend, being a Neapolitan, called it* uno sfizio, *which means "done for fun." We called it* Tortino di zucchine no. due *("number two") and substituted Fontina or a similar cheese for the mozzarella.*

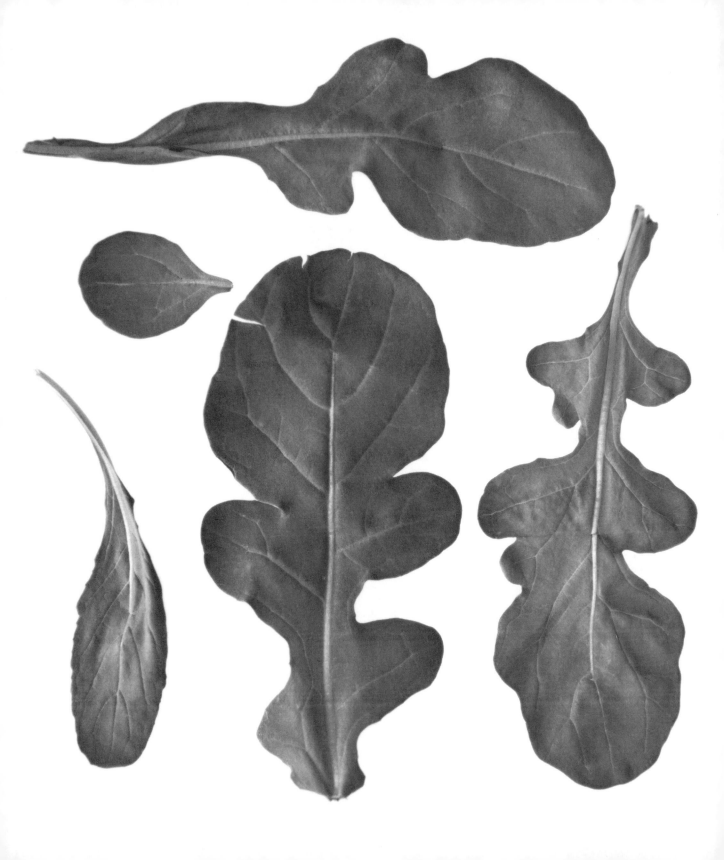

salads

INSALATE

Salad is an important part of the everyday meal all over Italy. Neapolitan markets are full of stands with all sorts of greens: bunches of lettuces, arugula, chicory, and purslane. Nowadays even the fashionable radicchio, which is a specialty of Treviso in northern Italy, sticks its red head out among the greenery. Salads in Italy are not eaten at the beginning of a meal but at the end before the cheese and fruit, which are also customary, especially with dinner.

Tomato Lovers

There is no need to remind you how passionate Neapolitans are about tomatoes. They put them in almost everything, but in moderation and not with the same exaggeration that I found when I came to the United States. I hated Italian restaurants where all the food was drowned in tomato sauce. Now these restaurants have become quite refined and gone back to more authentic Italian food. I always say that food evolves constantly, therefore we have to accept innovations, and if they are good, this makes sense. The Neapolitans have always been parsimonious, their cuisine being a "cuisine of the poor." Their food has always been controlled, without excess. The emphasis has always been on fresh flavors, and the most flavorful things are seasonal.

There are two schools of thought about which is the best grade of maturity in a tomato used in a salad. Some Neapolitans prefer the good, red San Marzano tomatoes that in the United States come only canned, or some greenish, still unripe ones. When we lived in Naples, this was the subject of many discussions between my father and his Neapolitan friends. Papa preferred the immature ones, but not everyone agreed, so we prepared the salad both ways, and everybody was happy.

A word of advice: Do not store your tomatoes in the refrigerator, they will lose all their flavor. I buy a few at a time and keep them in a basket. They are also ornamental!

Tomato Salad | **POMODORI AD INSALATA**

This recipe, a typical Neapolitan salad, is an ode to the tomato. At the market, tomatoes are sold freshly picked. But they also come from the *orto* (the kitchen garden), or from the many pots decorating the balconies of Naples. The Neapolitan writer Vittorio Gleijeses, author of the marvelous book *A Napoli si Mangia Cosi,* says that this salad "must be prepared with enthusiasm, because it represents summer, the sun and its color. Its freshness and perfume can be the happy epilogue of the day."

6 servings

3 tablespoons extra-virgin olive oil

Salt to taste

1 pound fresh tomatoes

½ cup basil leaves

1 sprig Italian parsley

1 cucumber, peeled and thinly sliced (optional)

In a salad bowl, mix the olive oil with some salt.

Slice the tomatoes. If they are large, cut the slices in half. Add them to the bowl and toss gently.

Chop the basil and parsley together and add them to the tomatoes along with the cucumber slices. Mix the salad just before serving.

NOTE *Chopping basil together with parsley prevents it from blackening.*

In Naples, this salad is used as a base for other ingredients. Neapolitans like to add a touch of garlic, a red onion sliced very thin, olives, or even anchovies or canned tuna.

Greens with Mint Vinaigrette

MISTICANZA

This salad combines various greens and vegetables. I do not understand all the fuss about the mixture of greens now sold in bags in supermarkets. It is expensive and most of the time looks tired and limp. Buy greens and mix them yourself; believe me, it will be much fresher than the mix you can buy.

6 to 8 servings

DRESSING

1 garlic clove, very finely chopped

2 to 4 fresh mint or basil leaves, chopped

¼ cup extra-virgin olive oil

1½ tablespoons wine vinegar

SALAD

8 radicchio leaves

5 or 6 endive leaves

4 or 5 romaine leaves

4 or 5 chicory leaves

10 to 12 arugula leaves

1 small fennel, trimmed and thinly sliced

1 carrot, thinly sliced

2 ripe but firm tomatoes, sliced or cubed

In a salad bowl, combine the garlic, mint, olive oil, and vinegar. Mix well.

Tear the greens into bite-size pieces and add with the fennel, carrot, and tomatoes to the bowl. Toss just before serving.

Red Cabbage Salad | **INSALATA ROSSA**

In wintertime, when lettuce was a little scarce, my mother used to make this salad we all liked a lot. I have modernized it by using balsamic vinegar, which was totally unknown in Naples at the time. This salad is better if prepared a day ahead.

6 servings

¼ cup extra-virgin olive oil

3 tablespoons balsamic vinegar

1 garlic clove, chopped

1 small onion, chopped

2 thin slices fresh ginger, peeled and chopped

2 tablespoons raisins

1 small head red cabbage, shredded

In a salad bowl combine the olive oil, vinegar, garlic, onion, ginger, and raisins. Mix well.

Add the cabbage to the dressing. Toss and let the salad sit in a cool place overnight.

Eggplant Salad | **INSALATA DI MELANZANE ALL'AMALFITANA**

The people of Campania love eggplants almost as much as tomatoes. This is an unusual salad with a strong garlicky flavor. Try to pick up medium "male" eggplants. You can identify them by looking at the tip—it's pointed.

6 servings

3 medium eggplants

¼ cup extra-virgin olive oil

Juice of half a lemon

1½ teaspoons chopped fresh oregano, or ½ teaspoon dried

2 garlic cloves, chopped

Salt to taste

Freshly milled pepper to taste

2 sprigs Italian parsley, chopped

Cut the eggplants lengthwise in 4 wedges each. Blanch the wedges in boiling water for 5 minutes. Drain and cool.

In a serving bowl, combine the olive oil, lemon juice, oregano, garlic, salt, and pepper. Mix well. Add the eggplant and toss to coat. Add the parsley just before serving.

White Bean Salad | **INSALATA DI FAGIOLI**

During the winter, it is cold in Naples. Robust salads made with dried beans, chickpeas, and lentils are a common fare. They are served cold or lukewarm as ideal accompaniments to many dishes, especially fish. The beets give this salad a nice red color.

6 servings

1 cup dried white beans

2 dry bay leaves

1 small red onion, finely chopped

¼ cup extra-virgin olive oil

3 tablespoons wine vinegar

Salt to taste

Freshly milled pepper to taste

2 large beets, boiled, peeled and diced (see page 54 for directions)

6 small red potatoes, boiled in their skin and cut in half or quartered

Place the beans in a skillet with cold water. Bring to a boil and simmer for 10 minutes. Drain and rinse with cold water.

Put the beans back in the skillet. Cover with water, add the bay leaves and bring to a boil. Simmer for 45 minutes, or until the beans are soft but not mushy. Drain and discard the bay leaves.

In a serving bowl, combine the onion, olive oil, vinegar, salt, and pepper, Mix well, add the beans and toss again. Add the beets and potatoes. Toss and serve.

NOTE | *Pre-cooking the beans for 10 minutes makes the overnight soaking unnecessary.*

Instead of white beans, you can use chickpeas or lentils. With the lentils, you can skip the pre-cooking step. They will cook in much less time—20 to 30 minutes.

Potato Salad with Bell Peppers and Arugula

INSALATA INVERNALE

Neapolitans need to have salad on the table every day. In winter they become very inventive, using whatever is available. This salad is sometimes made with dried tomatoes.

6 to 8 servings

1 garlic clove, mashed with a garlic press

3 tablespoons extra-virgin olive oil

Lemon juice to taste

2 baking potatoes, boiled, peeled and cut into pieces

1 green bell pepper, roasted, peeled, cored, and cut into strips

1 yellow bell pepper, roasted, peeled, cored, and cut into strips

1 small bunch arugula, stems trimmed

In a salad bowl combine the garlic, olive oil, and some lemon juice.

Add the potatoes and peppers and toss. When ready to serve, add the arugula. Toss the salad at the table and serve.

Salad with Tuna and Cranberry Beans

INSALATA DI TONNO E SPOLICHINI

For this salad you need fresh beans called *spolichini* in Naples. They are sold in their speckled red pods at farmers markets and some supermarkets in the United States. In Italy, Sunday dinner is not plentiful because the main, larger meal is usually served in the middle of the day. This salad is a perfect accompaniment to light Sunday evening meals such as eggs or pizza.

6 servings

2 pounds fresh cranberry beans

1 (6-ounce) can tuna packed in olive oil

1 small onion, chopped

1 tablespoon capers, drained

1 tablespoon chopped fresh Italian parsley

Juice of half a lemon

Pod the beans and blanch them for a few minutes. Drain.

In a bowl from which you can serve, put the tuna with its oil. Add the onion, capers, parsley, and lemon juice. Add the beans, toss well and serve.

Salad with Blanched Vegetables | **INSALATA CON VERDURE**

One of the many salads my mother made was this recipe with blanched or boiled vegetables. In Italy vegetables are often served as a salad, especially broccoli, cauliflower, string beans, and zucchini. The vegetables are blanched and simply dressed with oil and lemon and are an excellent accompaniment to grilled meat or fish.

6 to 8 servings

2 tablespoons extra-virgin olive oil, plus more for drizzling

3 tablespoons white wine vinegar

Salt to taste

Freshly milled pepper (optional)

1 garlic clove

1 cup loosely packed fresh basil leaves

2 sprigs Italian parsley

2 medium potatoes, boiled, peeled, and cut into small cubes

½ pound string beans, blanched and cut into bite-size pieces

10 to 12 broccoli florets, boiled

1 cup black olives, pitted

2 tablespoons capers, drained

1 small head Boston or other lettuce, trimmed

3 hard-boiled eggs, cut into wedges

In a food processor place 2 tablespoons of the olive oil, the vinegar, salt, pepper, garlic, basil, and parsley. Chop very finely. Set aside.

In a mixing bowl combine the potatoes, string beans, broccoli, olives, and 1 tablespoon of the capers. Add the dressing and toss well.

Line the bottom and sides of a salad bowl with the lettuce leaves. Place the vegetables in the middle. Sprinkle with the remaining capers, garnish with the eggs, and drizzle with olive oil.

Salad with Romaine, Marinated Artichokes and Beets

INSALATA DI LATTUGA, CARCIOFI SOTT'OLIO E BARBABIETOLE

When in season, red beets are often added to salads for flavor and color. They also go well mixed with oranges, dressed with olive oil and a touch of vinegar. Do not toss this salad until you are ready to serve it. The combination of ingredients looks very pretty.

6 to 8 servings

8 to 10 leaves of romaine or other green lettuce, torn into bite-size pieces

1 (5-ounce) jar marinated artichokes, drained (see note)

2 beets, boiled and peeled

3 or 4 tablespoons extra-virgin olive oil

2 tablespoons white wine vinegar

Freshly milled pepper to taste

Put the greens in a salad bowl. Cut the artichokes in wedges and place them in the center. Cut the beets in wedges and arrange around the artichokes.

In a small bowl, combine the olive oil, vinegar, and a pinch of pepper.

Just before serving, pour the dressing over the salad but do not mix until ready to serve.

NOTE   *I often substitute marinated mushrooms for the artichokes.*

My mother, who never threw anything away, used the oil from the artichokes or mushrooms to dress this or other salads.

Desserts

I DOLCI

Neapolitans prefer substantial desserts. In view of their proverbial poverty, they want to be completely satiated when leaving the table. When the *dolci* arrive, they must be rich and inviting. In all parts of Italy, desserts are served at the table only on festive occasions or for Sunday dinner. Everyday meals usually end with some cheese and fruit.

It is also common for people to go to a café in the afternoon to meet friends and relatives for the ritual espresso that is often ordered together with a pastry, such as a filled pastry called *sfogliatella* or a *baba* (Rum-Soaked Yeast Cake). Pastries are the absolute passion of the Neapolitans, no matter the social status, perhaps because to eat them is considered an indulgence.

The art of baking in the region of Campania has a long history. The Neapolitans are very imaginative people—this is visible in the variety, shapes, colors and garnishes of their cakes, cookies, and confections.

Ricotta Semifreddo with Chestnuts | **SEMIFREDDO DI RICOTTA E CASTAGNE**

In the province of Avellino, chestnuts and hazelnuts abound. At the beginning of winter, when chestnuts are in season, we used to go to a friendly farmer and pick, roast, and eat them. This dessert is made with a chestnut cream which was available year-round—my mother made several jars of it while the chestnuts were in season. You can find chestnut cream in Italian stores and some supermarkets.

6 to 8 servings

1½ pounds whole-milk ricotta, drained

3 tablespoons honey

1 (16-ounce) can chestnut cream

Nocello (Italian walnut- and hazelnut-flavored liqueur), such as Fra Angelico

6 to 8 candied chestnuts (optional)

In a food processor fitted with a plastic blade, combine the ricotta and honey. Process until smooth.

Fill individual goblets, alternating spoonfuls of the ricotta mixture with the chestnut cream. Add 1 tablespoon or less of the liqueur to each goblet and garnish with a candied chestnut, if using them. Refrigerate until well chilled.

NOTE *If you want to roast chestnuts in the fall, cut a slit on the round side of every chestnut. Place the chestnuts on a baking sheet and bake in a preheated oven at 375 degrees F for 30 minutes, or until they crack. Peel when the chestnuts are still warm.*

Vanilla Ice Cream with a Coffee Jolt | **SAMOCA AFFOGATO**

I serve this dessert at impromptu dinners. In Naples we had to plan it in advance because we didn't have ice cream, the main ingredient, in the freezer—we didn't even have a freezer! But nowadays it is a cinch to make, and everybody likes it.

6 servings

1 pint vanilla or coffee ice cream, or a mixture of the two

3 jiggers Sambuca Romana or Anisette liqueur

2 jiggers coffee liqueur

18 coffee beans

Pirouette cookies (optional)

Place the ice cream in individual glasses or bowls.

In a cup, combine the liqueurs and pour in equal parts on the ice cream. Garnish with a coffee bean. If serving Pirouette cookies, insert 2 into each serving.

NOTE *Any ice cream can make a great* affogato. *Just choose the flavor you like and "drown" it with a liqueur of your choice.*

Coffee Semifreddo | **CREMOLATA SEMIFREDDO AL CAFFE**

Semifreddo literally means "semi-cold." It is a chilled but not necessarily frozen dessert. Neapolitans, like all Italians, have a passion for coffee and these sorts of desserts. The famous *tiramisù* is a *semifreddo*. As an added bonus, they can be prepared in advance and are easy to make.

6 to 8 servings

6 egg yolks

1 cup sugar

¾ teaspoon potato starch or cornstarch

1 cup freshly brewed espresso, chilled

1 cup milk

1 ounce bittersweet chocolate, grated

1 teaspoon vanilla extract

3 tablespoons Sambuca Romana or Anisette liqueur

1 cup heavy cream, whipped

Coffee beans (optional)

In an enamel pot, beat the egg yolks and sugar. Slowly whisk in the starch, espresso, and milk, stirring until the mixture is smooth and liquid. Cook over low heat, stirring constantly until the mixture thickens. Do not boil. Remove from heat. Whisk in the chocolate, vanilla, and liqueur. Cool.

Reserve ½ cup of the whipped cream for garnish. Fold the remaining whipped cream into the coffee mixture, then spoon it into individual goblets. Garnish with a dollop of the reserved cream and a few coffee beans. Refrigerate until ready to serve.

Coffee Granita with Whipped Cream

GRANITA DI CAFFÉ CON PANNA

On a summer night, after dinner, sitting at a panoramic café overlooking the Gulf of Naples, there is nothing more pleasant than a *granita di caffé con panna*. This is what we did when we lived in Naples, and for us kids, it was paradise. Not only because of the *granita*, but because we were allowed to stay up late and even go for strolls with our friends as long as we were within our parents' sight. Nowadays, when I prepare this dessert, I think of those carefree days just prior to World War II and my *granita* tastes even better than the one I remember. It is an easy dessert and a wonderful conclusion to a good dinner.

6 servings

½ cup sugar

1 tablespoon unsweetened cocoa

3 cups hot strong espresso

1 cup heavy cream

In a mixing bowl combine the sugar and cocoa; slowly add the coffee, stirring with a whisk.

Pour the mixture into a shallow dish. Place in the freezer. As soon as ice crystals start to form around the edges, stir the mixture. Freeze again and repeat the stirring every 30 to 40 minutes until it reaches a granular consistency.

When ready to serve, whip the heavy cream. Spoon the granita into tall glasses and top each with the whipped cream.

NOTE *I sometimes add a splash of Sambuca liqueur to the coffee. Brewed decaffeinated coffee can also be used, but not instant coffee.*

Coffee Custard

COVIGLIE NAPOLETANE

Coviglie are a specialty of the Neapolitan *patisserie*. They are usually served in elegant little silver bowls resembling old-fashioned champagne glasses. Another coffee-flavored dessert that is easy to make, this recipe, which my mother learned to make when we were living in Naples, is the classic version. Of course I use Mamma's custard—because it's the best!

6 servings

1 cup heavy cream

One recipe Basic Custard (recipe on page 294), substituting 1 cup espresso for 1 cup of the milk

6 coffee beans, or a dusting of ground espresso coffee

Whip the cream and gently fold it into the cooled custard. Place in individual bowls and chill.

Serve each bowl topped with a coffee bean or dusting of ground coffee.

Basic Custard

CREMA DI MAMMA

I call it *crema di mamma*; my cousins call it *crema della zia* (aunt's custard); friends call it *crema della Signora Raffaella*, my mother's name. This custard is so good and so foolproof to make that everybody who has tasted it has asked for the recipe. This basic custard works well as a filling for cakes and can be combined easily with other ingredients. The best pot in which to make this *crema* is a copper zabaglione pot, but you can also use an enameled pot.

Makes 2 cups

4 egg yolks

¾ cup sugar

3 tablespoons all-purpose flour

2 cups milk

2 strips lemon zest

1 teaspoon pure vanilla extract

In a saucepan combine the yolks, sugar, and flour. Mix with a wire whisk until smooth. Slowly add the milk, stirring, until the mixture liquefies. Add the lemon zest.

Place the saucepan over medium-low heat and cook the custard, stirring constantly, until it starts to thicken and a few bubbles appear on the surface. Let it bubble 2 or 3 times, but be careful that it does not boil.

Remove from the heat and stir in the vanilla. Transfer to a bowl and cool.

NOTE *My mother always used a vanilla bean, which she added at the same time as the lemon zest. When finished, she would remove the bean, rinse it, let it dry and store it in a jar full of sugar. It was reused many times.*

For chocolate custard, mix 2 tablespoons of unsweetened cocoa with a few tablespoons of the hot custard and mix until smooth. Add the remaining custard and a pinch of ground cinnamon and whisk until smooth.

Mascarpone Semifreddo with Strawberries

SEMIFREDDO DI MASCARPONE ALLE FRAGOLE

This is a rather modern recipe. I didn't even know that in Campania they were making mascarpone cheese with buffalo milk, the same used for their famous mozzarella. But during one of my last visits to my extended family there, I had a delicious semifreddo with strawberries, which was indeed made with local mascarpone. You can also use other berries or fruits, pears are an especially perfect match, so don't be afraid to experiment.

6 servings

1 pound strawberries, hulled and sliced lengthwise

¼ cup sugar

8 ounces mascarpone cheese

⅓ cup Amaretto liqueur

6 amaretti cookies, crumbled

In a mixing bowl combine the strawberries and 2 tablespoons of sugar.

In another bowl combine the remaining sugar, the mascarpone, and Amaretto. Mix well.

Fill 6 goblets with the strawberry mixture. Add a large spoonful of the mascarpone mixture and sprinkle amaretti crumbs over all.

Refrigerate but take out before serving; it should be served at room temperature.

Trifle

ZUPPA INGLESE CASA MIA

Zuppa Inglese is a well-known Italian dessert, similar to an English trifle, but how many people know the reason for the Italian name, which literally translated means "English soup"? Well, it seems the salacious Roman waiters of the famous Cafe Greco in Rome's Via Condotti gave the name to the dessert. It was at the time of the Grand Tour when it was de rigueur for English gentlemen to come to Italy to round out their education. They used to frequent renowned coffee houses where they ordered a rum and custard-filled sponge cake called *pizza dolce* (sweet pizza). To the amusement of the waiters, they would ask for more rum to soak the *pizza dolce* in. The Italian waiters, ever so obliging, would consent, and at times the cake almost became a soup, therefore they started to call it *zuppa Inglese*.

Although *zuppa Inglese* is considered more of a southern specialty, you can find it in cafés and patisseries all over Italy. Many people garnish the dessert with whipped cream. In my opinion this dessert is rich as it is and does not need any additions. It is a good idea to make the sponge cake one or two days in advance; it will be easier to slice and also tastes better. Since the sponge cake needs to be cut into slices, I use a standard-size loaf pan to have more even slices.

6 to 8 servings

2 cups Basic Custard (recipe on page 294)

2 tablespoons unsweetened cocoa

1 Sponge Cake (recipe on page 297)

Rum

A sweet orange or hazelnut or almond liqueur

¼ cup confectioners' sugar

Cinnamon for dusting

Divide the custard into 2 parts and combine one part with the cocoa. Stir well to avoid lumps.

Cut the sponge cake into thin slices. Place one layer at the bottom of a shallow serving dish. Drizzle generously with rum. Spoon some of the yellow custard over the slices. Smooth with a spatula and top with another layer of cake. Sprinkle generously with liqueur, and evenly spread some of the chocolate custard over. Smooth with a spatula. Continue layering, finishing with slices of cake. Chill.

Take the *zuppa* out of the refrigerator to bring to room temperature 30 minutes before serving. Meanwhile combine the confectioners' sugar with the cinnamon and dust the *zuppa* with this mixture just before serving.

NOTE   *The reason why this dessert should be prepared one or two days in advance lies in its alcohol content. During the chilling process, the alcohol evaporates but the flavor increases and blends perfectly.*

Sponge Cake | **PAN DI SPAGNA LUCIANA AMORE**

I have to thank my cousin Luciana, who lives in a charming village in the province of Benevento, for giving me this recipe for an easy sponge cake. Unlike the traditional recipe, this one adds a little bit of baking powder and never fails.

6 to 8 servings

2 tablespoons all-purpose flour

Pinch of sugar

4 eggs, separated

¼ teaspoon lemon or vanilla extract

¾ cup sugar

¾ cup all-purpose flour

1 teaspoon baking powder

Preheat the oven to 350 degrees F. Lightly butter a 9-inch cake or springform pan. Mix the flour with a pinch of sugar and dust the pan with it, making sure that the bottom and sides of the pan are evenly covered.

Beat the egg yolks and add the lemon or vanilla extract and ¾ cup of sugar. Continue beating until the mixture is fluffy and lemon-colored.

Mix the flour and baking powder and stir into the yolk mixture. The batter will be dense.

Beat the egg whites until stiff. Fold one third of the whites into the batter mixture and gently mix until the white is absorbed. Add the rest of the whites, a little at a time, and gently, but swiftly, fold into the mixture. Pour into the prepared pan.

Bake for 45 minutes without opening the oven. If a toothpick inserted in the middle of the cake comes out clean, the cake is done, otherwise bake a little longer. Cool on a wire rack and unmold.

Ricotta Wheat Pie | **PASTIERA NAPOLETANA**

This is undoubtedly the most famous Neapolitan dessert. It was a tradition to serve *la pastiera* at the Easter dinner, but because it has become so well-known all over Italy, you can now find it served almost every day, especially in the south.

The ingredients are full of symbolism. Wheat represents the union of vegetable and animal life; flour stands for wealth; ricotta for abundance; egg for rebirth; sugar for sweetness; and the orange flavor is the perfume of Campania. You can find canned wheat and *fior d'arancio* (orange water) in Italian specialty stores and some supermarkets.

6 to 8 servings

1 batch Simple Pie Dough (recipe on page 299)

1 (14-ounce) can wheat (*grano per pastiera*), or 1 cup dry wheat (see note)

1½ cups milk

Zest of half a lemon in large strips, plus zest of half a lemon, finely chopped

½ teaspoon cinnamon

1 cup plus 1½ tablespoons sugar

1 pound whole-milk ricotta, drained

2 tablespoons orange water or orange liqueur

6 eggs, separated

2 tablespoons candied fruit, finely diced

1 tablespoon candied orange peel, finely diced

1 cup Basic Custard (recipe on page 294) (optional)

Butter a 10-inch springform pan. Roll out three quarters of the dough into a circle large enough to cover the bottom and sides of the prepared pan. Let the dough overhang slightly, trimming excess with scissors.

If watery, drain the wheat from the can. Heat the milk in a heavy saucepan but do not boil. Add the wheat, the strips of lemon zest, ¼ teaspoon cinnamon, and 1½ tablespoons sugar. Cover the saucepan and simmer over very low heat until the milk has been completely absorbed, about 45 minutes, stirring often to prevent scorching. Transfer the mixture to a large plate. Remove the lemon peel and discard. Cool.

Preheat the oven to 350 degrees F.

Place the ricotta in a food processor. Stir in the 1 cup of sugar, the remaining ¼ teaspoon cinnamon, the chopped lemon peel, and orange water. Process to mix well, then add 1 yolk at a time and process after each addition. Transfer the mixture to a bowl. Add the candied fruit, orange peel, and custard. Stir well. Add the cooled wheat mixture.

Whip the egg whites until stiff and fold them into the ricotta mixture. Pour into the prepared shell dough.

Roll out the remaining dough and cut into ½-inch strips. Top the *pastiera* in a criss-cross pattern. Fold the overhanging dough over and pinch all around the edge, in a decorative fashion.

Bake for about 1 hour and 15 minutes. If the top starts to brown too much, cover loosely with aluminum foil.

NOTES *If using dry wheat, place it in a pot and add 4 cups water and 1 tablespoon butter. Cook at a simmer for about 2½ hours, adding more water if necessary. Proceed as described in step 2.*

Simple Pie Dough | **PASTA FROLLA SEMPLICE**

This is a basic pie dough, equally suited for savory (vegetables, meat, fish, etc.) and fruit pies. Eliminate the sugar when used for savory pies.

Makes 1 double crust 9-inch pie

2 cups all-purpose flour

¼ cup sugar

1 stick (4 ounces) butter, cut into ½-inch cubes

3 tablespoons solid vegetable shortening, chilled

1 large egg

½ cup or more ice-cold water

In a food processor fitted with a steel blade, place the flour and sugar. Process a few seconds. Add the butter and shortening. Process until the mixture resembles coarse meal. Add the egg, process just to blend and start adding the cold water a little at a time. Stop as soon as a ball starts to form on the blades.

Remove the dough from the processor and with floured hands, form a ball. Cut the ball into 2 parts, shape into 2 balls, flour them lightly and wrap in plastic wrap. Chill for 1 hour or more. This dough can be frozen.

Use as instructed in your recipe.

Chocolate Walnut Cake | **TORTA CAPRESE**

A real specialty from the island of Capri, this recipe is from the book *Great Italian Desserts* by my friend Nick Malgeri.

6 to 8 servings

6 ounces bittersweet chocolate, chopped

1½ sticks unsalted butter, room temperature

⅔ cup sugar

6 eggs, separated

1⅓ cups shelled walnuts

⅓ cup all-purpose flour

Confectioners' sugar for dusting

Butter a 10-inch cake pan and fit the bottom with a piece of parchment paper or wax paper.

Preheat the oven to 350 degrees F.

Place the chocolate in the top of a double boiler over simmering water. Stir occasionally until the chocolate melts. Cool.

Beat the butter with half of the sugar until soft. Stir in the melted chocolate and the egg yolks, one at a time.

In the bowl of a food processor, combine the walnuts and 1 tablespoon of the remaining sugar. Chop quite finely. Stir the walnuts into the batter. Add the flour and combine.

Whip the egg whites until they hold soft peaks, then gradually add the remaining sugar. Continue whipping until glossy and stiff. Fold into the batter.

Pour the batter into the prepared pan, smooth the top and bake for 40 minutes, or until a toothpick inserted in the middle of the cake comes out clean. Cool the cake in the pan for 10 minutes. Invert onto a serving platter. Cool completely. Dust with confectioners' sugar just before serving.

NOTE   *Nick recommends not chilling the cake, even if made the day before.*

Mixed Nut Pie | **NOCCIOLATA**

The filling for this pie is made with a mixture of crunchy nuts, a favorite ingredient of the Neapolitans. The nuts come from the countryside around Avellino. Chocolate and honey, on the other hand, are foreign influences in many recipes from Campania.

6 to 8 servings

¾ cup hazelnuts

¾ cup almonds

¾ cup walnuts

1 batch Simple Pie Dough
(recipe on page 299)

1 teaspoon sugar

Zest of an orange, chopped

½ cup honey

¼ cup brown sugar

½ stick unsalted butter, melted

3 eggs

1 teaspoon vanilla extract

½ teaspoon almond extract

1 cup bittersweet chocolate,
coarsely chopped

1 tablespoon pine nuts

Preheat the oven to 500 degrees F for 10 minutes.

On a baking sheet, spread the hazelnuts and almonds. Place the walnuts on the sheet at a little distance so that they remain separate. Put the baking sheet in the oven and immediately switch off the heat. Let cool completely in the oven.

Meanwhile prepare the pie dough according to the recipe.

Remove the nuts from the oven. Set the walnuts aside. Place the other nuts on one long side of a kitchen towel, cover the nuts with the other end and roll your hands over it. This will dislodge the skins from the nuts. Shake the skins off and place all the nuts in the bowl of a food processor. Add 1 teaspoon sugar and chop coarsely. Add the orange zest and mix well.

Transfer the nut mixture to a bowl and add the honey, brown sugar, and melted butter. Mix well. Add the eggs, one at a time, and mix thoroughly. Stir in the vanilla, almond extract, and chocolate.

Preheat the oven to 350 degrees F. Butter a 10-inch pie pan.

Roll out or press the prepared dough, as thin as possible, to cover the bottom and sides of the prepared pan. Add the filling, smooth the top and sprinkle the pine nuts over all. Pinch the edge of the dough all around.

Bake the pie until a toothpick inserted in the center comes out clean, about 45 to 50 minutes. Cool on a rack before serving.

NOTE   *This pie can be made one day in advance. Keep it in a cool place but do not refrigerate.*

Orange Cake

TORTA ALL'ARANCIA

This is a delicate and simple cake from the rustic countryside of Campania, where oranges are plentiful. I bake it in a Turk's head pan and when serving, I often fill the middle with strawberries or blueberries, dressed with a little honey and orange juice.

6 to 8 servings

2 sticks unsalted butter, at room temperature

1¼ cups sugar

6 eggs, separated

1½ cups all-purpose flour

2 teaspoons baking powder

Zest of 1 orange, grated

2 tablespoons Grand Marnier or Contreau liqueur

⅓ cup milk or orange juice

⅛ teaspoon cream of tartar

Confectioners' sugar

Preheat the oven to 350 degrees F. Butter and flour a 10-inch Turk's head (bundt) pan.

Cream the butter, gradually adding the sugar until the mixture is soft and fluffy. Add the egg yolks, one at a time, blending well after each addition.

Sift together the flour and baking powder and add to the butter mixture. Mix well. Stir in the orange zest, liqueur, and milk or orange juice. Mix well.

In a separate bowl, combine the cream of tartar with the egg whites and whip the mixture until stiff. Fold into the batter blending quickly but gently in order not to break the bubbles of the egg whites.

Pour the batter into the prepared pan. Bake 1 hour, or until a toothpick inserted in the middle of the cake comes out clean. Cool the cake and sprinkle with confectioners' sugar before serving.

NOTE *In Sorrento, from where the best lemons of Italy come, this cake is made with lemon instead of orange.*

Pear-Hazelnut Upside-Down Cake

TORTA SOTTOSOPRA DI PERE E NOCCIOLE

When we lived in Naples, we were often invited during the summer to spend a weekend in the countryside. I remember that upon our arrival, we were dispatched with baskets and a grown-up in tow to pick pears and apples. Pears are not only used in cakes, but pears and cheese is a favorite Italian dessert. There is a proverb about pears that shows how much they are appreciated: *"al cafon non far sapere quant'e buon formaggio e pere"* ("Don't let the peasant know how good is cheese and pear"), meaning that if the peasant learns to appreciate these good things himself, he will not bring them to the market anymore.

8 to 10 servings

1½ sticks unsalted butter, room temperature

4 or 5 pears (preferably Anjou), peeled, cored, and cut into eighths

½ cup brown sugar

1 cup toasted hazelnuts, coarsely chopped

¾ cup sugar

2 eggs

1 teaspoon vanilla extract

1¾ cups all-purpose flour

2 teaspoons baking powder

1 cup hazelnuts, finely ground

½ cup milk

Melt 1 tablespoon of the butter in an ovenproof 10-inch skillet. Add the pears and sauté over medium heat until slightly brown, about 8 minutes. Transfer the pears to a platter with a slotted spoon. Wipe the skillet clean and set aside.

In a small saucepan, combine 3 tablespoons of the butter and the brown sugar. Cook over low heat stirring until melted.

Preheat the oven to 350 degrees F.

Butter the skillet in which the pears cooked. Spread the brown sugar mixture at the bottom. Arrange the pear slices in concentric circles on top. Sprinkle with the coarsely chopped toasted hazelnuts.

Combine 1 stick of butter and the sugar, and beat until fluffy and creamy. Add the eggs, one at a time, beating after each addition. Add the vanilla.

In a separate bowl, combine the flour, baking powder, and ground hazelnuts. Add this mixture, a little at a time, to the egg mixture, alternating with the milk. Spread the batter evenly over the pears. Bake for about 1 hour. Cool for only 10 minutes and then invert the cake onto a serving platter.

NOTE *Other fruits, especially apples (Cortland, Golden Delicious, Granny Smith) can be used for this recipe in place of the pears.*

Apple Cake with Coconut and Walnuts

TORTA ALLE MELE, NOCE DI COCCO E NOCI

When I was a child, it was a treat to have a piece of coconut, which was sold by vendors from Africa on the beautiful Via Caracciolo lining the shore of downtown Naples. Yet one Christmas we received as a present four whole coconuts! This cake was born as a result of that gift. With shredded coconut being readily available, I make it often today. It is a cake rich in exotic flavors, softened by the juices of the apples and the crispness of the nuts.

6 servings

2 or 3 unpeeled green apples (such as Granny Smith), diced

¼ cup raisins

1 cup walnuts, coarsely chopped

½ cup shredded unsweetened coconut

1½ cups all-purpose flour

1 teaspoon baking powder

1 teaspoon ground cinnamon

1 teaspoon ground nutmeg

2 eggs

¾ cup sugar

1½ sticks unsalted butter, melted

2 tablespoons Nocino or Amaretto liqueur

Confectioners' sugar

Butter and flour a 9-inch cake pan. Preheat the oven to 350 degrees F.

Mix the apples with the raisins, walnuts, and coconut in a medium bowl and set aside.

In a separate bowl, combine the flour, baking powder, cinnamon, and nutmeg.

In a mixing bowl beat the eggs and sugar. While beating, add the butter and liqueur. Add the flour mixture and stir. Add the fruit mixture and stir well.

Scoop the dough into the prepared pan, smooth the top, and bake for 45 minutes, or until a toothpick inserted in the middle of the cake comes out clean. Cool and unmold. Dust with confectioners' sugar just before serving.

Chocolate-Glazed Coffee Cake | **TORTA AL CAFFÈ CORRETTO**

During beautiful summer nights in Naples, it was almost a ceremony to go to the café, meet friends and enjoy a good *caffè corretto*, a cup of espresso that has been "corrected" with a liqueur such as Sambuca or Anisette. This cake is reminiscent of those delightful tastes and smells.

6 servings

12 ounces bittersweet chocolate

2 tablespoons Sambuca or Anisette liqueur

1 tablespoon instant espresso coffee granules

1½ pounds unsalted butter, at room temperature

1½ cups sugar

6 eggs, separated

¾ cup flour

GLAZE

4 ounces bittersweet chocolate

2 tablespoons Sambuca or Anisette liqueur

Preheat the oven to 350 degrees F. Butter and flour a 9-inch cake pan.

Place the chocolate, liqueur, espresso, and 1 tablespoon of the butter in the top of a double boiler. Place over simmering water and stir until the chocolate is melted, then remove from the heat and cool.

In a mixing bowl cream the butter and sugar. Add the egg yolks, one at a time mixing well after each addition, and then little by little add the flour. Add the chocolate mixture and mix well.

Beat the egg whites until stiff and fold into the batter. Pour into the prepared pan.

Bake for 45 minutes to 1 hour, or until a toothpick inserted in the middle of the cake comes out clean. Cool and unmold upside down.

Prepare the glaze by melting the chocolate in a double boiler. Add the liqueur, mix well and glaze the cake with it. Cool the cake completely before slicing.

NOTE   This cake may collapse slightly in the center and crack at the top. Reserve a little bit of the glaze so you can fix these eventual spots using a little spatula.

Lattice Pie with Custard and Ricotta

PIZZA CAMPAGNOLA DI CREMA E RICOTTA

This is a specialty from the countryside around Avellino and Benevento. Often in Italian, a cake is also called a pizza, however, it is a *pizza dolce* (sweet pizza). This is a little different from the usual Italian ricotta cake or pie found in the United States, because it also contains custard.

8 to 10 servings

1 batch Simple Pie Dough (recipe on page 299)

1 batch Basic Custard (recipe on page 294)

2 cups whole-milk ricotta, drained

¼ cup unsweetened cocoa

¼ cup sugar

1 tablespoon chopped orange zest

½ cup candied mixed fruits (optional)

½ teaspoon cinnamon

1 teaspoon vanilla extract

Confectioners' sugar

Butter a 10-inch pie pan. Prepare the pie dough according to the recipe. Reserve ¼ of the dough. Roll out remaining dough into a circle large enough to cover the bottom and sides of the prepared pan. Place in the pan.

Prepare the custard and set aside.

Preheat the oven to 375 degrees F.

In a food processor, place the ricotta and process for a few minutes. Add the cocoa, sugar, orange zest, candied fruit, cinnamon, and vanilla. Process until well mixed.

Combine the ricotta mixture with the custard and pour in the prepared pie shell.

Roll out the remaining dough, cut into strips and make a lattice top for the pie. Bake 1 hour. If the top tends to brown too much, cover loosely with aluminum foil. Cool. Sprinkle with confectioners' sugar when completely cold and serve.

Rum-Soaked Yeast Cakes | **BABA AL RUM**

Baba al rum, as it is called in Naples, is of course of French origin. Probably introduced by one of the famous chefs working for an aristocratic family, it has become one of the most well-loved Neapolitan desserts. My friend Nick Malgeri, who is much better at desserts and pastries than me, gave this recipe to me; it is from his splendid book *Great Italian Desserts*. I have simplified it a bit and use muffin pans, so my babas are not as big as usual.

Makes 15 to 20 babas

SPONGE

½ cup milk

1 envelope active dry yeast

¾ cup all-purpose flour

DOUGH

3 eggs

½ teaspoon salt

2 tablespoons sugar

1½ cups all-purpose flour

1 stick butter, melted and cooled

2 tablespoons unsalted butter for the pans

SYRUP

2 cups sugar

½ cup dark rum

FOR THE SPONGE Bring the milk to lukewarm in a small saucepan. Remove from the heat. Sprinkle the yeast on the milk and let stand for 5 minutes. Whisk until smooth and stir in the flour. Cover the sponge and let rest for 20 minutes.

FOR THE DOUGH Beat the eggs, salt, sugar, and flour in a medium bowl. Beat in the sponge, then add the cooled butter and mix well.

Butter muffin pans. With a pastry bag, pipe the dough into the muffin cups about half full. Cover the pan loosely with buttered plastic wrap and allow proofing until the dough rises to the top of the cups.

Preheat the oven to 375 degrees F.

Bake the babas for 10 to 15 minutes, or until golden and baked through. Cool on a rack.

FOR THE SYRUP Combine the sugar and 3 cups water in a pan and bring to a boil. Add the rum and bring the syrup back to a boil.

Release the babas from their molds and soak them a few at a time in the hot syrup. If the syrup is not very hot, the babas will not absorb it well and may remain dry in the middle. Transfer the babas to a noncorrosive plate to cool. Serve the same day.

Honey-Glazed Fritters | **STRUFFOLI**

This is an ancient dessert originating from the Jews living in Italy in Roman times. Therefore I was not surprised when I was served a similar confection called *teiglach* at a Rosh Hashanah dinner. In Naples, they called it *struffoli*, which means "cotton wads." As children, we loved this dessert because it looked so festive with its garnish of candied fruits and almonds.

4 eggs, at room temperature

3 tablespoons sugar

½ cup extra-virgin olive oil

1 tablespoon liqueur, preferably orange

3 cups all-purpose flour, plus more as needed

Canola oil for deep-frying

1½ cups honey

3 to 4 tablespoons almonds, blanched

2 tablespoons diced citron

¼ cup candied orange peel, diced

6 red candied cherries, or a mixture of red and green, halved

Place the eggs and sugar in a food processor, mix for a few minutes, then add ¼ cup of the olive oil and the liqueur. Process to mix well. Start adding the flour a little at a time until a ball forms on the blades. Transfer the dough to a floured board and knead until smooth and pliable, adding more flour when necessary.

Break off pieces of dough and roll with your hands into long, thin, round strips. Cut each strip into small pieces the size of chickpeas. Keep the pieces on a lightly floured board until ready to continue.

In a skillet combine the canola oil and ¼ cup of olive oil. Heat to the smoking point and start frying the pieces of dough until golden. Drain on paper towels placed on a wire rack.

In a large skillet heat the honey until it changes color. Add the fried pieces of dough and stir gently with a slotted spoon until all the pieces are well coated. Add the almonds and citron towards the end.

Wet a large platter and transfer the honey mixture to it. When cool enough to handle, wet your hands and shape the mass into a mound. Scatter the orange peel all around and garnish with the cherries.

NOTE   *My mother, with my help, used to shape each little piece of dough to make it look like a chickpea. The Neapolitans, on the other hand, make the balls the size of hazelnuts. It is up to you, but I prefer it my mother's way.*

Cinnamon-Dusted Donuts | **ZEPPOLE DI SAN GIUSEPPE**

The feast of Saint Joseph is a national holiday in Italy. After Mass everybody goes to their favorite coffeehouse to have an *aperitivo* and *zeppole*. In Naples this is a must. In my family the *zeppole* were made in large quantities because my father's name was Giuseppe (Joseph).

About 50 pieces

1 cup water

½ stick butter

Zest of 1 lemon or 1 small orange

Pinch of salt

1 cup all-purpose flour

5 eggs

4 tablespoons sugar

Oil for deep-frying

½ teaspoon cinnamon

In a heavy skillet place the 1 cup water, butter, zest, and salt. Bring to a boil, remove from the heat and add all the flour at once. Mix vigorously until smooth. Return the skillet to the heat and cook over medium heat until the dough starts to detach from the sides of the skillet. Transfer to a mixing bowl and continue beating until the dough has cooled.

Add the eggs, one at a time, plus 2 tablespoons of sugar. Mix well and transfer the mixture to a pastry bag fitted with a star tip. Pipe the pastry on individual pieces of parchment paper or aluminum foil in circles with a hole in the center.

In a large skillet, pour enough oil to come up just under one inch of the edge of the pan. Heat the oil and drop the *zeppole* in, a few at a time, peeling them off the paper. Fry on both sides until golden. Drain on paper towels. Cool.

When ready to serve, combine 2 tablespoons sugar and the cinnamon, dredge the *zeppole* in this mixture, or sprinkle them with it. Set on a plate and serve.

Almond Biscotti

BISCOTTI ALLE MANDORLE

These classic *biscotti* are made everywhere in Italy. My grandmother Nonnina, as we affection-ately called her, used to make them all the time. She would always have them ready for visitors. The beverages varied depending on the person to whom the cookies were served. Tea or hot chocolate for the ladies, some special wine for others. My father always managed to be the one serving "the others," so he would dip his cookies in the *Vino Cotto*, which he loved.

Makes 24 cookies

3 cups all-purpose flour plus ½ cup for kneading

2 teaspoons baking powder

4 eggs

1 cup sugar

1½ sticks unsalted butter, melted

3 tablespoons olive oil

1 teaspoon almond extract

1 teaspoon vanilla extract

1 cup skinned almonds, lightly toasted and coarsely chopped

Preheat the oven to 350 degrees F.

Sift the flour and baking powder together.

In a mixing bowl, combine the eggs and sugar. Beat for 5 minutes, then add 1 stick melted butter. Mix briefly and add the olive oil, almond extract, vanilla, and chopped almonds. Gradually add the flour mixture and beat until well combined.

Line a baking sheet with parchment or wax paper and brush lightly with melted butter.

Transfer the dough to a floured board and knead for 5 to 8 minutes, adding more flour if necessary. Shape the dough into two 14 × 2-inch loaves. Place on the pre-pared baking sheet. Bake until golden, about 25 minutes. Cool on a rack.

Reduce over temperature to 275 degrees F.

Cut the loaves diagonally with a serrated knife into 2-inch slices. Return the slices to the baking sheet and bake for 10 minutes. Turn and continue baking for 10 more minutes. Cool completely before storing in airtight containers.

NOTE   *You can also use hazelnuts, peanuts, or walnuts instead of almonds.*

ITALIAN

ENGLISH